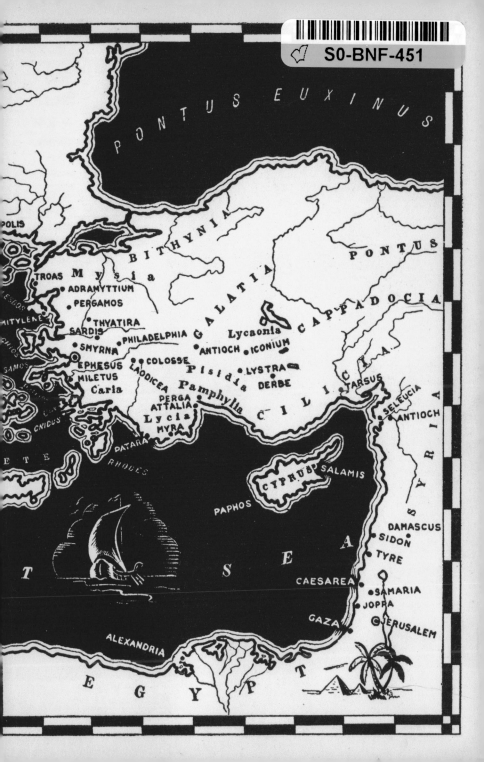

PONTUS EUXINUS

BITHYNIA

PONTUS

GALATIA

CAPPADOCIA

POLIS

TROAS Mysia

ADRAMYTTIUM

PERGAMOS

MITYLENE

THYATIRA

LESBOS

SARDIS

Lycaonia

CHIOS

SMYRNA

PHILADELPHIA

ANTIOCH ICONIUM

EPHESUS

COLOSSE

Pisidia

LYSTRA

SAMOS

MILETUS

LAODICEA

DERBE

CILICIA

Caria

Pamphylia

TARSUS

PERGA

SELEUCIA

CNIDUS

ATTALIA

ANTIOCH

Lycia

SYRIA

MYRA

C R E T E

PATARA

RHODES

CYPRUS SALAMIS

PAPHOS

DAMASCUS

SIDON

S E A

TYRE

CAESAREA

SAMARIA

JOPPA

GAZA

JERUSALEM

ALEXANDRIA

E G Y P T

*On Whom*

*the Spirit Came*

# On Whom
# the Spirit Came

## A Study of the Acts of the Apostles

by

MILES W. SMITH

ἐπλήσθησαν πάντες πνεύματος ἁγίου
They were all filled with the Holy Ghost
—Acts 2:4

## THE JUDSON PRESS
*Philadelphia*

CHICAGO                    LOS ANGELES

# ON WHOM THE SPIRIT CAME

FIRST EDITION

"A glorious band, the chosen few
  On whom the Spirit came,
Twelve valiant saints, their hope they knew,
  And mocked the torch of flame;
They met the tyrant's brandished steel,
  The lion's gory mane,
They bowed their necks the stroke to feel:
  Who follows in their train?"

*—Reginald Heber*

# Preface

*I*T MAY not be amiss to set down here the practical purposes which this book aspires to serve. Although the following pages treat in considerable detail the entire contents of the Acts of the Apostles, the book is not offered as a comprehensive commentary. Numerous commentaries, some for advanced students and some for students gaining their first acquaintance with the Bible, are already available. A few of the most helpful ones are listed in the Bibliography. Furthermore, although the following pages are not deficient in scholarship (at least, so the author fondly hopes!), matters of a purely critical nature have been passed over briefly. The critical problems have their importance, but a discussion of them likely would discourage those readers for whom this book is chiefly intended. In brief, this volume attempts but little more than to retell, for the benefit of the average reader, Luke's story of the expansion of Christianity between the years A.D. 29 and 64—three and a half decades of tremendous significance for all subsequent time.

We best appreciate the world's indebtedness to Luke when we take account of the fact that his history is practically our only source of information concerning Christian activities and achievements during those momentous years. Luke tells us how the gospel was carried throughout the Roman Empire, and how finally it was preached even in Rome, the imperial city. The letters written by the apostle Paul, of course, contribute to our understanding in numerous ways, but in themselves they are of too personal and occasional a nature to provide us with an over-all, objective picture of the Christian development and outreach during that period. Indeed, much that is found in the Pauline epistles would be inexplicable apart from the historical outline furnished by The Acts. As for the traditions which gained currency in the early church, they seem frequently to be secondary, rather than primary, sources of historical information; that is to say, they seem in many instances to be inferences arrived at through a study of the Scripture records.

Let it be reiterated, then, that this book attempts to give the story *as Luke has related it*. Accordingly, account is taken of Luke's point of view and of his purpose in writing. It is essential that we should know well what Luke has written before we attempt to pass any judgment upon his work. As will speedily become apparent to the reader, the author holds that Luke was a competent, careful, and conscientious historian, to whom the Holy Spirit gave a true insight into the spiritual significance of the events which he chronicled.

Some modern scholars have given much attention to what they judge to be a contradiction between Luke's account and two or three statements made by Paul in his epistles. They have insisted that in matters having to do with Paul's life, Paul's own statements should have the preference. It might be answered—and this without any impugning of Paul's veracity—that an impartial observer sometimes sees events more clearly than one who is involved in the heat and turmoil of them. Be that as it may, the difficulties undoubtedly have been exaggerated; they might disappear entirely if we possessed fuller knowledge. Luke nowhere claims that he has told everything. Like every author who is under the necessity of keeping the length of his book within a reasonable limit, he had to select those events which bore most directly upon his purpose. In a discussion of the difficulties encountered in connection with a somewhat similar problem, the harmonizing of the four Gospel accounts of the life of Christ, Dr. John A. Broadus once remarked that the burden of proof rested always upon those who were minded to challenge the Scripture records as they stand. So long as a single possibility remains that the records might be harmonized if we possessed fuller knowledge, we have no right to charge that they are in error.

Numerous attempts have been made to weave together in one connected narrative all that Luke wrote and all that Paul wrote. Such a composite writing, however wisely prepared, proves somewhat unsatisfactory. It suffers the same shortcomings as do all combinations of the four Gospels into one "complete" Gospel. A composite Gospel, although containing more material than any single Gospel, completely ignores the special purpose which each evangelist had in mind when writing; it destroys the evangelist's literary composition and obscures his literary style; it hides the evangelist himself, the Spirit-filled man from whom we would learn. It is for this reason that in the present writing only on rare occasions has Luke's account been supplemented by any of that wealth of material which can be drawn from Paul's epistles. The primary aim throughout has been to acquaint the reader with Luke's narrative.

In further pursuit of this aim, whenever reference has been made to deeds or sayings of Christ, Luke's Gospel, if possible, has been quoted. This has been done, first, because Luke's Gospel and The Acts belong together, they being but the two volumes of a single work frequently designated as Luke-Acts; and, second, because in this way the Lucan point of view is most consistently maintained.

In order that the book may be consulted easily by anyone who desires help on a particular Scripture passage, it has been plentifully supplied with topical headings. Except in the first chapter, each heading is followed by the corresponding Scripture reference. These references are in their natural order and comprehend the whole of The Acts. But it is hoped that the book will be read, not piecemeal, but as a whole, and read easily and rapidly, so as to catch that feeling of action and expansion which is so prominent in Luke's narrative.

Of course, the reading of this book is not intended to take the place of the reading of the Scriptures themselves. The student should keep his Bible open to the passage under discussion. What is offered here is not a substitute for the Scripture text, but an interpretation of it, an interpretation made possible by our steadily growing knowledge of the history and social customs of the first century. It will be helpful to refer frequently to the map which is provided or to some larger map of the Mediterranean region. Only by a careful tracing of Paul's missionary journeys can one gain an adequate knowledge of the manner in which Christianity was spread throughout the world of that day.

It is hoped that this book will prove useful as a text for leadership and missionary education classes, and as an elective course for church school classes made up of young people or adults. Questions for discussion appropriate to each chapter, as well as study and service projects, will be found in the Appendix. The Appendix contains also a chronology of the years covered by the book of Acts and a brief annotated bibliography.

All the Scripture quotations throughout, unless indicated otherwise, are given as they appear in the King James Version—not because the writer holds that translation to be the best, but because it is the translation which readers of this book are most likely to have at hand. However, in every instance where the American Standard Version or the recently published Revised Standard Version of the New Testament makes an important textual emendation or change in translation, attention is called to that fact. Quotations from the American Standard Version and the Revised Standard Version are made with the courteous permission of the International Council of Religious Education and Thomas Nelson & Sons, publisher. To save space, a few readily recognized abbreviations have been employed: KJV stands for the King James Version; ASV stands for the American Standard Version; RSV stands for the Revised Standard Version.

To avoid impeding the reader's progress, most of the Scripture references have been put in the footnotes. These references are not to be thought of as proof-texts. They are intended to aid the student in locating in his Bible any quotation which he may wish to examine in its context. Sometimes the reference will locate for him an incident to which attention has been directed. The other footnotes serve to give the reader additional information on points in which he may be interested, information which could not well be included in the body of the book without many lengthy digressions.

Let me express my indebtedness to the many wise and consecrated teachers under whom it has been my privilege to study, to the writers of the scores of books which I have consulted while engaged in this task, and to the good friends who have read this book in manuscript and in proof. I am grateful to these readers for their helpful suggestions. Although they deserve credit for much that is good in the book, they cannot be held responsible for any of the book's shortcomings. The views advanced are wholly my own.

This, then, is what The Acts, written by Luke so long ago, means to me. May others, with the help of this book, find in Luke's great history the same spiritual inspiration and practical help which I myself have found in it.

MILES W. SMITH

Philadelphia, Pa.
June 1, 1948

# CONTENTS

*Preface*

## CHAPTER 1

# The Acts: Authorship and Purpose

## LUKE 1:1-4; ACTS 1:1-5

*T*HE Acts of the Apostles recounts the brave exploits of Spirit-filled men who defied death itself in their zeal to bear witness to Jesus Christ. These men had found Jesus to be the supreme revelation of God's person, the all-convincing manifestation of God's righteousness and love. Accordingly, they had accepted Jesus as their Saviour and Lord, and they had become concerned that all men should know that it was by Him that God would judge the world.[1]

This chronicle of Christian witness-bearing is filled with stirring adventures and hairbreadth escapes, with mob violence and imprisonments, with perilous voyages and a shipwreck, with instances of amazing perseverance and unflagging loyalty culminating in martyrdom. The Acts tells of the growth of the Christian movement, of the missionary labors of Paul, and of the establishment of Christian churches throughout the Roman Empire. In The Acts we hear the thoughtful, yet impressioned, preaching of the apostles. We are given an intimate and revealing picture of the life within the early churches. We are shown what it means to be "filled with the Spirit." All this makes enthralling and profitable reading whether one's chief interest is in high adventure, in inspiring biography, in early Christian history, in the development of church polity, in the missionary program, or in world peace and brotherhood.

There is, however, a more important reason for studying

---

[1] Acts 10:42.

1

The Acts. The Holy Scriptures are a medium through which
God has spoken to the hearts of men in ages past, and they
are the principal medium through which God speaks to men
today. Always to be remembered is the announced fact that
the Scriptures, given by inspiration of God, are profitable
for doctrine, for reproof, for correction, for instruction in
righteousness.[2] Our approach to this book of Scripture, therefore, must be on a spiritual level. As we read it, we should
ask ourselves constantly: "What is it that God is saying to us
here? What is it that He would have us learn?" And, above
all, "What is it that He would have us be and do?"

When one begins the study of a book of Scripture (The
Acts equally with any other), there are certain questions
which come naturally to mind. They are, to mention but a
few: "Who wrote these words? When did he write them? To
whom did he address them? And for what purpose?" Although
it is not necessary to have complete and final answers to all
of these questions in order to be able to read the Bible with
intellectual enjoyment and spiritual enrichment, it is obvious
that the answers to these questions (if the answers can be
found) will furnish us with a key which will unlock the
meaning of many passages which otherwise would be obscure
or meaningless. Stating this fact in another fashion, the importance of our undertaking—our urgent need to ascertain
and carry out the will of God—puts us under obligation to
avail ourselves of all the help which a reverent biblical scholarship can give us. This first chapter, therefore, has to do with
the authorship and purpose of the book of Acts, and with
various other considerations of an introductory nature.

## The Title

The title of the book we are to study, the book which
stands fifth in the New Testament, is given in the King James
Version as *The Acts of the Apostles.* In the American Standard Version, the title is simply *The Acts.* In the recently published Revised Standard Version, the longer title, *The Acts
of the Apostles,* has been restored. The word "Acts," as used

2 2 Tim. 3:16-17.

here, denotes a record of historic events—of events, of course, in which the apostles had the most prominent part. In one respect at least, the shorter title more closely corresponds to the contents of the book. The account which The Acts gives is not limited to the labors of those men who made up the original company of apostles. We are told also of the work of Philip the evangelist, of Stephen the deacon, of Paul the missionary, and of numerous other early Christians.

Although *The Acts of the Apostles* is the title which appears upon our oldest and best manuscripts, it is not likely that this title originated with Luke, the book's author. If he gave the book any formal title, it probably was nothing more pretentious than *To Theophilus, Volume 2*. *To Theophilus,* because it was to that distinguished gentleman that Luke dedicated his work.[3] *Volume 2,* because The Acts, as even a little study will show, is but a continuation of the narrative begun in the Gospel by Luke.

Luke's writings, his Gospel and his Acts of the Apostles, constitute approximately one-fourth of the New Testament. Luke's Gospel, by recounting the life of Jesus from His birth to His ascension, gives us the beginnings of Christianity; The Acts then recounts the spread of Christianity from Jerusalem to Rome. Thus, we have in these two writings an orderly and comprehensive history of Christianity. The history, being much too long to be written upon a single scroll, was prepared in two parts or volumes. Many New Testament scholars, desiring to show the connection between the Third Gospel and The Acts, refer to Luke's history of Christianity as *Luke-Acts.*

It has often been remarked that whereas the historic title of the book is *The Acts of the Apostles,* it might have been entitled with equal or even greater appropriateness *The Acts of the Holy Spirit.* In his Gospel Luke gives many indications of his absorbed interest in the work of the Holy Spirit; in The Acts he gives to the work of the Holy Spirit a place of central importance. All that the apostles achieved, they achieved through the power of the Holy Spirit imparted to

3 Acts 1:1-5; cf. Luke 1:1-4.

them. They were, in truth, those "on whom the Spirit came." They were Spirit-filled, Spirit-impelled, and Spirit-empowered. As we read The Acts, therefore, we should be on the watch for these references to the Holy Spirit, not alone for the sake of a better understanding of the Spirit's work, but also for the sake of learning how we may gain divine direction and strength for our daily lives.

## The Author

As has been stated already, Luke-Acts was written by Luke. This is the unvarying tradition which has come down to us from antiquity. There is no sufficient reason for holding that Luke-Acts was published anonymously. Dibelius, arguing from the fact that Luke's work follows the pattern of all Greek historical writings, is confident that the manuscript originally bore the name of Luke, its author.[4] Indeed, the earliest reference to the authorship of The Acts (in the Muratorian Fragment, *circa* A.D. 170-200) asserts that the book was "compiled in order by Luke the physician." Irenaeus, Tertullian, and Clement of Alexandria likewise attribute the book to Luke. These early church fathers must have possessed some convincing evidence that Luke-Acts had come from Luke's pen, otherwise it is difficult to see why they should have credited him with being the author of so large and significant a work.

Luke was not one of the early followers of Jesus. Had it not been for his literary labors, he would have remained a little-known and relatively unimportant figure. His name Luke (or Lucas) is a shortened form of Lucanus, and like all such diminutives implies an intimate and friendly relationship. Luke was a Greek, not a Jew. This is indicated in Colossians 4:10-14, where he is not listed with those "who are of the circumcision," i.e., who are Jews; but is mentioned separately, and therefore as a Gentile.

Luke's name does not appear anywhere in the Third Gospel; neither does it appear in The Acts. In his writing, Luke modestly chose to keep himself in the background. He was

---

[4] Martin Dibelius, in *A Fresh Approach to the New Testament and Early Christian Literature* (Chas. Scribner's Sons, 1936), p. 64.

content if his words served to glorify Jesus Christ. In fact, Luke is mentioned by name in the New Testament only three times. All three of these references occur in epistles written by Paul. Luke is spoken of in Colossians 4:14; in Philemon 24; and in 2 Timothy 4:11. In the first of these passages Paul reveals his warm affection for Luke. He characterizes him as "the beloved physician." In Philemon 24 Paul includes Luke (Lucas) in a brief list of his "fellow-labourers." It was during his first Roman imprisonment that Paul wrote his letter to the Christians in Colosse and his more personal letter to Philemon, who was of that same city. Luke, as we see, was with Paul at that time. When Paul wrote his second letter to Timothy, he again was a prisoner in Rome. There is infinite pathos in Paul's words: "Only Luke is with me." Faithful Luke! Paul's devoted companion, standing by him to the end!

In The Acts there are four passages which Luke appears to have quoted from a travel diary—his own travel diary, so we believe, because the literary style of these passages matches perfectly Luke's own style of writing. They are Acts 16:10-18; 20:5-16; 21:1-18; and 27:1—28:16. These are the "we-sections" which have been so much discussed by scholars. Whereas Luke hitherto consistently had written of Paul and his companions in the third person, in these passages he makes an abrupt change in the pronouns. "They" becomes "we," "them" becomes "us," and "their" becomes "our." Some scholars have suggested that the author (or compiler) of The Acts, in these instances, quoted some early source which he had discovered, and that he overlooked the fact that in his source the pronouns were in the first person. Luke was too careful of his literary style to be guilty of any such blunder. The most natural explanation is that on the occasions described in these passages Luke personally was present. He participated in those events, and, therefore, rightly said "we."

These "we-sections" show that Luke joined Paul when Paul, on his second missionary journey, reached Troas. Luke accompanied Paul from Troas to Philippi in Macedonia. They show that Luke rejoined Paul, when Paul, on his third missionary journey, came again to Philippi. Luke then went with Paul up to Jerusalem. It appears that Luke remained in

Palestine during the two years that Paul was imprisoned in Caesarea. It was at that time, no doubt, that Luke gathered his material concerning the life of Christ and the beginnings of the Christian movement—the material which he employed to such good advantage when writing his Gospel and the early chapters of The Acts. When Paul was taken as a prisoner to Rome, Luke journeyed with him and shared the hardships of that voyage. All that we learn from these "we-sections" is in complete harmony with the references to Luke in Paul's letters.

Luke, then, was a Greek, a Gentile. He was a physician. His home was in Macedonia. He already was a Christian when he met Paul, or he became a Christian as a result of that meeting. Thereafter, he was Paul's travel companion. He was with Paul during both of Paul's imprisonments in Rome. Anything more than this is only conjecture. It has been suggested that he was one of the Seventy sent out by Jesus [5]; that he was one of the Greeks who came to Philip with the request, "Sir, we would see Jesus" [6]; and that he was the un-named companion of Cleopas on the walk to Emmaus. [7] All of these suggestions are contradicted by Luke 1:1-4. In that passage (it should be read in one of the modern translations), Luke states that he himself was not an eyewitness of the events in the life of Christ, but that he received his information concerning those events from men who had been eyewitnesses of them. The idea that Luke was a painter as well as a physician has no support other than a very dubious tradition.

There is, however, another way of becoming acquainted with Luke. It is through his writings. Buffon's famous utterance is true: *Le style est l'homme meme* ("The style is the man himself"). Luke's writings show that he had a profound regard for the truth. They show that he possessed broad sympathies and was moved by humanitarian impulses. Luke's Christianity was devoid of bigotry and provincialism.

[5] Luke 10:1-24.

[6] John 12:20-23.

[7] Luke 24:13-35.

## The Purpose

Something of the purpose which Luke had in writing Luke-Acts has already been indicated. Many writings of greater or lesser reliability had appeared.[8] Luke undertook the larger and more difficult task of writing a comprehensive and really trustworthy history of Christianity. He went to the original sources. He examined the records. He questioned those who had been eyewitnesses. He set down the facts only after he had fully verified them. He arranged his material in accordance with a well-considered plan. In volume 1 he related the beginnings of Christianity; in volume 2 he told how Christianity had been spread throughout the Roman Empire. He told his story in an interesting fashion. His narrative is animated, often exciting. He did not preach, but was content to let the facts speak for themselves.

Luke wrote his history in Greek, the literary language. He could do this easily, because Greek was his native tongue. He aimed, by his book, to commend Christianity to all thoughtful readers throughout the Greek-speaking world. He was at pains to show that the Christian movement, far from being in any sense anarchistic, was humane and peace-promoting. Christianity was a religion of reconciliation with God, of morality, brotherhood, and love. Pilate, the Roman procurator, had found no fault in Christ. Christ's followers—Peter and John, Paul and Silas, and many others—had been brought before Roman governors and magistrates, and always they had been found free of any conspiracy against the Emperor.

It should be kept in mind that the dedication to Theophilus, with which the Gospel opens, is in reality the dedication of the entire two-volume work. The briefer dedication to Theophilus at the beginning of The Acts merely repeats and reaffirms the original dedication. The Acts then picks up the story from the precise point where the Gospel leaves off. All that is said, therefore, in the dedication of the Gospel, both as to the purpose in Luke's mind and as to the historical

8 Luke 1:1-4.

method which Luke employed, applies with equal force to The Acts.

Because Luke-Acts comes to a close with Paul a prisoner in Rome and awaiting trial, some have wondered if Luke, being so intimate a friend, may not have written this work in the hope that it might secure Paul's release. Theophilus evidently was a man of importance, one who could intercede with the Emperor on Paul's behalf. Whether or not this idea is tenable depends, in part, upon the date when Luke-Acts was written. It may be well, therefore, to give attention next to the date of Luke's writing.

## The Date

If Luke wrote with Paul's forthcoming trial in mind, Luke-Acts cannot be dated any later than A.D. 61,[9] For in that year Paul's first Roman imprisonment came to an end. This view, of course, necessitates holding that the Gospel of Mark was written some years prior to A.D. 61, for Luke drew upon Mark's Gospel when writing his own. In support of this early date for Luke-Acts, it may be argued that Luke would have reported the outcome of Paul's trial if the trial already had been held. If Luke-Acts was not written until after Paul's martyrdom, it is surprising, to say the least, that Luke gives no account of it.

It is possible, of course, that Luke had come to the end of his second scroll, and that he planned to write a third scroll in which he would tell of Paul's release from prison, his later missionary journeys, and finally his martyrdom. The contemplated third volume may never have been completed, or, if completed, may have become lost almost immediately. If we here are dealing with a part of a three-volume work, the date would be some years later.

Although no less a scholar than Harnack has argued that The Acts was written during the lifetime of Paul,[10] many

[9] On this date, and other dates appearing hereafter, see in the Appendix "A Chronology for The Acts."

[10] Adolf Harnack, in *Date of The Acts and the Synoptic Gospels*, trans. J. R. Wilkinson (Putnam, 1911) , pp. 91, 124, 162.

recent scholars hold to a later date. The dates proposed range from A.D. 75 to 95. These writers believe that Luke-Acts, on close reading, shows evidence that its author possessed knowledge of certain later happenings, such as Paul's martyrdom, the destruction of Jerusalem, and developments in church organization and polity. Some argue that The Acts is a relatively late compilation of earlier sources. Dr. Goodspeed lists fifteen arguments for dating the book as late as A.D. 90. He feels that the cumulative force of these fifteen arguments is convincing.[11] He explains the fact that The Acts ends with Paul a prisoner in Rome by saying that Luke had fully accomplished his purpose when he had related how the gospel had been carried to Rome, the capital of the world.

Perhaps this question of date cannot be settled finally at this time. An early date for The Acts (e.g., A.D. 61) seems to be coming back in favor. In support of an early date is the fact that The Acts contains no references to Paul's letters. We know that shortly after Paul's death they were collected, copied, and widely circulated. If Luke-Acts was not written until the late decades of the first century, it is difficult to understand why Luke made no use of them. They contain much material that he could have used to fill in details of his narrative. Luke must have known that Paul had written letters to various churches, but these letters apparently had not yet gained more than a local circulation. It remained for later Christian leaders to recognize the historical and spiritual importance of the Pauline letters.

## The History

Inasmuch as Luke has been called a historian and his writing a history, it is in order to mention here the historical dependability which characterizes The Acts. There is today an abundance of documentary and archaeological evidence in support of Luke's statements. Wallace and Dana give the following excellent summary of the situation:

"Recent archeological discoveries have confirmed more

11 Edgar J. Goodspeed, in *An Introduction to the New Testament* (University of Chicago Press, 1937), pp. 191-197.

and more the accuracy of the writer of Acts. Even in minute details, he has been proven to be correct. He describes accurately the social customs of the various peoples mentioned; the rapidly changing civil affairs of Jews, Greeks, and Romans; the territorial divisions and the locations of cities; the peculiar names and titles of different officers in widely distributed districts and towns; and many other particulars requiring accurate knowledge and conscientious care in recording. It is hardly conceivable that a writer so accurate in the smallest details could have been either careless or unfair in the truth of events narrated as historical fact. That his book reveals a practical religious aim and discloses artistic literary ability should not impeach the trustworthiness of the writer as a historian. It is just this that renders him not merely a chronicler but truly a historian." [12]

[12] J. Sherman Wallace and H. E. Dana, in *The New Testament: An Introductory Study*, p. 70. Copyright, The Judson Press, 1942.

CHAPTER 2

# The Commission and the Promise

ACTS 1:1-26

*L* UKE, in his first volume (his Gospel), had told only of the life and work of Jesus Christ. Jesus' birth, ministry, crucifixion, and resurrection were the historic events which had initiated and inspired the Christian movement. That men had hope of eternal life by reason of those verifiable facts of history was the "good news" which the apostles had been heralding abroad.

Being a skillful writer, Luke had concluded his Gospel at a point which left the reader eager to learn what followed. The risen Christ had appeared to His disciples on numerous occasions. He had given them a Great Commission: "that repentance and remission of sins should be preached in his name among all nations, beginning at Jerusalem." [1] And He had made them a Great Promise: that they should receive in their lives a new power from God. He had said: "Behold, I send the promise of my Father upon you: but tarry ye in the city of Jerusalem, until ye be endued with power from on high." [2] This enduement with spiritual power would fortify the apostles against the dark days which lay ahead, and would enable them to spread the "good news" far beyond the boundaries of Judea and Galilee. It was clear that another glorious chapter was to follow.

[1] Luke 24:47. Cf. Mark 16:16; Matt. 28:18-20.

[2] Luke 24:49. Note, in Matt. 28:18, that Jesus possessed "all power." The power was His to bestow upon whom He would. Note, in Mark 16:17-18, the mention of "signs" which would indicate that the new power had been received.

11

In his second volume (The Acts), Luke gives his account of the early days of the Christian church. After a brief dedication which matches the dedication of his Gospel, he takes up the story at the point where his Gospel had left off. In his introduction to The Acts (Acts 1:1-14) there is only so much recapitulation of events recorded in the Gospel as will insure that the reader knows of the missionary commission which the Lord gave His followers and of His promise to them of the spiritual power they would need. The Acts then tells how that promised power (the Holy Spirit) was bestowed upon the disciples; how the Christian church, under the Holy Spirit's direction, gradually took shape; and how the gospel, through the witnessing of the apostles and the many unnamed followers of the Lord, was spread throughout the world of that day. In the first twelve chapters of The Acts the apostle Peter is the most prominent figure; in the later chapters the apostle Paul comes to the fore. We are told how Paul, despite persecution, carried the gospel from city to city, from the continent of Asia to the continent of Europe, and finally to the imperial city of Rome, where the story ends.

We now have before us the two themes which will hold our major and continuing interest throughout this study; namely, the work of the Holy Spirit and the missionary work of the churches. Until the Holy Spirit has done His quickening (vitalizing, regenerating) work in our hearts, we possess no true life. Furthermore, apart from the Holy Spirit's indwelling presence and ever-available help, our lives are doomed to frustration, our greatest efforts prove futile. Christianity is a missionary religion. With such an origin and history, it could not be otherwise. These two themes, the Spirit's power and the Christian mission, are not to be regarded as foreign to each other. In their deeper meanings, they are inseparable. Hence, we see the force of what two great scholars have said concerning The Acts. One of them (Jülicher) gave as the theme of the book, "the history of the power of God in the apostles"; the other (Harnack) said that the book tells of "the power of the Spirit of Jesus in the apostles, manifested most impressively in the expansion of the gospel."

## The Dedication (Acts 1:1-5)

Luke dedicated The Acts, as he had dedicated his Gospel, to Theophilus, of whom we know nothing beyond what the Scriptures tell us here and in Luke 1:1-4. The name Theophilus, by derivation, yields a beautiful meaning: either "Friend of God" or "Beloved of God"; but since the name was of common occurrence in that day, this meaning is not a sufficient reason for doubting that a real person was addressed. That Luke addressed Theophilus as "most excellent" [3] implies that he was a person of rank, probably a Roman nobleman. But Luke-Acts, though addressed to Theophilus in particular, was meant to have a wider reading. It is, in reality, a masterly defense of Christianity before the eyes of the entire civilized world.

In his dedication Luke makes reference to his "former treatise." [4] He summarizes the contents of that volume by saying that it recounted "all that Jesus began both to do and to teach, until the day in which he was taken up." Two words in that expression, "began" and "until," deserve attention. Both words emphasize the fact that what had been told already was by no means the end of the story. The reader of The Acts would learn of many more wonderful works, wonderful works done through the power of the risen and ascended Christ, now come to dwell, in a new manner, in the hearts of His devoted followers.[5]

3 In Luke 1:3. Two Roman governors are so addressed, Felix (in Acts 23:26 and 24:3) and Festus (in Acts 26:25).

4 "Former treatise" is, literally, "first treatise." But since the word "first," then as now, was often used loosely and when only two objects were in mind, its occurrence here is not proof that a third volume was contemplated. However, it certainly does not preclude a projected third volume, as a correct use of the Greek word for "former" would have done.

5 Luke had made it clear that the Spirit of the Lord had been upon Jesus, and also had been in all that Jesus had done and said (Luke 3:22; 4:1; 4:18-19, etc.). The mention of the Holy Spirit in the dedication of The Acts is, in a sense, an announcement of the book's theme. For clear theological thinking, the Second and the Third Persons of the Trinity must be distinguished; but inasmuch as Christ's spirit was the Holy

There was one matter of which Luke would remind the reader, for unless it were remembered, what was to follow would not be fully understood. It was that Jesus (before He ascended into heaven and during that forty-day period when, by His appearances to His disciples, He gave them so "many infallible proofs" of His resurrection) had bidden His disciples to remain in Jerusalem until a promise which the heavenly Father had made to them had been fulfilled. They were to receive such a baptism, so it had been promised, as the world had never seen before. They were to be baptized with (literally, in) the Holy Spirit.[6] That baptism was to come upon them before many days had passed.

## The Question about the Kingdom (Acts 1:6-8)

When Jesus spoke of this promise to the disciples (it was on an occasion when the entire company of disciples was present), they asked Him if He meant that the time was at hand when the kingdom of Israel would be re-established. That they should ask such a question shows that they were still thinking of a temporal kingdom. They had not yet grasped the full significance of what He had taught respecting the spiritual nature of God's reign.

Jesus declined to answer the question. He did not wish them to be unduly concerned about "times" and "seasons." The Father would bring all things to pass in full accordance with His own will. Let the disciples substitute for curiosity a wholehearted devotion to the missionary task committed to them. Let them wait until they were filled with the Holy Spirit. Then, when they were properly and adequately em-

Spirit, the terms Spirit of Jesus and Holy Spirit are practically synonymous. If Jesus could say, "I and my Father are one" (John 10:30), and also, "If a man love me, he will keep my words: and my Father will love him, and we will come unto him, and make our abode with him" (John 14:23), it behooves us not to draw too sharp a distinction between the presence of the Holy Spirit in the believer's heart and the presence there of the risen, ever-living, and indwelling Christ.

6 John the Baptist had foreseen this baptism in the Holy Spirit, a baptism far more wonderful than the baptism which he himself had administered. See Luke 3:16.

powered for Christian service, let them go forth and bear witness to Christ "in Jerusalem, and in all Judea, and in Samaria, and unto the uttermost part of the earth."

Note the ever-widening character of the Christian mission. The disciples, in their witness-bearing, were to go out from Jerusalem, where the Christian movement had had its beginnings, into Judea, the surrounding countryside; then into Samaria, where they would encounter men of a different race; and, finally, out into the vast Gentile world, out to the uttermost part of the earth. This world-embracing task was so vast and so difficult that even stout-hearted men would be tempted to say, "Impossible"; but the disciples, and those who would follow after them, were to receive the help which they would need. They would be given power, spiritual power, the power of the Holy Spirit. How much that would mean, they could know only after their hearts had been filled with the Spirit.

## The Ascension of Our Lord (Acts 1:9-12)

Luke had told in his Gospel of Jesus' ascension into heaven.[7] That account necessarily had been brief, for whereas that event marked the close of Jesus' earthly ministry, it also prepared the way for the new era. The account of the ascension, logically, belonged in The Acts fully as much as in the Gospel. Luke, accordingly, gives in this first chapter of The Acts a somewhat fuller account of it.

The ascension occurred shortly after Jesus had promised power to His disciples, and when they were gathered with Him upon the Mount of Olives. Luke's simple, but convincing, statement tells us all that we really need to know: "While they beheld, he was taken up; and a cloud received him out of their sight."

Our Lord's resurrection had been announced by heavenly messengers; and, similarly, here at the ascension two angelic beings are seen. They inform the disciples that they are to go into the city, but that their going need not be in sorrow, for Jesus would return. He would return from heaven in the same manner that they had seen Him ascend into heaven.

7 Luke 24:50-53.

This hope of the Lord's return filled the hearts of the disciples with joy,[8] and it has had an inspiring and sanctifying influence upon the lives of believers throughout all the centuries since that day.

This concludes the introduction to The Acts. When we consider this introduction as a whole, and especially when we consider it in the light of the purpose of The Acts, it becomes evident that Luke would have us know that we, as followers of Christ, have been given a mission, and also have been promised the spiritual help which we need for the discharge of it. With the task so clearly stated and with the help promised so adequate, we surely are without excuse if we forget the Christian mission or fail to give ourselves wholeheartedly to it.

## The Disciples in the Upper Room (Acts 1:13-26)

Following their Lord's ascension, the disciples returned to Jerusalem. Amazed by what they had seen, and puzzled, no doubt, by what they had heard, they made their way to the upper room which had become their meeting-place. It apparently was that same upper room in which Jesus had led them in the observance of the Passover feast and in which He had instituted the Lord's Supper.[9]

Acts 1:13 is of interest because of its list of the apostles. This list may be compared with the lists given in Matthew 10:2-4; Mark 3:16-19; and Luke 6:14-16. Peter, as always, is mentioned first. Judas, the brother of James, is not to be confused with Judas Iscariot, the betrayer of our Lord, who already had gone to his horrible death. With the eleven apostles, and sharing with them both in their worship in the upper room and in their worship in the Temple,[10] were Mary the mother of Jesus, Jesus' "brethren," [11] and a number of faithful women. [12] Take note that Jesus' "brethren" were present. We conclude that Jesus' resurrection and His sub-

8 Luke 24:52.

9 Luke 22:7-20.

10 Luke 24:53; Acts 2:46.

11 Matt. 12:46-50; 13:54-56.

12 Luke 23:49.

sequent appearances had at last dispelled their doubts and convinced them of His messiahship. They have now joined themselves wholeheartedly with the believers.

The remaining verses of this chapter need not detain us long. Peter, addressing the entire Christian company (one hundred and twenty were present), pointed out that Judas' betrayal of Christ had been in accordance with what the Holy Spirit had declared through the Scriptures. The Davidic passage to which Peter referred is Psalm 41:9. In citing this verse, Peter was but echoing our Lord's own words as recorded in John 13:18.

Peter then proposed that they choose someone to take Judas' place, in order that the apostolic group of twelve might again be complete. The following qualifications were laid down. The person to be chosen was to be one who had been a follower of Jesus, and who therefore possessed personal knowledge of all that had taken place from the time of Jesus' baptism by John to the time of Jesus' ascension. Above all, he was to be one who could bear testimony to Jesus' resurrection. Now observe the democratic procedure which was followed. After due consideration, two names were placed in nomination. The first was that of Joseph Justus (or Joseph the Just), also called Barsabas (that is, son of Sabas); the other was that of Matthias. So far as could be humanly judged, both of these men were qualified to be apostles. A choice had to be made between them, and here the group wisely resorted to prayer. They prayed that their choice might be God's choice. Whether they then cast their ballots or cast lots is not wholly clear; but however it was, Matthias was chosen. It has been remarked that the election was of combined human and divine wisdom; that the assembly selected two, and of these two God selected one. Thereafter, Matthias was numbered with the eleven apostles.

All this, however, was but a human provision, a prudent looking forward to the future, a serious-minded preparation for the missionary task which the apostles knew lay ahead of them. The promised empowering of the Holy Spirit was soon to be received. Thus does God recognize and bless our human efforts at his service.

CHAPTER 3

# The Gift of the Holy Spirit

ACTS 2:1-41

JESUS' ascension took place on the fortieth day following
His resurrection. Ten days later came the Jewish feast of
Pentecost. On that feast day (a Sunday), the spiritual power
which Jesus had promised to His disciples was bestowed upon
them. Because this gift of the Holy Spirit is of epochal significance, we shall give it our principal attention in this chapter.

*The Holy Spirit Bestowed (Acts 2:1-3)*

Pentecost was the second of the three chief Mosaic festivals,
the Passover being the first and the feast of Tabernacles being
the third. It was observed on the fiftieth day following the
second day (the sabbath) of the Passover.[1] Originally, it celebrated the completion of the grain harvest. Whereas the Jews
in celebrating the Passover expressed their gratitude for their
deliverance from bondage, in celebrating Pentecost they expressed their gratitude for their own land and for the yield
of their fields.[2] It was, therefore, a sacred and joyous occasion, a wholly appropriate time for the spiritually exhilarat-
ing event which was to occur. In yet another respect we see

---

[1] "Pentecost" is derived from the Greek name of the feast, *pentecostos*
meaning fiftieth. The Hebrews called it the feast of weeks, because it
came seven weeks (a "week" of weeks) after the Passover.

[2] For the origin of Pentecost and for its Old Testament observance,
see Ex. 23:14-17; 34:22; and Deut. 16:9-12. But keep in mind that these
two ancient Jewish feasts have now taken on a new and Christian significance. The Passover season was the time of our Lord's crucifixion and
resurrection; Pentecost, the time of the bestowal of the Holy Spirit.

the wisdom of the divine timing. Pentecost, that year as always, had brought to Jerusalem a great many devout Jews from both near-by and more distant lands. These religious pilgrims, on returning to their homes, would herald far and wide the happenings of that day.

The coming of the day of Pentecost found the disciples "all together in one place."[3] They were assembled, not because they had been led to expect some unusual occurrence on that special day, but because they had been remaining together all the while in Jerusalem, in careful obedience to the charge which Jesus had laid upon them.[4] These days of waiting, as we have learned, had not been spent in idleness, but in "prayer and supplication."[5] There is a sense, therefore, in which it may be truthfully said that the Holy Spirit came upon the apostles in answer to their prayers. We may well believe that there would have been no outpouring of the Holy Spirit if they had failed to pray, or if they had been less faithful in their obedience to Christ's commandment.

The "one place" where they were all assembled, apparently, was that upper room which they had made their headquarters. Because of the statement that they worshiped daily in the Temple, because of the large number of disciples, and because of the size of the crowd which quickly assembled, some scholars have supposed that the disciples were worshiping at the time in one of the courts or chambers of the Temple. Artists frequently have so depicted the scene. But this transfer of locale from the upper room to the Temple is unnecessary. The miracle, in the first instance, may have been experienced only by the apostles. The crowd to which Peter preached may have assembled in the street before the house.

On this day of Pentecost, then, and in the familiar place where they had been praying, the bestowal of the Holy Spirit took place. A tremendous spiritual energy was suddenly manifested. In fulfillment of Jesus' promise, the Holy Spirit came upon the disciples. The Spirit came in a manner which the disciples could hear, see, and feel. There was a roar, like that

3 Acts 2:1, RSV.
4 Acts 1:4.
5 Acts 1:14.

of a mighty blast of wind, and there were tongues, like flames of fire, that rested upon the heads of the apostles. As the Holy Spirit took possession of them, they felt themselves shaken, exalted, and empowered.

Luke, in his account, succeeds in conveying to us something of the excitement of the moment. He supplies us with all of the essential details, and he does so in a manner which displays his profound insight into the supernal truth. Accordingly, let us look closely at his carefully chosen words.

It will be observed at once that Luke does not attempt a description of the Holy Spirit. Language is not equal to the task of describing Deity. He limits himself to telling what the *effect* of the Spirit's coming was upon the apostles; he records only those things which they heard, saw, and experienced. In doing so, he never once fails to distinguish between that which is no more than material substance and that which is in essence wholly spiritual. The apostles heard a sound, a sound which registered not only upon their ears but also in their deepest awareness. This sound resembled that of "a rushing mighty wind," but it was no earthly wind that they heard. This was the Wind of Heaven, the Breath of God, the Holy Spirit; the Holy Spirit was blowing upon them, was catching them up, was sweeping them along, was irresistibly impelling them.[6] At the same time that they heard this sound, their eyes reported a sensation of light, such as is caused by an intense fire. Though it was no earthly fire, this that they beheld resembled fire in yet another respect. It leaped up in that peculiar way which flames have. It spread as fire spreads, until these "cloven tongues like as of fire" were resting upon all of them. This was the Fire of Heaven, the Flame of God, the Holy Spirit; the Holy Spirit, consuming, yet purifying, and being communicated to first one and then another until all of the apostles were afire with a new spirit and zeal.[7]

All this—so Luke would have us understand—was nothing less than an experience of the presence and power of God

[6] On the Holy Spirit as the impelling force in the life of Jesus, note the uncommonly strong expression in Mark 1:12: "And immediately the spirit driveth him into the wilderness."

[7] On the Holy Spirit as a purifying fire, see Isa. 6:6-7.

Himself. All who knew aught of the Old Testament Scriptures would recognize this heavenly Wind and this heavenly Fire as signs of God's presence. Beyond such analogies, such similarities without identity, our language cannot go with respect to God.[8] But Luke's words, despite this human limitation, are fully sufficient to warn us against the mistake of thinking that what took place within the apostles was nothing more than a humanly contrived marshaling of enthusiasm and courage. This new power which the apostles felt within themselves had not been a growth or slow accumulation; it had come upon them suddenly. Furthermore, it had come to them from without. It was not a product of their subconscious minds, for a man's subconsciousness, however deeply it may be buried, is still a part of the man himself. This was something "wholly other." This was God!

Now, it may well be that this experience (if we may borrow the terms of the psychologists for a moment) came to each apostle through the portal of his subliminal self, for is not that the door at which the patient Christ is ever knocking?[9] Certainly, the divine power took hold of the apostles at the point of their deepest, truest being. Where else could God have approached them so directly and compellingly? Where else can the Divine Spirit and the human spirit meet? But the spiritual experience—let it be repeated—was not self-generated. Its initiation was in the purpose of God, whose mercy always precedes man's supplication [10]; and its manifestation took the form of a "divine invasion" of the human personality—one of those gracious revelations and blessings which man cannot account for, but which nevertheless move him to exclaim, "This is wholly of the goodness and mercy of God!"

Because all this, for the apostles, was fundamentally an inner experience and not a matter primarily of external signs and wonders, it had far more meaning for them, and for all subsequent generations of believers, than it would have had otherwise. Signs and wonders, for a time, are an occasion for

8 On wind and fire in association with the presence of God, see Ex. 13:21; 19:18; 1 Kings 19:11-12; etc.

9 Rev. 3:20.

10 1 John 4:19.

astonishment. Then they are stored away upon that mental shelf to which all of life's unexplained mysteries are relegated. Soon thereafter they are forgotten. But being in the realm of religious mysticism, the descent of the Holy Spirit has kinship with all the other direct experiences of the presence of God which the saints of all ages have reported to us.

## The Speaking in Tongues (Acts 2:4-13)

Luke's restrained statement is: "They were all filled with the Holy Ghost, and began to speak with other tongues, as the Spirit gave them utterance." The Spirit whom God had bestowed upon the apostles immediately produced in them an overmastering desire to testify to "the wonderful works of God." Spirit-inspired testimony is concerned always with the goodness of God, especially as it is revealed in Jesus Christ.[11] Whereas the apostles previously had lacked confidence and courage, they now began to bear witness to Christ with great joy and boldness.

The Holy Spirit who had descended upon the apostles had come upon them in order to be their Helper. When the apostles began their witnessing, they discovered, to their amazement, that one result of their having been filled with the Holy Spirit was that they were able, on this occasion at least, to speak in languages other than their customary Aramaic.[12] The purpose of the miracle is evident. The apostles were enabled by it to bear effective testimony to the thousands of Jews and proselytes who had come from districts where other languages were spoken, and who were then in Jerusalem for the observance of the feast.

The sound of all this[13]—the sound, that is, of the apostles'

---

[11] John 15:26.

[12] Luke's expression, "with other tongues" (especially in this context), will not admit of any other interpretation. That the reference is to other languages is established by vss. 6-8.

[13] The expression, "when this was noised abroad," which appears in vs. 6 of KJV, is an inaccurate translation which later versions have corrected. Doubtless word of this event did spread quickly, but it was the noise which, in the first instance, attracted the crowd.

cries of excitement, exultation, praise, and testimony—was heard outside the house, and a curious crowd quickly gathered. The many different lands from which these sojourners in Jerusalem had come make an impressive list. Even more impressive is the effect which this Spirit-inspired testimony had upon these men from the far parts of the world. They heard these humble Galileans speaking other languages. They understood perfectly what they were saying. But even tongues inspired by the Holy Spirit avail nothing at all when men shut their ears and refuse to listen. Although most of the crowd recognized that a miracle had taken place, there were some who professed to believe that this earnest testifying by the apostles was nothing more than the deluded antics of drunken men.

Luke tells in The Acts of two other occasions on which Spirit-filled men spoke with other tongues. The passages are Acts 10:46 and 19:6, and they will receive attention in due course. It may be stated here, however, that we shall find in them only fading echoes of this first speaking with tongues. This leads us to wonder if this gift of tongues was not designed chiefly to meet the special situation on the day of Pentecost. Such speaking with tongues as took place later— in the church at Corinth, for example—was less edifying, because less understandable. The apostle Paul discusses this speaking in tongues in 1 Corinthians, chaps. 12-14. It is a gift of the Spirit, he says, but it is far from being the greatest of the Spirit's gifts. It is neither so useful, nor so much to be desired, as the Spirit's gift of love.

Before leaving this subject for the time being, it may not be unwarranted moralizing to point out that it was man's overweening ambition, displayed in the building of the tower of Babel, which produced the original confusion of tongues. Differences in language have led to misunderstandings and to strife between nations. The reception of the Holy Spirit into the heart, however, tends to overcome the language barrier and to unite men within the kingdom of God. Love finds ways of making its message known. The language of love, always and everywhere, is much the same.

*Peter's Sermon on the Day of Pentecost  (Acts 2:14-41)*

On this occasion, as on numerous others, Peter was the spokesman for the apostles. His sermon to the assembled throng should be read and pondered. It is called a sermon, but it is not so much a sermon in the present-day literary sense of that term as it is an earnest testimony to Jesus as the promised Messiah. In this respect, Peter's sermon is typical of all the sermons preached by the apostles. Apostolic preaching, today as then, bears witness to Jesus Christ.

Peter was addressing Jews who knew and believed the Old Testament Scriptures. He very wisely, therefore, based his argument upon them. Jesus had said of the Scriptures, "They are they which testify of me," [14] and Peter so employed them in his sermon. He showed his hearers that the things which had taken place were in fulfillment of them. If his hearers were sincere in their professed devotion to the Scriptures, logic would compel them to acknowledge that Jesus of Nazareth, whom they had rejected and crucified, was none other than the Christ, the Anointed of God. All Spirit-inspired preaching, in addition to being Christ honoring, is also based upon the Scriptures.

The three Old Testament passages which Peter effectively employed are Joel 2:28-32; Psalm 16:8-11; and Psalm 110:1.[15] The spiritual exhilaration and the ecstatic cries of the apostles were not due to drunkenness, as some had maliciously charged, but were the results of that outpouring of the Holy Spirit which the prophet Joel had declared would take place in connection with the coming of the day of the Lord. As for the resurrection of Jesus (that historic event which Peter's hearers were unwilling to believe, but to which all of the apostles bore witness [16]), had it not been prophesied by David in the Sixteenth Psalm? David, when he wrote of a resurrection, could not have had reference to himself, for, as everyone

[14] John 5:39.

[15] These passages are quoted, not from the Hebrew Scriptures on which our English Old Testament is based, but from the Septuagint, a very early translation of the Hebrew Scriptures into Greek. This fact explains the few and unimportant variations in wording.

[16] See especially vs. 32.

well knew, no resurrection had followed his death. The reference could only be to that Righteous One whom God had promised David to raise up from among his descendants. Jesus' resurrection and ascension to the right hand of God proved Him to be that Promised One, the Messiah, the One whom God had appointed to be Judge and Ruler over all. David, by the Holy Spirit, must have foreseen something of this, for in yet another Psalm he had written, "The Lord said unto my Lord, Sit thou on my right hand." [17] That is, "The Lord" (Yahweh, God) "said unto my Lord" (the Messiah, Jesus Christ), "Sit thou on my right hand" (the place of highest honor). In that he did not write "*the* Lord," but "*my* Lord," it was clear that David himself had made it a personal matter. He was laying his own crown at Jesus' feet.

Peter, with a Spirit-inspired directness and courage, concluded his sermon by charging his hearers, both as a nation and as individuals, with having crucified the Son of God. God, however, had raised up Jesus and had exalted Him above all. The truth of Peter's words filled many of his hearers with dismay. They saw the enormity of their guilt, and they besought Peter and the other apostles to tell them if there was any way by which they might escape the wrath of God. Peter's answer was brief, yet adequate. He told them that they needed to repent; that is to say, to have a change of mind with respect to sin. Whereas they had loved sin and sought it, they now needed resolutely to turn away from it and to endeavor to live righteously. They needed also to be "baptized in the name of Jesus Christ for the remission of sins."

Repentance, of itself, does not remove the guilt of sin; one's sins need to be forgiven by Jesus Christ. In being baptized, the repentant ones would be confessing Jesus Christ as their Saviour and Lord; they would be showing to all beholders that they were looking to Him for forgiveness of sins and for guidance and strength to live nobler lives in the future. They would also be identifying themselves as members of the Christian fellowship. If they were willing to do these things, Peter said, they might then count upon experiencing

[17] Peter no doubt recalled that Jesus once had used this passage to confute his critics. See Luke 20:41-44.

a work of grace in their hearts in accordance with God's invitation and promise. This work of grace would be a work of the Holy Spirit. They would receive the Holy Spirit's priceless gift of cleansing and moral renewal.

Now that we are hearing for the first time the preaching of an apostle, we shall do well to pause a moment that we may take the fullest possible account of what it was that Peter, freshly filled with the Spirit, preached on that day of Pentecost. What was the good news which he heralded? What was it that he announced? Can we distinguish his message (Greek, *kerygma*) from his thoughts about that message? Can we go behind the man—his personality, preaching style, and vocabulary—and discover the message which God had given to him and had charged him to deliver?

If we had only this one apostolic sermon we might find it difficult to differentiate the message itself from those accompanying expressions which were called forth by the special circumstances existing at that time. But when we compare Peter's sermon with Stephen's sermon and with Paul's sermons, as we shall have opportunity to do later, we discover that all the apostolic preaching had an identical theme. The striking resemblances between the sermons of Peter, Stephen, and Paul are not due to the fact that Luke had no knowledge of what these witnesses actually said, and therefore in writing of them was compelled to cast all their sermons in the mold of his own mind; the resemblances occur because all of these men felt called upon to deliver the same message. The message which they had in common and which they sought to deliver faithfully (we here attempt no complete definition) was this: that Jesus was the Christ, the Son of God; that He had been manifested, crucified, raised from the dead, and exalted to God's right hand; and that men, by repenting of their sins and believing on Him, can have forgiveness and eternal life.

Observe that this was not a preaching of the Mosaic law; neither was it a preaching, as we might have expected from the apostles, of that higher and more exacting standard of morality which Jesus had set forth in His Sermon on the Mount. It was an announcement of a way of salvation made

possible by a divine interposition in human affairs, seen in
certain events which had taken place in known and recorded
history, but which in their significance transcended all history. By reason of those historic, yet transcendent, events, and
only by reason of them, did men have hope of salvation.

This, then, was the message, the message to which the
Gospels (yet to be written) would give a fuller expression.
This was, and is, that "Word from the Beyond for our human
predicament." This is the Word which must be uttered, else
there is no true preaching at all. In the delivering of the
message, to be sure, there will be differences of emphasis,
even as we discern differences of emphasis in the four
Gospels. The manner of proclamation will vary in accordance with the circumstances and times, and in accordance
also with the hearers (whether they be Jews or Gentiles),
but always central in the herald's announcement will be the
fact that God has opened for man a way of salvation—a
way which cannot even be rightly discussed apart from Him
who by His incarnation, His death upon the cross, and His
glorious resurrection, made it possible. Of these events and
of these evidences of divine grace, we can only say: "This is
the Lord's doing; it is marvelous in our eyes." [18]

So much for Peter's sermon. To the apostles' great joy,
there were some three thousand who that day accepted Jesus
Christ. These three thousand were baptized, and the company
of believers thereby was greatly increased in number and in
influence. God had fulfilled His promise, the promise that
His Word, if faithfully preached, would not return unto Him
void.[19] Other blessed results of the bestowal of the Holy Spirit,
some of them mentioned in the closing verses of Acts 2, will
be considered in the next chapter.

18 Ps. 118:23.
19 Isa. 55:11.

CHAPTER 4

# The First Fruits of the Spirit

ACTS 2:42–4:22

*T*HE tree is known by his fruit." [1] The heaven-born sagac-
ity of this brief word uttered by our Lord searches our
hearts. It gives us an index to our true characters. It also
suggests to us an approach which we may profitably employ
in our quest for a fuller knowledge of the Holy Spirit. We
may take account of the "fruit" which the bestowal of the
Holy Spirit produced, first in the lives of the apostles, and
then in the lives of the other believers, now increased in number by the addition of the three thousand who had turned
to Jesus Christ following Peter's sermon on the day of Pentecost.

## The Christian Fellowship (Acts 2:42-47)

At the same time that the Holy Spirit was filling the hearts
of the believers with joy and confidence, and impelling them
to bear glad testimony to Jesus Christ, the Spirit was drawing
these believers together and uniting them in a unique Christian fellowship. All the believers, so Luke informs us, "continued stedfastly in the apostles' doctrine and fellowship, and
in breaking of bread, and in prayers."

The four parts of this statement invite separate attention.
They are the more important because they characterize the
situation not on that day only, but throughout the weeks and
months that followed. The new believers, naturally, wished
to learn more about the Christ to whom they were indebted

1 Matt. 12:33; Luke 6:44.

28

for their salvation, and they asked the apostles to instruct them. The apostles, accordingly, told them of Christ's ministry, death, and resurrection; and they made clear to them the kind of life which Christ demands of all His followers. In this passage the word "doctrine" means no more than instruction. The systematizing of thought, the formulation of a consistent theology, the propagation of the historic dogmas—all of that came later in the stream of Christian history.

The word "fellowship" reflects a growing sense of togetherness and of belonging. The converts were received as additions to, as members of, the existing Christian group. They, like the original members, accepted the apostles as their leaders. Jesus, when at Caesarea Philippi, had informed His disciples of His intention to bring into being the church.[2] Now, here in Jerusalem, under the Spirit's promptings, we see the church beginning to take shape. Prior to the giving of the Holy Spirit, the church could not assume its proper pattern; until its members were actuated by the Holy Spirit, it could not display its most distinctive characteristics.

These early believers broke bread together. Verse 46 adds that they did so "from house to house." The reasons are obvious. No one dwelling could now contain the whole company of believers. Besides, it was only fair that the different families should take turns in preparing and serving these meals. The frequent occasions on which the believers thus ate together made for sociability, better understanding, and democracy. Luke says nothing expressly of any observance of the Lord's Supper, and we must be on our guard lest we read back into his account something which was not meant to be there. These were communal meals, not observance of the Lord's Supper as such. The Lord's Supper did not possess then, and should not possess now, the sacramental character which it later acquired. What is most probable is that the early believers, having in mind Christ's words spoken in the upper room, endeavored to make every meal together, every breaking of bread and drinking of the cup, a memorial of His death on their behalf.

Finally, they prayed together—at stated times, no doubt,

2 Matt. 16:18.

both in the Temple and in their own homes, and also whenever the Spirit moved them to pray, wherever they might be. These things they did, not occasionally, but regularly. They "continued stedfastly" in the doing of *all* of them. Thus, their fellowship together was strengthened.

Luke tells us something more: "All that believed were together, and had all things common; and sold their possessions and goods, and parted them to all men, as every man had need." This sharing of possessions for the sake of helping the less fortunate, like the fellowship which the believers had one with another, was prompted by the Holy Spirit. It is probable, of course, that these believers expected that Christ would return soon. Had not His return been promised by the angels? [3] And were there not many signs which indicated that judgment upon the nation was near at hand? The time of grace, during which the gospel might be preached and men might believe unto salvation, was therefore brief. Whatever they would do, they must do quickly. But this idea must not be overworked. It must not be implied, for example, that the believers shared their possessions because they thought that all money and property would soon be valueless due to the end of the age. So to account for their charity is to deprive them of all proper credit for one of their most Christian impulses. Their sharing was inspired by a Spirit-awakened feeling of brotherhood, of brotherhood with the needy equally with those of their own economic status.

This kind of living always commends itself to all beholders. The neighbors of these believers, seeing their "gladness and singleness of heart," their devotion to Christ, and their readiness to give help to the needy, were much impressed. Who is not impressed when the witness of unselfish living is added to the witness of the spoken word! In addition, the "many wonders and signs" done by the apostles[4]—what some of these wonders and signs were we shall learn presently—called forth a proper and salutary fear of God in the hearts of all be-

---

[3] Acts 1:10-11.

[4] This was not the first use by the apostles of divinely bestowed power. Jesus, in the course of his ministry, had instructed them and trained them in anticipation of this hour. See Luke 9:1-2, 10.

holders. The result was that the number of believers was increased yet more.

Luke's statement of this fact deserves notice: "The Lord added to the church daily such as should be saved." To be sure, the word for "church" does not appear in the oldest and best manuscripts: the more accurate translation being, "The Lord added to their number day by day those who were being saved" (RSV); but the idea of the church undoubtedly is implicit in the passage. Observe that here the church is defined only in relation to its spiritual nature and motivation. Only those who have experienced in their hearts the regenerating power of the Holy Spirit are qualified for membership in it; only those who "walk not after the flesh, but after the Spirit" [5] display the kind of life which is becoming in a church member. This being the nature of the true church, it becomes evident, as Luke implies, that only the Lord can add members to it. Only the Lord, by His redeeming grace, can qualify a person for membership in it. This does not mean that those already members of the church have no responsibility in the matter. What it does mean is that their responsibility lies within the area of witness-bearing. If they will bear witness to Christ faithfully by word and by life, the Lord will honor their witnessing by adding to their number those whom He has saved.

## The Healing of the Lame Man (Acts 3:1-26)

It was during those early days of the church's history, when the hearts of the believers were still fully surrendered to the power of the Holy Spirit, that the healing of the lame man occurred. Peter and John were going up to the Temple to pray, for they had not yet come to understand that the new revelation of God in Jesus Christ had fully superseded the Temple and its ordinances. It was mid-afternoon. At the entrance to the Temple's inner court, beside the Gate Beautiful,[6] they found a crippled beggar. In the practical help which

[5] Rom. 8:1.
[6] Josephus states that the Gate Beautiful was of Corinthian bronze adorned with plates of silver and gold.

they were able to give him—they healed his lameness and led him to believe on Jesus Christ—we see another gracious fruit of the Spirit.

How easy it would have been for the two apostles to have "passed by on the other side"! [7] How many that day had done that very thing, or at most had merely tossed the beggar some small coin! Peter, however, took a personal interest in the man, unprepossessing though his appearance was. He stopped to talk with him.

"Look on us," Peter said.

Hope sprang up in the beggar's heart, then as quickly faded, for Peter added: "Silver and gold have I none."

But wait! The apostle has not finished.

"What I have, that give I thee."

There was something that Peter could and did give to the lame man, something that all the money in the world could not have bought. He gave him healing for his lameness and such an acquaintance with the Lord Jesus Christ as filled his heart with thanksgiving and praise to God. The beggar had a religious experience as well as a physical cure, for it was the Spirit of Christ, working through Peter, that had enabled him to walk.

Where the Holy Spirit dwells, there we find sympathy for all who suffer or are in need; there we find giving to the limit of one's ability. Surely it does not need to be said that this incident furnishes no excuse for the failure to give money when money is needed and one is able to give it. We are but stewards of whatever wealth we may have, and "it is required in stewards, that a man be found faithful." [8] At the same time, this incident should remind us that even as man cannot live by bread alone, [9] so it is equally impossible for man to live by money alone. The poor need money, but even more they need our personal interest and help. How they would welcome some small evidence of our friendliness! How they would welcome an opportunity to become self-supporting once more! Perhaps there would not be so many empty pews if our

7 Luke 10:31-32.
8 1 Cor. 4:2.
9 Deut. 8:3; Luke 4:4.

churches were more mindful of the lame of every sort lying
at their very doors.

The healing of this man who had been a cripple from the
time of his birth, naturally, drew a crowd, and Peter used the
opportunity to preach Christ to those who assembled. Observe
how careful Peter was to make it clear that the miracle was
not the result of any magic power which he possessed. It had
been wrought by the power of the ever-living Christ, a divine
power for which he had been merely a channel.[10] Observe
also the resemblances between this sermon and the sermon
which he had preached on the day of Pentecost. Jesus, whom
Peter's hearers had denied and crucified, had been none other
than God's "Holy One and the Just"; i.e., their Messiah. In
proof of this was the fact that God had raised Him from the
dead. The terrible thing which they and their leaders had
done, had been done in ignorance. Yet it had been in accordance with their Scriptures, which had foretold that the
Son of God would be subjected to indignities and sufferings.
Accordingly, they were not left without hope. The divine call
to them—kindly, and at the same time peremptory—was: "Repent ye therefore, and be converted." Only by so doing would
they find forgiveness for their sins and enjoy the messianic
blessings, "the times of refreshing," which were to accompany
the return of Jesus Christ from heaven.

Peter, by quoting Deuteronomy 18:15-19, showed his hearers that Moses had foretold that God, in some later day, would
raise up a Prophet, to whose words they were to give implicit
obedience. Not only Moses, but all the other prophets, from
Samuel on, had given warning of the things which had come
to pass. Peter's hearers had participated in these events, for
they were the "children . . . of the covenant" which God of
old had made with their fathers. Here Peter quoted Genesis
12:3. It was in accordance with God's historic promise that
they had been the first to have the opportunity to believe on
God's Servant, Jesus. The result of this scriptural preaching

10 In keeping with the customary Jewish usage, the "name" of Christ
(vs. 16) is regarded as equivalent to Christ Himself. When the beggar
displayed "faith in his name," he was in reality laying hold upon Christ,
in all of Christ's regenerating and strengthening power.

was that many were converted. The total number of believers, augmented by three thousand on the day of Pentecost, now came to be about five thousand.[11]

Perhaps this is the place to inquire if there is not need today for a new emphasis upon preaching as a divinely appointed means of winning men to the Lord Jesus Christ. Peter had faithfully proclaimed God's Word, that Word of which God had said: "It shall not return unto me void, but it shall accomplish that which I please, and it shall prosper in the thing whereto I sent it." [12] God's faithfulness to His promise had been demonstrated both in the case of Peter's sermon on the day of Pentecost and in the case of his sermon in the Temple court. Some years later, Paul will write in a letter to the Romans: "Whosoever shall call upon the name of the Lord shall be saved." Then the Spirit will move him to add: "How then shall they call on him in whom they have not believed? and how shall they believe in him of whom they have not heard? and how shall they hear without a preacher? and how shall they preach, except they be sent?" [13]

## The Arrest of Peter and John (Acts 4:1-22)

Peter's preaching greatly angered the Temple authorities. They were particularly incensed because Peter had declared that God had raised Jesus from the dead. They had supposed that the crucifixion of Jesus would put an end to all talk about Him. Now He was being preached as having risen from the dead! The only thing that they could do was to have Peter and John arrested and thrown into prison. Since by that time it was late in the day, they arranged to put them on trial in the morning.

On the morrow, Peter and John were brought for trial before a distinguished, but unscrupulous, company. Annas and Caiaphas were present; Annas, the former high priest, and Caiaphas, the reigning high priest. The same Annas and

11 Acts 4:4.
12 Isa. 55:11.
13 Rom. 10:13-15.

Caiaphas who had condemned Jesus! Also John and Alexander, who probably were sons of Annas, and numerous other relatives of the high priest. Important Sadducees, all of them. These Jewish rulers did not deny that a miracle had occurred, but they did demand to know "by what power, or by what name" Peter had wrought it.

Peter knew that these men had the power, if not the legal right, to send him to his death, even as they had hurried Jesus to the cross. But through the help which the Holy Spirit gave him, Peter answered them truthfully and boldly.[14] The beggar owed his healing, Peter said, to Jesus of Nazareth, whom they had crucified, but whom God had raised from the dead. Peter's words, so it immediately appears, were not so much a defense of himself as they were a testimony to Jesus Christ. Jesus was none other than that Stone which they, the builders, had rejected, but which God had raised to the head of the corner, the place of highest honor. Peter here was quoting Psalm 118:22. In Jesus' name, and in His name only, was there salvation.

The high priests were now at a loss to know what to do. They took note of the fact that Peter and John were not learned men, yet they had spoken courageously and pointedly. Although they had not denied that they had been associated with Jesus, the hearing had not yielded any ground sufficient for holding them in prison. The man who had been lame from birth was present as a living proof that God had wrought a miracle through the apostles. Besides, the sympathy of the people seemed to be strongly with Peter and John.

So the captain of the Temple, the priests, and the Sadducees did the only thing they could think of to do under the circumstances. They ordered their prisoners released, but before freeing them, they threatened them with bodily harm if they continued asserting that Jesus was the Christ. They tried to browbeat the apostles into silence. Peter's reply showed a wisdom and fortitude born of the Holy Spirit:

14 Jesus had promised to give help to His disciples whenever, in consequence of their witnessing to Him, they found themselves in such a predicament. See Luke 12:11-12.

"Whether it be right in the sight of God to hearken unto you more than unto God, judge ye. For we cannot but speak the things which we have seen and heard."

This was but the first of the many persecutions which the early followers of Christ had to endure; and, sad to relate, there are still lands where the faithful preaching of Christ either is forbidden or else brings upon one's head a crushing weight of persecution. But truth cannot be put down by force. We are fortunate in that we live in a land where a man's religious convictions are treated with more respect. Or should we say, with more indifference? But this fact, strangely enough, has not resulted in any increase in Christian boldness. It seems rather to have lulled us into complacency. The Christian church cannot successfully meet the issues of the present day if it remains content with its present half-hearted allegiance to Christ.

## CHAPTER 5

# The Early Church and Its Life

## ACTS 4:23—5:16

THE Scripture passages now to be considered are like a row of windows, small but fully opened, through which we may catch glimpses of what went on within that first church in Jerusalem. Because what we see is typical of much that we cannot see, these brief scenes furnish us with a true index to the manner of life which characterized the early believers.

The organization of the church was still of the simplest sort. It recognized the apostles as its proper leaders. Its only ordinances were baptism and the Lord's Supper. Those who professed faith in Christ were baptized, and were received as members of the Christian fellowship. For their Scriptures these believers had the Old Testament. Being Jews, they continued their attendance upon the Temple ceremonies; and, until persecution made it no longer possible, they worshiped also in the synagogues. It appeared for a time that Christianity might become a sect within Judaism, but this was not to be. We speak of Christianity, but the followers of Christ had not yet come to be called Christians.[1] They spoke of themselves modestly as followers of "the way"[2]; that is to say, of the way of life which Christ had made known.

These early Christians were distinguished by a beautiful, Spirit-inspired brotherly love. They lived together harmoniously. They worked together happily. They sought to mani-

[1] Acts 11:26.
[2] Acts 9:2; 19:9, 23; 22:4.

fest the same Spirit that they had seen in Christ, and by that Spirit they were prompted to give help to those in need.

## The Church at Prayer (Acts 4:23-31)

When Peter and John were released from prison, after having been threatened with many dire things if they continued their preaching of Christ, they at once returned to their Christian brethren and reported to them all that had taken place. Probably the church was already assembled, having been engaged in prayer for their safe return. Peter's account moved the congregation to thanksgiving, and some member of it put into words the prayer which was in every heart. This prayer is of interest to us, not only because it gives us our first opportunity to hear the early church at prayer, but also because of its unusual character.

Their prayer is offered to God, whom they address as the Omnipotent Sovereign,[3] Maker of heaven and earth. This prayer, like the apostolic preaching, is scriptural in its mood, its background, and its phraseology. What had taken place brought to mind the opening verses of the Second Psalm. In them David had been moved by the Holy Spirit to write of the furious, but futile, wrath of the ungodly. All that such ungodly men could do had been foreseen, even that which they had done against God's anointed Servant,[4] Jesus the Messiah. Then when men had done their worst, God, by His sovereign power and with a single stroke, had brought to naught all their boasted might and all their cunning devices. The Psalm had received its supreme fulfillment right there in Jerusalem when Jesus had been brought for trial before Herod and Pilate, and when both Jews and Gentiles had clamored for, and participated in, His crucifixion. But God had over-

[3] The Greek word in vs. 24 (translated "Lord" in the KJV) is *despota,* and it should be rendered in some such manner as above.
[4] In vs. 27 read (with the ASV) "holy Servant," rather than "holy child." On the Messiah in the role of a Suffering Servant, see Isa. 53 and the other so-called Servant passages. Both Messiah (Hebrew) and Christ (Greek) mean The Anointed One. To say that Jesus is the Christ (or to put the names together, Jesus Christ) is equivalent to saying that Jesus is the One whom God anointed to be Saviour and King.

ruled the wrath of men by raising Jesus from the dead.

The release of Peter and John, accordingly, was but another striking evidence of God's ability to deliver His faithful servants. Since they who prayed were servants of a God of such wisdom, power, and love, they were well content to leave their lives and all earthly things to His ordering. They merely asked the Lord,[5] in view of the threats that had been made against the lives of Peter and John, to give those apostles such strength as would enable them to continue their ministry, preaching the Scriptures ("thy word") as fulfilled in Christ with all boldness, and ministering to the sick in the name of Jesus and with whatever healing power He might impart to them. It is noteworthy that they do not ask that any of them should be spared from persecution, but only that they may fulfill their mission at whatever cost. This was prayer in the spirit of their Master, who had said, "Not as I will, but as Thou wilt." [6]

We worship a prayer-hearing God. His answer to this prayer was immediate and evident to all. It came in the form of an experience resembling that on the day of Pentecost. That pentecostal experience, it will be recalled, likewise had occurred following prayer. This time, the "place was shaken" (cf. the "sound from heaven as of a rushing mighty wind" heard on the day of Pentecost); and once more "they were all filled with the Holy Ghost." They were not promised any freedom from persecution, but the knowledge that God had heard their prayer and this new bestowal of the Holy Spirit gave them courage to continue their witnessing in the face of the rising persecution.

*The Church Caring for the Poor (Acts 4:32-35)*

Verses 32 to 35 furnish us with another general description of the life within the church. It may be compared with the statement in Acts 2:42-47. Again, the sincerity and unanimity of purpose: "the multitude of them that believed were of one heart and of one soul." Again, the sharing of possessions in

5 Here in vs. 29 *kurios*, the usual word for "Lord," is used.
6 Luke 22:42.

a desire to give practical help to the needy: "they had all things common." Again, the glad and effective witnessing to "the resurrection of the Lord Jesus." This kind of living, then and always, pays spiritual dividends: "great grace was upon them all."

Verses 32 to 35, and also the passages next to be studied, make it evident that in that early Christian company there were many who were poor. Some had been reduced to hopeless poverty by various social injustices. Others, in their desire to devote their entire time and strength to witnessing for Christ, had left their customary work and had speedily come to want. Still others discovered that when their loyalty to "the way" became known, they could no longer earn their living in their accustomed manner. They found themselves ostracized; they suffered persecution. The early church faced a difficult situation in this matter, but love found a way of meeting it.

Love's way of doing this was so simple that we are in danger of failing to perceive how Christlike and truly efficient it was. Those who had wealth in excess of their actual needs contributed according to their ability, and the apostles distributed among the poor the sum thus raised. Some who possessed houses and lands sold them and the proceeds were added to the common fund. Thus these Christians undertook to share as brethren whatever hardships might befall any of their number.

They were, as has been said, "of one heart and of one soul." We may think of them, therefore, as constituting one large family, a family, indeed, in which each member was mindful of all the others. No one felt that anything he owned was something to be selfishly enjoyed.[7] He stood ready to share his possessions with anyone whose need was greater than his own.[8]

[7] Consider the example which Christ had set for them in this matter. He had voluntarily surrendered all that was rightfully His as equal with the Father, had humbled Himself, and had become obedient unto death (so Paul explains in Phil. 2:5-11). See also 2 Cor. 8:9.

[8] It has been well said that nothing is truly our own until it has been shared with all the world.

What we see in the early church, then, is a voluntary sharing. It resembles, but is not the same as, socialism or communism. No one was compelled to share his possessions; he was under no restraint save that of love. Indeed, it is difficult, if not impossible, to see how a society in which all things are shared, can ever succeed apart from a true Christian spirit in the hearts of its members. But let it be added at once that no form of social organization can properly be called Christian, if there is absent from it this willingness on the part of its members to share whatever they may have with those less fortunate than themselves.

## Barnabas' Gift to the Poor (Acts 4:36-37)

Among those who aided the poor in this practical fashion was a man named Joses (Joseph). He was a Levite, and he was a native of Cyprus. The spirit of this man was so inspiring that the apostles gave him a new name. They called him Barnabas,[9] and it is by this latter name that we know him best.

We are told that Barnabas sold a field (it may have been his entire Cyprus estate) and brought to the apostles the money he received for it. It is not said that Barnabas' contribution was the largest one made. In fact, it is mentioned only because it was typical of many other splendid gifts, and because Luke wishes to introduce us to this earnest, capable Christian who, at a later point in the story, will figure prominently as Paul's missionary companion.

It has been suggested that Barnabas, having made this gift, was no longer cumbered with business affairs, and therefore was free to devote himself to the widest possible missionary service. Be that as it may, his inspiring example affords a striking contrast to the Great Refusal made by the rich young ruler of whom Luke had told in his Gospel.[10] When Jesus

[9] The name Barnabas is Aramaic, and means "son of consolation" or "son of exhortation." In such expressions, "son of," in accordance with Hebrew usage, means merely "the one who"; in this case, "the one who gives encouragement."

[10] Luke 18:18-24.

tested that young man's character, saying to him, "Yet lackest thou one thing: sell all that thou hast, and distribute unto the poor," he turned away sorrowful. If that was what discipleship meant, he would have none of it; he loved his wealth too much! Seeing this, Jesus was moved to comment, "How hardly shall they that have riches enter into the kingdom of God!"

*The Sin of Ananias and Sapphira (Acts 5:1-11)*

In contrast to Barnabas' singlehearted devotion to Christ (a devotion which found expression in generous assistance to the poor), stands also the foolish and, as it proved, fatal deception attempted by Ananias and Sapphira his wife.[11] This dishonest couple coveted for themselves such commendation as had been bestowed upon Barnabas, but they were not willing to practice the self-denial which would make them deserving of it. When Ananias had sold some property, he brought a sum of money to the apostles to be put into the common fund. In presenting the money, he made it appear that he and his wife were giving up everything which they possessed. Perhaps he hinted that in return it would be the duty of the church to see that they never came to want. But secretly they had withheld for their personal use a substantial part of the money they had received. Apparently they were not willing to trust their brethren with all their money, judging them—it may be—to be possessed of that same covetousness which they perceived within themselves.

It must be understood that Ananias and Sapphira had been under no compulsion to sell their property either in whole or in part. The church had passed no rule requiring them to do this. Nor had the church said that when property was sold, the whole of the proceeds had to be given to the common fund. All this is made clear by Peter's statement in verse 4:

[11] If it should be asked why this story was included in the record, the answer is that it was included because it was true. We are shown the early church, not as we might wish to have seen it, but as it actually was: brave yet far from perfect, strong yet not free from instances of hypocrisy.

"Whiles it remained, was it not thine own? and after it was sold, was it not in thine own power?" What Ananias and Sapphira had done, they had done of their own volition. Their sin lay in their deliberate misrepresentation. When giving only a part, they had pretended they were giving all. By lying to the apostles, they sought to gain credit for a generosity they had not practiced, to win praise for a brotherliness they had not felt.

The hypocrite's acting is never so convincing as he imagines it to be. Peter discerned Ananias' deception at once. He had no sooner pointed it out than Ananias fell dead. When Sapphira came in, she told the same story that her husband had told, showing how premeditated and well rehearsed their lies had been. On learning of the fate which had overtaken her husband, and of the failure of all their scheming, she too fell dead. In these sudden deaths the Christians saw evidences of a judgment of God, a terrifying judgment which had been visited upon the pair because of their deception. The wages of sin, always, is death. Because those wages sometimes are not paid until a late hour of the day, a man may think that he is escaping the consequences of his wrongdoing. But not so! In the case of Ananias and Sapphira, the judgment fell swiftly. Peter, it must be noted, did not strike them down. They brought the judgment upon their own heads.

Does it seem to us that the judgment was unjustifiably severe? May it not be that every sin, even the so-called "little sins," are graver in their consequences than we like to think? And should we not keep in mind how important it was that the life of this first church should be established on a secure and honest foundation? Let us remember also that their sin was not done in ignorance or on sudden impulse. It was premeditated, and it was committed in the face of all the marvelous manifestations of the Holy Spirit which they had witnessed. Peter spoke truly when he said: "Thou hast not lied unto men, but unto God." Ananias and his wife had "agreed together to tempt the Spirit of the Lord"; professing obedience to the Holy Spirit, they had been guilty of hypocritical pretense.

*The Continued Growth of the Church* (*Acts 5:12-16*)

In Acts 5:12-16 we come upon another of those interesting passages in which Luke undertakes to summarize a multitude of happenings which he has neither the time nor the space to relate in detail. Whenever the Christians went up to the Temple for prayer, they were wont to congregate in that court known as Solomon's Porch. It was there that Peter had preached Jesus and the resurrection for the first time within the Temple precincts. If the fate of Ananias and Sapphira frightened off some of the less honest inquirers about Jesus, and if the threats made by the Sanhedrin deterred some of the less courageous among the would-be believers, there were many, nevertheless, who did find life in Christ. The number of Christians increased greatly.

One reason for this rapid increase in numbers was the helpful ministry carried on by the apostles. So mightily did the Holy Spirit dwell within them that they were able to work many gracious miracles of healing. Especially moving was the sight of those who brought their sick or demon-possessed friends to the apostles in the hope that they might be healed. Some of them had come even from villages a considerable distance from Jerusalem. Thus the Holy Spirit, working through the apostles and the church as a whole, created there in Jerusalem a scene not unlike that in Galilee when the Lord Himself had ministered to the sick of body and the tormented of mind.[12]

Some who came had little or no understanding of the source of the apostles' power. They knew only their desperate need and the fact that the apostles had healed others. Such faith as they possessed oftentimes was mixed with a superstitious belief in magical powers. It was so with those who thought there might be some healing virtue even in Peter's shadow. But at the least, this was a beginning of faith, a seed from which a truer, larger, more healing faith might grow. Faith won its sure reward. They found the healing that they sought.

12 See Luke 4:40-41.

## CHAPTER 6

# The First Fires of Persecution

Acts 5:17—7:60

WE MAY be sure that the apostles were under no illusion as to what lay ahead of them. Jesus, when with them in the upper room, had warned them of the cost of discipleship: "If they have persecuted me, they will also persecute you. . . . But all these things will they do unto you for my name's sake, because they know not him that sent me."[1] They had seen Jesus' enemies relentlessly pursue Him and revile Him; then they had seen those enemies hang Him upon a cross. They knew that they, being His disciples, could expect no better fate. Yet, with amazing courage, they continued their witnessing. They bore testimony to Christ, not because they thought their words might escape the ears of the Temple authorities, and not because they thought the members of the Sanhedrin would show them any more consideration than they had shown to the Lord Himself, but because they were genuinely loyal to Christ and because His Spirit had fully taken possession of their hearts. The arrest of Peter and John, and the demand by the Sanhedrin that they should cease their preaching, had given them added warning, but had in no way silenced them. They were prepared to bear their testimony, even though it might cost them their lives.

### The Apostles Imprisoned and Delivered (Acts 5:17-32)

It was inevitable, therefore, that the Sanhedrin, sooner or later, would take steps to put a stop to the apostles' preach-

1 John 15:20-21.

ing. They were speaking with great boldness, and by their words and healing ministries were winning the support of an ever increasing number of people. Clearly, the situation admitted of no further delay.

There were two reasons why the apostles' preaching infuriated the members of the Sanhedrin. The apostles were charging that they, the high court of the Jews, had with malice aforethought put to death an innocent man, and that that man, Jesus, had been none other than the Anointed One, the Messiah, whom God had sent. They felt that they could not ignore or dismiss lightly so serious a charge. Furthermore, the apostles not only preached that Jesus was the Christ, but offered in proof of that fact evidence that God had raised Him from the dead. Most of the members of the Sanhedrin belonged to the party of Sadducees, and the Sadducees had as one of their tenets the impossibility of any resurrection from the dead.[2] They felt that on both these counts they were being discredited, and that they needed to do something at once to regain, if possible, their standing in the eyes of the people.

They therefore ordered the arrest, this time not of Peter and John only, but of all the apostles. The Twelve were speedily apprehended and lodged in prison, and a meeting of the Sanhedrin was called for the next morning. Thus, the issue was joined. The members of the Sanhedrin, by arresting the apostles, were hurling their defiance into the face of God —the God who had revealed Himself in Jesus Christ, and who in the Holy Spirit was leading the apostles out into a worldwide service. The plight of the apostles would indeed have been desperate had not God been minded to show these Jewish rulers how futile were their plans, how impotent was their rage. That night God, who is never without someone ready and able to do His bidding, sent one of His heavenly messengers to release the apostles. The angel opened the prison doors, led out the apostles, and bade them continue their preaching of the spiritual life which men could find in Jesus ("all the words of this life"). And this the apostles did, so soon as it was morning and people began to assemble in the Temple.

2 Luke 20:27.

When the Sanhedrin came together, they called for their prisoners to be brought before them. The officers presently returned and reported, in great perplexity, that their prisoners had disappeared. This, despite the fact that they had found all the prison doors securely locked and all the guards where they had been stationed! While the high priest and those associated with him were still wondering to what limits this business might grow, someone reported that he had just seen the apostles in the Temple. They were preaching and teaching the people in their customary fashion. The Sanhedrin then directed the captain to take with him a company of his soldiers and to bring the apostles into court. The captain did so, but he was careful to do them no bodily harm. So great was the number of the Christians that he was somewhat fearful that he and his men, when arresting the apostles, might be stoned.

When the apostles had been brought before the Sanhedrin, the high priest made three charges against them. First, that they had been preaching about the one whose name was not to be mentioned,[3] as they had been straitly charged not to do. Second, that by their teaching they were stirring up the entire population of Jerusalem.[4] Third, that they were saying that the members of the Sanhedrin were guilty of having murdered a certain man.

Then Peter, speaking not only on his own behalf but also on behalf of all the apostles, declared: "We ought to obey God rather than men." This was, in substance, what he had said to the Sanhedrin before.[5] It left them at a loss for a reply.

3 Following the crucifixion of Jesus, the Jewish leaders looked upon Him as one accursed, and they refused to speak His name. They hoped, by a conspiracy of silence, to erase every memory of Him from the minds of men. Note that here they do not say, "Did not we straitly command you that ye should not teach *about Jesus?*" but "Did not we straitly command you that ye should not teach *in this name?*" Note also in vs. 28 that they do not say "bring *Jesus'* blood upon us," but "bring *this man's* blood upon us."

4 Evidence, from the lips of their enemies, that they were carrying out the first part of the commission that had been given to them. They had been faithfully witnessing "in Jerusalem." See Acts 1:8.

5 See Acts 4:19-20.

But Peter's words were more than an example of clever dialectics; they were a straightforward announcement that the
apostles had made up their minds as to where the will of God
lay, and were prepared to obey God's will at any cost. Then
Peter—not with bravado, but nonetheless with great courage
—reiterated what he had said on other occasions: that the one
whom they had murdered,[6] God had raised from the dead,
and had exalted to be the Prince and Saviour through whom
alone Israel could find forgiveness of sins. The apostles, Peter
declared, were but bearing a truthful witness to what had
taken place, a witness confirmed by the Holy Spirit whom
God had imparted to them, and would impart to anyone who
would believe.[7]

### Gamaliel's Counsel to the Sanhedrin (Acts 5:33-42)

Peter's plain speaking aroused the Sanhedrin to a rage
greater even than before. They were "cut to the heart," but it
was not such a piercing of heart as would move them to repentance; instead, it made them more determined than ever
to do away with the apostles. That their lives were spared on
this occasion was due, under God, to the intervention of
Gamaliel.

Gamaliel was the most learned and influential teacher of
that day. Later Jewish literature made this grandson of the
great Hillel to be the first of the seven famous rabbis who
were honored with the higher title of rabban. At one time
Gamaliel had had among his pupils a young man named Saul.[8]

[6] In referring to the crucifixion, Peter employed in vs. 30 an expression
("whom ye slew and hanged on a tree") found in the Old Testament,
which he could adapt to his purpose. Cf. Gen. 40:19; Deut. 21:22; Josh.
10:26. Whereas the reference here is to crucifixion, the Roman method
of execution, the Jews hanged only those who already had been put to
death. The purpose of the hanging was not to cause cruel suffering with
ultimate death, but, by displaying the dead bodies, to give warning to
other malefactors.

[7] One of the important works of the Holy Spirit, both in Himself and
in the person of those into whom He enters, is to bear testimony to
Christ. Cf. John 15:26.

[8] Acts 22:3.

Whereas the Sanhedrin was made up largely of Sadducees, Gamaliel was a Pharisee and the spokesman in the Sanhedrin for the Pharisaic party. Although the Pharisees had bitterly opposed Jesus, charging Him with disregard for the laws of Moses, they had up to this time taken no steps against the apostles.

When the apostles had been removed from the room, Gamaliel addressed the Sanhedrin. Probably he found a measure of satisfaction in the fact that the Sadducees were coming off second best in their dealings with the apostles. At any rate, he advised the Sanhedrin to consider well what it was doing before it took action against the apostles. This he said, not out of any love for Christ and His followers, and not out of any real concern to see justice done. With the detachment and calm of a scholar, he advocated patience. Leave the matter in God's hands, he said. If their work was of God, the Sanhedrin could not stop it; if it was not of God, it would speedily come to naught. In proof of the latter statement, he reminded his hearers of two of the many messianic movements which had arisen in Israel, that by Theudas and that by Judas of Galilee. In both instances, when the leader had been slain, his followers had scattered and had been heard from no more. It was only reasonable to expect that the same thing would happen in the case of the followers of the Nazarene, now that their leader had been crucified. For all his wisdom, how little Gamaliel really knew! Beyond his recognition of God as supreme in history, it is not possible to find in his words anything more than a counsel of prudence and opportunism.

The Sanhedrin heeded Gamaliel's counsel. It felt that it could not proceed without the support of the Pharisees. But before releasing the apostles, it got what satisfaction it could out of having them sorely beaten for their disobedience. Then they again served notice on the apostles that they must cease their preaching of Jesus. With their backs bloody from the beating they had received, the apostles rejoined their relatives and friends. The stuff they were made of is evidenced by the fact that they rejoiced that they had been counted worthy to suffer this pain and this shame for the sake of Christ. And they continued "to teach and preach Jesus Christ" daily in every house open to them, and also publicly in the Temple!

## Relief Work Systematized (Acts 6:1-7)

Among the early Christians were a number of Greek-speaking Jews. Probably they had come originally from outside Palestine. In certain of their religious views they were less strict than the Palestinian Jews. In their synagogue services they read from the Septuagint, a Greek translation of the Hebrew Old Testament. For this reason they were spoken of as Hellenists or Grecians. Some little time after the events recorded in the fourth and fifth chapters of The Acts, these Hellenists complained that certain widows of their company, sorely in need of help, either were being discriminated against or else were being overlooked completely in the distribution of relief.

How much truth there may have been in this charge, it is impossible to tell. Perhaps the apostles, burdened with many responsibilities, quite accidentally had overlooked some of these widows; perhaps the Hellenists spoke more out of fear of what might happen some day than out of knowledge of any actual neglect. Suspicion of any sort can be easily aroused. At any rate, the apostles dealt with the situation immediately. Far from taking offense at the complaint, they proposed a plan which would make discrimination or oversight impossible in the future. They asked the church to select seven Spirit-filled, trustworthy, and really capable men to have charge of the distribution of relief. Such an arrangement would enable the apostles to devote themselves more completely to prayer and preaching, while the administering of relief would be no less capably carried on.

The plan proposed met with unanimous approval, and the church chose for this purpose seven men "of honest report, full of the Holy Ghost and wisdom." The names of these seven men, who later came to be called "deacons," [9] are given

9 These seven are not here called deacons (diakonoi), but the name was derived from the expression used to describe the service which these

in verse 5. It is significant that all of them, as their names clearly show, were Hellenists. They therefore could talk with the needy among the Hellenists in their own tongue, and could be counted upon to treat all Hellenists fairly. It is as though the apostles said to the complaining members: "You have mistrusted us, but see how completely we trust you. We are putting into the hands of some of your own number the entire matter of administering relief. We know that they will deal fairly with all." That spirit will go a long way toward removing any friction there may be in a church.

The seven men who had been elected were formally set apart, or ordained, for their special work. The apostles prayed for them, and by laying their hands on them signified their appointment. We know from later Scriptures that these men not only cared for the poor, but also, like the apostles, witnessed for Christ at every opportunity. Of two of these deacons, Stephen and Philip, we are to hear more.

These wise arrangements freed the apostles for more continuous and widespread testifying. In consequence, "the word of God increased; and the number of the disciples multiplied in Jerusalem greatly." Included among these new converts were many priests. They represented the first believers to be won from among the ranks of the Sadducees.

## The Witnessing and Martyrdom of Stephen (Acts 6:8–7:60)

Stephen is described as a man "full of faith and power"— the power being that of the Holy Spirit whom he had allowed to take possession of his life. Through the Spirit he was able to do "great wonders and miracles among the people." We are not told what these miracles were, but one evidence of the Spirit's presence in his life was seen in the convincing character of the testimony which he bore to Jesus Christ.

There were a number of synagogues in Jerusalem. One of them was composed of "Libertines, Cyrenians, and Alexan-

men were to render. There is nothing in the passage to suggest that the church was setting up an episcopacy with lower and higher ecclesiastical ranks. The office continued because the need continued, and because the arrangement proved a wise and helpful one.

drians, and of them of Cilicia and of Asia." [10] Stephen, being
a Hellenist, quite likely belonged to this synagogue. Saul, who
became Paul the apostle, came from Tarsus in Cilicia. Therefore there is at least a possibility that he also attended this
synagogue. When Stephen bore testimony in this synagogue
to Jesus Christ, some of its members of Pharisaic persuasion
disputed his statements, but they could not successfully refute his Spirit-inspired utterances. Was Saul, the brilliant
young rabbi who had studied under Gamaliel, one of those
who essayed to match words with Stephen and who failed
ignominiously in the attempt?

The leaders of this synagogue, when defeated in debate,
resorted to dishonesty and falsehood. They summoned unscrupulous men who, for pay, spread the report that they had
heard Stephen speak disparagingly of the Mosaic law and
blasphemously of God. Stephen, no doubt, had said that God
had given through Christ a revelation which superseded that
which He had given through Moses. It was not difficult to dis-
tort such a statement and to make it sound anarchistic and
blasphemous. This report, maliciously and persistently circulated, soon stirred up those of the people who were influenced by the teachings of the Pharisees with respect to the
importance and sanctity of the law. A crowd accordingly set
upon Stephen and took him before the Sanhedrin for trial.

This renewal of activity by the Pharisees boded ill for the
Christians. The Pharisees had been Jesus' most bitter enemies
throughout His ministry. They had charged repeatedly that
He had violated the laws of Moses. The Sadducees did not
turn against Jesus and join forces with the Pharisees until
comparatively late in His ministry. Then, until this preaching
by Stephen, the Pharisees had taken no active part in the persecution of the Christians. Perhaps their inactivity was due to

10 The Libertines were Jews who had been Roman captives, but who,
having bought their freedom, had returned to Jerusalem. The Cyrenians
and Alexandrians were Jews from the north coast of Africa. Like the
Libertines, they were more tolerant of Greek customs than were the
Palestinian Jews. The provinces of Asia and Cilicia were located in what
is now called Asia Minor, another region where Greek influence was
dominant.

the policy of watchful waiting recommended by Gamaliel; perhaps they enjoyed seeing the discomfiture of the Sadducees when the apostles preached the resurrection of Jesus. The Sadducees had instituted the persecution and had been coming off second best. Now the Pharisees were aroused. They saw to it that Stephen was brought before the Sanhedrin, and they demanded that the Sanhedrin deal severely with him.

The false witnesses who testified against Stephen brought against him the very same charges that had been made against Jesus. It may be that the realization of this fact enheartened Stephen, for the members of the council, watching Stephen closely to see what effect his arrest and these charges might have upon him, saw in him no least sign of fear, no least wavering of purpose. Indeed, such was the radiance of his spirit that it shone forth. It transfigured his face with a light so spiritual that his countenance resembled that of an angel.

Stephen's address before the Sanhedrin is reported at greater length than any other in the book of ACTS. It was not so much a defense of his conduct as it was a warning to Israel. Their long history as a people, so Stephen declared, had been characterized by repeated acts of unbelief. Now that they were confronted with the supreme issue, with God in Christ, they again were displaying their hardness of heart, their unwillingness to believe.

All the many references Stephen made to events in the nation's history would be understood by his hearers. He did not need to state in so many words the application of each reference to the situation in which they stood. The application was implied, and perceived. It amounted to this: that from the beginning of their history they had rejected the leaders whom God had sent to them. Had they not rejected Moses, and had they not rejected also that Prophet whose coming Moses had foretold?[11]

The uneasiness and mounting anger of the Sanhedrin must have been apparent. Stephen, seeing that he would not be permitted many more words, became prosecutor instead of defendant. He brought the Sanhedrin for judgment before

11 Acts 7:35, 37.

the bar of God. Speaking with the fire of an Old Testament prophet and in words reminiscent of their messages, he suddenly cried: "Ye stiffnecked and uncircumcised in heart and ears, ye do always resist the Holy Ghost: as your fathers did, so do ye." [12] They had added to their other sins this greatest sin, that of betraying and murdering the Just One whom God had sent unto them. Not he, Stephen, but they themselves were the violators of God's law!

The rage of the Sanhedrin then went beyond all bounds. But Stephen, facing death, was granted a vision of "the glory of God, and Jesus standing on the right hand of God." This transcendent vision gave him strength for what was to follow. He had time only to declare what he had seen, for the members of the Sanhedrin (the court was now in great disorder) rushed upon him, roughly hurried him outside the city, where they set about cruelly stoning him to death.

Stephen, who had undergone the same false accusations as his Lord, and who had suffered many of the same indignities, now showed how fully he was possessed by his Lord's Spirit. He called upon God, saying, "Lord Jesus, receive my spirit." Then, falling upon his knees, he prayed for those who were stoning him, crying loudly enough for all to hear: "Lord, lay not this sin to their charge." The stones were beating upon him. His pain was blotted out by a merciful unconsciousness, succeeded straightway by the sleep of death.

Thus Stephen became the first of the followers of Christ to suffer martyrdom.

12 Acts 7:51.

CHAPTER 7

# The Gospel in Judea and Samaria

ACTS 8:1-40

*T*OSS a pebble into a pond and the point where the pebble disappears from view immediately is surrounded by concentric circles. These ripples slowly widen until, if they do not lose their momentum, they reach the farthest shore. Some have used this familiar physical phenomenon as an illustration of the way in which the gospel, first heard in Jerusalem, became known in Judea and Galilee, and ultimately in the most distant lands of that day. This illustration, though interesting, is far from adequate.

We need to keep in mind that the apostles were impelled to carry the gospel afield by a command which their risen Lord had given them. They did not question His authority; they could not mistake the meaning of His explicit words. He had said: "Ye shall receive power, after that the Holy Ghost is come upon you: and ye shall be witnesses unto me both in Jerusalem, and in all Judea, and in Samaria, and unto the uttermost part of the earth." [1] No combination of natural circumstances will explain satisfactorily the spreading of the gospel throughout the Roman world. The gospel was spread by conscious effort. It was established throughout the Empire by a group of men who remembered the commission which their Lord had given them, and who were determined to show themselves obedient to it whatever the cost might be. Their consecrated living and their faithful witness-bearing were made effective for evangelization by the Holy Spirit.

[1] Acts 1:8.

55

The illustration falls short in another respect. Whereas the ripples caused by the tossed stone become feebler and less clearly marked the farther they move from the center of the disturbance, this apostolic witnessing became bolder, clearer, and more convincing the farther afield the bearers of the good news went. These first Christian missionaries went "from strength to strength." The ability of Christ to meet the needs of every land became more apparent with each new triumph of the gospel. The gospel which the apostle Paul carried ultimately to Rome was no last echo of the teachings of a provincial Jewish cult, but the gospel well-formulated in its theological expression, well-established in its program of service, and incontestably missionary in its world outlook. It was Christianity full-orbed, universal, and triumphant.

## The Believers Scattered by Persecution (Acts 8:1-4)

Strange as it may seem, persecution contributed to this early evangelistic outreach. It compelled many of the believers to leave their Jerusalem homes, to flee for their lives; but wherever they went, they told of Christ. They had not invited persecution. They no doubt would have avoided it, if they could have done so with honor. But when the persecution proved inescapable, they sought to endure it bravely. They endeavored to turn to the glory of God even the persecution which scattered them abroad.

The leader in this new wave of persecution, the most severe which the Christians had yet experienced, was a young man[2] named Saul—that Saul whose other name was Paul, the name by which we know him best. Saul had witnessed the stoning of Stephen; in fact, he had participated in it.[3] He had taken charge of, had kept watch over, the clothes (the outer robes) which the Sanhedrin dignitaries had thrown off in order that they might cast their stones with greater force and accuracy.

Though Paul did not realize it then, Stephen's Spirit-in-

[2] If the traditional date of Paul's birth, A.D. 1, be accepted as correct, Paul would be about 34 years of age at this time—a "young man" in the eyes of the elders who made up the Sanhedrin.

[3] Acts 7:58.

spired witnessing, his courage, his forgiving spirit, and his uncomplaining acceptance of martyrdom were leaving upon him a lasting impression, one which would bear fruit in a later day. A Jerusalem mob, by and by, would hear Paul tell how he had confessed to the Lord his part in the death of Stephen: "When the blood of thy martyr Stephen was shed, I also was standing by, and consenting unto his death, and kept the raiment of them that slew him." [4]

Paul, having approved the stoning of Stephen, now became the instigator of a general persecution of Christians. What he did, of course, he did with the endorsement and support of the Sanhedrin. So sorely did he harass the Christians of Jerusalem that practically all of them, with the exception of the apostles, were compelled to seek refuge in various districts of Judea and Samaria. How it came about that the apostles were allowed to remain in the city is not clear. Perhaps the leaders of the Sanhedrin were a little afraid of the apostles. Perhaps they thought that so long as the apostles remained in Jerusalem it would be possible to keep a close watch over their activities. Perhaps the apostles thought that they would be dishonoring Christ if they joined the other believers in flight. However it was, while "devout men" were lamenting the death of Stephen and arranging his burial, Paul "made havoc of the church." Entering into the homes of those suspected of being Christians, he arrested many—women as well as men— and had them committed to prison. That some of those arrested were put to death is implied in Paul's statement: "I persecuted this way unto the death. . . ." [5] But God can overrule the fury of wicked men. Paul, thinking to stamp out the Christian movement, succeeded only in spreading the fire.

This was that very scattering of the Christians which Christ had foretold. But tragic though it was, it served to save the early church from becoming localized and permanently settled in Jerusalem. Of this persecution, Dr. Philip Schaff wrote: "This bloody baptism of the church resulted in the birth of a Christian world. It was a repetition and prolongation of the crucifixion, but it was followed by a resurrection."

4 Acts 22:20.
5 Acts 22:4.

## Philip Preaches Christ to the Samaritans (Acts 8:5-13)

The persecution had this outcome only because those who were scattered abroad by it did not leave their faith behind them. In every district into which they came, they bore witness to Jesus Christ. One who did this was Philip; not the apostle Philip, but that other Philip who had been chosen as a deacon[6] and who also was called an evangelist.[7] Philip went down to the city of Samaria and preached Christ there. He possessed the Holy Spirit, and through the Spirit's power he was able to work numerous miracles. He not only healed some sufferers of their ailments, but also, through his telling of the good news of Christ, brought great joy to many of the Samaritans.

We must not overlook the significant fact that Philip, by this preaching in Samaria, had carried the gospel beyond the borders of Judea. He had introduced it into Samaria, which, though near-by, was virtually a foreign land. This outreach was in obedience to Christ's command. At the same time, it was an exemplification of the essential difference between Judaism and Christianity. Whereas Judaism, historically and sentimentally has kept its gaze fixed upon Palestine, Christianity, like its Lord, looks out upon the world. With the one Jerusalem is the goal; with the other only a starting point.

## Peter and John Are Sent to Samaria (Acts 8:14)

Word that these Samaritans had become Christians soon reached the apostles in Jerusalem, and it seems to have occasioned both surprise and concern. Would the Christian company welcome these newly won followers of Christ? It must be remembered that they were, in the eyes of the Jews, despised Samaritans.

No doubt there was some discussion among the Christians of Jerusalem as to how sincere the Samaritan converts were in their profession of faith in Jesus Christ, and likewise some discussion as to how well they understood what it meant to

6 Acts 6:5.

7 Acts 21:8.

walk in "the way." At any rate, the Jerusalem church (as many of its members, that is, as had survived the persecution) appointed two of the apostles, Peter and John, to go to Samaria. They were to investigate the matter, and when they had ascertained the facts they were to do whatever seemed to them best.

Note the confidence which the church had in the good judgment of Peter and John. But note also that the church "sent" them; that is to say, the church laid this task upon them. Peter had no such authority over the other apostles and over the churches as has been claimed for him by Roman Catholic theologians. The greatness which Peter possessed did not reside in any office to which he had been appointed, or in any special prerogatives which had been granted to him; it lay rather in his devotion to Christ and in his willingness to serve Christ in whatever way he could.

## The Samaritans Receive the Holy Spirit (Acts 8:15-17)

When Peter and John arrived in Samaria, they found that although some of the Samaritans had professed faith in Jesus Christ and had been baptized, they had not experienced in their lives any manifestations of God's power. So Peter and John prayed[8] that the Holy Spirit might come upon them in some such manner as He had come upon the company of disciples on the day of Pentecost. That would establish the status of these Samaritan converts. If the Holy Spirit came upon them, it would be conclusive proof that God had accepted them on equal terms with the Jewish Christians. Furthermore, the Holy Spirit would enable them to bear a more effective Christian witness. As it was, they were impotent as Christians; they were deficient both in spiritual understanding and in spiritual vigor.

After they had prayed, Peter and John laid their hands on these Samaritan converts and each of them received the Holy

_____

[8] Observe how great a change the Holy Spirit works in a man's heart. Here was John praying that a blessing might come upon the Samaritans —the very people on whom, but a short time before, he would have called down fire from heaven. See Luke 9:54.

Spirit. What the visible manifestations were, if any, we are not told. It is likely, however, that they were so exhilarated by the new power which came into their lives that they shouted and sang for joy. Because the subject is difficult, yet of utmost importance, it may be well at this point to give further attention to these gifts of the Holy Spirit.

We find, on careful reading of the Scriptures, that it is possible to distinguish three kinds of bestowals of the Holy Spirit. We note, first, that every person who believes receives the Holy Spirit. It is the Holy Spirit who cleanses and renews the believer's life. In doing this, the Holy Spirit operates directly upon the motives which produce conduct.[9] This work of the Spirit is not in view in the passage we have been studying, for these Samaritans had already believed when Peter and John arrived in their city.

What the Samaritan believers had not received was such an enduement of power as had come upon the apostles and those assembled with them on the day of Pentecost. Such a bestowal of the Holy Spirit—we may call it the second type—was what these Samaritans needed before they could witness boldly for Christ and be strong to endure persecution. On this occasion the Holy Spirit was received through the laying on of the apostles' hands. But the laying on of hands was not essential (see Acts 10:44), where the Holy Spirit was bestowed unexpectedly and even before the converts had been baptized—a telling argument against the contention that baptism is essential to salvation. Bestowals of the Holy Spirit of this second type were peculiar to the early church, and occurred in situations where the converts were in special need of such help and encouragement.

The third type of manifestation of the Holy Spirit was closely related to the second; in fact, was an outgrowth of it. It was, however, distinctly inferior to it. As a result of being filled with the Holy Spirit, as already described, some were able to speak with tongues, others were able to prophesy and work miracles. But Paul pointed out, in 1 Corinthians, chaps. 12-14, that these spiritual gifts, while valid and to be desired, were not to be so highly regarded as the simple Christian

9 John 16:7-14; Titus 3:5.

grace of love. Gifts, such as miracles, tongues, healings, and prophesyings, belonged to a passing phase of Christianity; they were open to grave abuses, and subjected the one who possessed them to great temptation. The Holy Spirit, however, abides forever, and His power does not diminish. His power is available to any believer who will let Him use his life to the glory of Jesus Christ.

### Peter Rebukes Simon Magus  (Acts 8:18-25)

Among the Samaritans who had professed belief and had been baptized was a magician named Simon.[10] The world of that day was filled with magicians, mediums, fortunetellers, and other folk of that stripe, all of whom were ready to take advantage of the ignorance and superstition of the people. This Simon represented himself as "The Great Power of God." That he had given himself such a title suggests that he was something of a messianic pretender. He supported his preposterous claims by his tricks and by such bits of scientific lore as the ancient magi had acquired. By one unscrupulous means or another, he had gained a sizable following.

It is impossible to tell how much, if anything, he had meant by his profession of faith. No doubt he had been much astonished by the miracles wrought by Philip. He could do nothing of *that* sort! If Simon was in any measure sincere, it is evident from what follows that he had only a most meager knowledge of what is involved in being a Christian.

Then, when he saw men and women receive the Holy Spirit through the laying on of the apostles' hands, he—magician that he was—coveted that power. Perhaps he could buy the secret of it from the apostles!

But when Simon offered to buy this power of bestowing the Holy Spirit, Peter was rightly indignant. Such power as Peter had displayed had not come from himself, and it most certainly was not a trick. The power had come from Christ, and it was not something that could be bought and sold. Peter, with his characteristic vigor, denounced Simon. His words,

10 To distinguish this Simon from Simon Peter, he is frequently called Simon Magus. The word *magus* means magician.

"Thy money perish with thee!" were fully justified. In trying to buy with money gifts of a spiritual character, Simon had disclosed a fundamental lack of understanding and a wholly mercenary purpose. Black though the magician's heart was, there was still hope for him. But as Peter made clear, he would have to come to Christ by the way of sincere repentance and prayer. Peter's denunciation frightened Simon into asking Peter to pray for him.[11] But there is no record that Simon himself ever asked the Lord to forgive him for the many times he had imposed upon the people, or that he ever asked the Lord to give him the understanding and strength to lead a true Christian life.

As Peter and John made their way back to Jerusalem, they took advantage of their travel opportunity and preached the gospel in the Samaritan villages through which they passed. Thus, Peter and John, as well as Philip, had a part in the carrying of the gospel to the Samaritans. These men had caught enough of the true spirit of the gospel to rise above racial prejudice; they had undertaken to carry out Christ's command to tend his sheep, those "other sheep . . . which are not of this fold," of which Christ had spoken.[12] This, mark well, was before Peter's housetop vision,[13] which showed him even more clearly that he was to be Christ's ambassador to the Gentiles.

*Philip Instructs and Baptizes an Ethiopian* (*Acts 8:26-40*)

There was yet more work for Philip to do. This lay preacher and Hellenist had preached to the half-Jewish Samaritans; he was now to take the gospel to one of a wholly different race, to an Ethiopian.[14] An angel of the Lord directed Philip to make his way along the road running from Jerusalem down

---

[11] Simon Magus, instead of praying for forgiveness, as Peter had bidden him do, asked Peter to pray for him. Peter, gladly, would have done that, but there are some prayers which each must offer for himself.

[12] John 21:15-17; 10:16.

[13] Acts 10:9-20.

[14] The land of Ethiopia, not to be confused with Egypt, corresponded roughly with present-day Abyssinia.

to Gaza. Philip obeyed, and the reason why he was sent along that road speedily became evident. On it he encountered a person of more than ordinary importance. This man was the court treasurer under Candace,[15] queen of Ethiopia. As was not uncommon among members of the court in lands ruled by a queen, he was a eunuch. What is more important, this Ethiopian was a worshiper of Jehovah; he was a Jewish prose- lyte. Having been up to Jerusalem to worship, he was now returning to his own land. As he rode in his chariot, he studied the fifty-third chapter of Isaiah, and he had come in his reading to what is now the seventh verse.

Philip, emboldened by the Holy Spirit, approached the chariot of this dignitary and asked him if he understood the meaning of the words he had read. The man confessed his inability to understand the prophet's message, and invited Philip to explain it to him. When the Lord sends a man on a mission such as Philip's, he also prepares in mind and heart the one to whom the man is sent.

Philip was able to explain the meaning of the prophet's words. Whatever the passage may have meant in its original utterance and historical context, it had now received its ulti- mate and highest fulfillment in the humiliation and self-offer- ing of Jesus Christ. When Philip employed this passage to explain the nature of Jesus' atoning ministry and death, the Ethiopian, who already believed in God, found it easy to be- lieve on Jesus Christ, God's Suffering Servant for man's re- demption.

All the while that they had been talking together thus earnestly, Philip had been riding with the Ethiopian in his chariot. When presently they came to a deep stream or pool of water, the Ethiopian asked if he might be baptized.[16] Philip

15 Not a personal name, but a class name applied to Ethiopian queens; cf. the use of Pharaoh as a designation for all Egyptian kings.

16 Vs. 37, since it is not found in the oldest and best manuscripts, has been omitted from the newer translations. No doubt Philip, before bap- tizing the Ethiopian, called upon him to make a public profession of his faith in Christ, but we are not to think, as some have done, that the words of vs. 37 give a baptismal ritual or ceremonial already in force in Christian circles. Such theological formulations came at a later date.

was glad to do this. He led the Ethiopian down into the water, and there, upon his profession of faith in Christ, baptized him. Now that Philip's mission was accomplished, the Spirit of the Lord "caught away" Philip; that is to say, sent Philip elsewhere.[17] The eunuch, though he saw nothing more of Philip, went on his way rejoicing. A man had been won to Christ, an earnest, studious, influential man, who would carry the gospel with him to his faraway home in Ethiopia.

Philip is next found at Azotus, the ancient Ashdod. From Ashdod, Philip journeyed northward, preaching in all the coast cities until he came to Caesarea. Now that the gospel had been thus effectively proclaimed in Samaria and the surrounding regions, the hour was near for the conversion of Paul. Once Paul's great energy had been redirected, he would carry word of Christ unto "the uttermost part of the earth."

[17] On the Spirit of God as a transporting force, cf. 1 Kings 18:12; 2 Kings 2:16; Ezek. 3:1; and Ezek. 8:3.

## CHAPTER 8

# The Chief Persecutor Converted

## ACTS 9:1-31

*T*HE ninth chapter of The Acts introduces us to a new and most important section of Luke's narrative. In it, Paul is the principal figure. His experiences are reported with a wealth of detail—a clue, it may be, to Luke's purpose in writing Luke-Acts. Not that there is a complete break. The closing verses of the ninth chapter, as well as most of chapters ten, eleven, and twelve, are concerned with Peter. But from this point on, Paul is the more prominent person. It is to the recounting of his missionary labors that the remainder of The Acts is devoted.

In writing of Paul one has at hand a vast amount of relevant material. In addition to what Luke tells us concerning Paul, we have Paul's own letters. Though we do not possess all the letters which he wrote, those which have been preserved make up a very substantial part of the New Testament. These letters contain much material of an autobiographical nature. Whereas The Acts is concerned chiefly with what Paul said and did, the epistles reveal Paul's character—his feelings, motives, spiritual conflicts, and triumphant faith. We truly know the man only when we see his heart. It would be both interesting and profitable to examine psychologically the changes which took place in Paul's character following his meeting with the risen Christ on the Damascus road; it would be equally interesting and profitable to survey the theological formulations which Paul developed on the basis of that same epochal experience. To do so, however, would extend this book beyond the permissible limits. The most that can be undertaken is to carry out the purpose originally announced for these studies; namely, to discover what Luke has to tell us about this man. We shall find that Luke describes him as a man who, when once he truly had come to know Christ, was impelled by the Holy Spirit to dedicate his life to missionary service.

### Paul's Early Years (Acts 21:39; 22:3-4, 27-28; 26:4-5)

A few words concerning Paul's early years may be introduced here. Acts 22:3-4 informs us that Paul's birthplace was Tarsus, a large city in the province of Cilicia in Asia Minor. Being located upon the Cydnus River only ten miles from the sea, Tarsus was an important port. It could boast of a prosperous trade in cloth and lumber. Tarsus was also the seat of a famous university. In that cosmopolitan and largely Greek-speaking city Paul spent his boyhood. There he received his first schooling, and there also he learned his trade of tent-making.

Paul had received at birth two names, one Jewish and the other Roman. His Jewish name was Saul. Being a Jew, he would be proud of that name, for it had been the name of Israel's first king. Being a free-born Roman citizen, he would be proud also of his Roman name. It was Paulus; or, to give it its more familiar English form, Paul.[1]

Paul secured a much better education than the average for those days. In addition to the acquaintance he gained in Tarsus with all that was best in the Greek culture, he was privileged to visit Jerusalem and to study there under the most distinguished of all Jewish teachers, Gamaliel. Paul was a Pharisee, and the instruction he received from Gamaliel had to do largely with matters pertaining to the Jewish religion.

Probably Paul was not in Jerusalem at the time of Jesus' ministry and crucifixion. If he had personally witnessed the crucifixion, it is likely that in his epistles he would have had more to say about the manner of it. As it is, he discusses the

---

1 Some scholars have suggested that Paul did not receive or employ this Roman name until after his converting of Sergius Paulus. That matter will be considered in connection with the study of Acts 13:6-12.

crucifixion only in its religious significance. Possibly Paul had returned to Tarsus before the crucifixion took place, and if there he heard about Jesus, he regarded Him merely as an impostor who very properly had been put to death by the Jerusalem authorities.[2]

But a year or two after Jesus' crucifixion we find Paul back in Jerusalem. By this time he had become an influential religious leader among the Jews, one well known to the members of the Sanhedrin.[3] He had heard the testimony of the Christian leaders, of Stephen in particular, and he had become convinced that the followers of Jesus, by reason of their peculiar views, were seriously interfering with the Jewish religion. He felt that he would be doing God a service if he rid the country of them. Therefore, he had approved the Sanhedrin's decree that Stephen should be stoned, and he had been on hand to see that decree carried out.

Paul's rage seems to have been directed chiefly at those Christians who had turned away from the ancient Jewish practices and customs. He was not greatly concerned about the apostles. Peter and John and men like them, he believed, remained at heart true Jews. Christianity, if left in their hands, was not likely to become anything more than a cult within the Jewish religion. But Christians like Stephen the Hellenist, men who possessed less Jewish background and training and who were strongly influenced by Greek customs

[2] Whereas most commentators take the view that Paul had not known Christ "after the flesh," but only as a risen, glorified Spirit, Joseph Klausner, the eminent Jewish scholar, maintains that it is difficult, if not impossible, to account for Paul's emotional experience apart from the view that he had witnessed the crucifixion of Jesus as well as the stoning of Stephen. The decision turns upon the interpretation given to 2 Cor. 5:16. See Klausner's *From Jesus to Paul* (Macmillan, 1943), pp. 312-316.

[3] Some have supposed, on the basis of Acts 26:10 (a passage which states that Paul gave his vote for the death penalty to be imposed upon the followers of Jesus), that Paul was a member of the Sanhedrin. The verse, however, does not necessarily imply this. The probability is that Paul was too young to be a member of the Sanhedrin. That body, however, recognized him as one of the most ardent and promising of the young rabbinic students, and was quite willing that he should take the lead in persecuting the Christians.

and habits of thought, were a source of grave danger. Such men would stop at nothing.

The early efforts to suppress the followers of Christ had served only to scatter them, and now that they were widely scattered they could not be watched easily. That was why Paul had asked the Sanhedrin for permission to hunt them out, to arrest them, and to bring them to trial. The Sanhedrin had approved Paul's plan, had granted him the requested authority, and had furnished him with such soldiers as he needed.

### Paul the Persecutor Is Stopped by Christ (Acts 9:1-7; 22:1-10; 26:9-15)

Thus it came about that Paul, accompanied by a number of soldiers, one day set out for Damascus. He had learned that there were Christians there, and he was determined to put an end to their activities. Damascus was one hundred and fifty miles distant from Jerusalem, a week's journey. The provincial synagogues there would recognize the authority of the Jerusalem Sanhedrin. The letters which Paul carried would introduce him to them and secure for him their co-operation in his bloody work of persecution. Paul's furious state of mind is aptly described in the statement that he was "yet breathing out threatenings and slaughter." Many writers have made much of the scenery which Paul saw on this journey. With his mind in such turmoil, it is unlikely that he gave heed to it. At any rate, it was not the scenery which stayed Paul in his mad career, but the Lord.

Before Paul reached Damascus, he came face to face with Jesus Christ! There on the highway, at noonday, Jesus confronted him. Jesus, whose followers he had been persecuting. Jesus, who had been crucified, but who had risen from the dead. Jesus checked Paul in mid-course; checked him for the sake of the Christians in Damascus, for the sake of Paul himself, and for the sake of the service which Paul could render to the kingdom of God.

There are in The Acts three accounts of Paul's conversion: the account here in the ninth chapter (which we may call

Luke's account, though, of course, Luke learned the manner of it from Paul's own lips) ; the account in the twenty-second chapter (Paul's own account, contained in his address to the mob when he stood, a prisoner, upon the castle stairs in Jerusalem) ; and the account in the twenty-sixth chapter (Paul's defense when brought before King Agrippa). All three of these accounts affirm that Paul, who likely had not seen Jesus during His earthly ministry, now beheld Him raised from the dead and glorious in majesty.

In an event of such epochal importance, each small detail is of interest. The "light from heaven" that shone round about Paul was not that of the hot Syrian sun, but a supernatural light marking the approach of the glorified Christ. Any effort at a naturalistic explanation (to state, for example, that Paul suffered a sunstroke) is but reading an extraneous and wholly unwarranted meaning into Luke's plain words. When Paul had fallen to the earth, he heard words which searched his soul: "Saul, Saul, why persecutest thou me?" There is tender sympathy in Christ's use of "Saul." Saul was Paul's Hebrew (perhaps boyhood) name. Paul was stopped, not by force, but by an irresistible love. To his astonished cry, "Who art thou, Lord?" Christ replied in words of utmost simplicity, "I am Jesus whom thou persecutest." The ASV and the RSV have omitted from this passage the words, "It is hard for thee to kick against the pricks," for these words do not appear here in the best manuscripts. The expression is found, however, in Acts 26:14, and undoubtedly was a part of Christ's speech to Paul. Paul had been acting stubbornly, like an ox kicking against the goad and only hurting himself by doing so.

The appearance of Christ blinded Paul, but in that instant he realized the mistake he had made; knew that instead of serving God he had indeed been fighting against God; saw that Jesus, far from being the arch-enemy of society, was in truth the Saviour of the world. Paul knew, from his own heart as well as from Jesus' words, that he had been persecuting the servants of the Lord of heaven and earth, the One whom he himself should have been serving with all the loyalty and faithfulness of which he was capable. He experienced a complete reversal of feeling and purpose. From that moment it became his chief ambition to make his entire life well pleasing to Jesus Christ. He became, by the regenerating power of the Holy Spirit, a new man.

We may discern in Paul's experience a divinely planned preparation effected through Spirit-directed persons. We shall not forget the faithful testimony borne by Stephen, nor the courage and confidence with which Stephen went to his death. Certainly, Paul had not forgotten those things. He had beheld the same faith and fortitude in the Christians whom he had arrested and brought to trial. He could not dismiss those memories from his mind. Furthermore (so we learn from his letters) he had for some time entertained misgivings as to the effectiveness of his efforts as a Pharisee to achieve personal righteousness through a strict observance of the law. He was finding it hard indeed to kick against these pricks of conscience. This being true, we must never forget our responsibility as Christians to point others to Christ. We must never think that what we can do toward achieving their salvation is unimportant. There is much truth in the often quoted words: "If Stephen had not prayed, Paul might never have been saved."

We shall be making a serious mistake, however, if we think of Paul's conversion as a wholly subjective experience. Not Paul only, but his companions also, saw the light out of heaven. They too were struck down by it.[4] Likewise, those who journeyed with Paul, as well as Paul himself, heard the heavenly voice, though apparently they were not able to distinguish the words which Christ spoke.[5] We shall be making an equally great mistake if we minimize in any way the part which Christ Himself had in Paul's conversion. The initiation and consummation of all things always are in the hands of God. The divine activity both transcends and makes possible all human activity. God teaches and man learns; God draws and man consents; God gives and man accepts.

The relationship between the human and the divine factors is well set forth in these words written by the late Dr. H.

[4] Acts 26:14.
[5] Acts 9:7.

E. Dana: "It is clearly evident that the Holy Spirit employs human agencies in the work of regeneration. The prayers and interest of Christian friends, the word of Christian testimony, and the impact of Christian example, are the instrumentalities the Holy Spirit commonly uses. With these, the Spirit produces the conviction upon which regeneration must be based. It is the divine Spirit of God Himself, however, who finally accomplishes the miracle of spiritual transformation." [6]

It is clear both from Luke's narrative and from Paul's epistles that Paul did not think of his conversion as the result of a seeking on his part to find God in Jesus Christ. He had rebelled violently against every suggestion that Jesus was the Christ. Neither did Paul attribute his conversion to any human circumstance or combination of human factors. He felt that he owed his salvation to the grace and intervention of Christ. Christ had appeared to him, had laid hold upon him, when he had been wholly bent upon persecuting the Christians.

We are sometimes puzzled by Paul's conversion. It seems to us unaccountable and largely contrary to all our present-day experience. But perhaps we err in thinking of it as exceptional; perhaps we should think of it as typical. Does not the risen Christ interpose Himself in the way of every man who is bent upon doing evil? Does He not confront every soul, and does He not speak words which search that soul to its depths? And may it not be that the heavenly light and the supernal voice of Christ there on the Damascus road were, in a sense, but a manifestation to the eyes and ears of men of what is implicit in every conversion, a dramatization of those spiritual things which are basic to all valid Christian experience and to all truly Christian theology?

*Paul Receives His Commission as a Christian* (*Acts 9:8-19; 22:11-16; 26:16-18*)

To Paul's query, "Lord, what wilt thou have me to do?" the Lord had replied, "Arise, and go into the city, and it shall be told thee what thou must do." But when Paul opened his

6 Published in *Adult Class* for April 2, 1944. Copyright, The Judson Press.

eyes (he had shut them instinctively against the light from heaven), he could see nothing at all. He was blind. It was necessary for his companions to lead him by the hand. He who had set out for Damascus with so much pride and boasting entered that city a chastened and completely humbled man. Christ extends His kingdom now, as then, by means of men whose lives He has changed. Paul found lodging with a man named Judas, whose house was on Straight St. That ancient street still runs through the city of Damascus from east to west. Once settled there, Paul spent the next three days in fasting and prayer. In the course of his praying, the Lord, by a vision, made known to him that he would shortly receive a visit from a Christian named Ananias.

This Ananias (to be distinguished, of course, from that Ananias of whom we read in ACTS 5:1-6) was both a devout Jew and an earnest Christian believer.[7] But when the Lord, again by a vision, made it known to Ananias that he should visit Paul, Ananias at first hesitated. He knew how zealously Paul had persecuted Christians, and it seemed to him that the Lord was sending him on a very dangerous mission. The Lord then gave Ananias assurance that Paul was a changed man, a man who had been divinely chosen for a special work. Paul was to preach Christ, not only to the children of Israel, but also to the Gentiles and their kings. When Ananias had sought out Paul's lodging place and had come into the room where Paul was, he addressed him as "Brother."

Paul heard with joy Ananias' statement that he had come to restore his sight and to impart to him the Holy Spirit. At the touch of Ananias' hands, what seemed to be scales fell from before Paul's eyes and he had his sight once again. At the same time, Paul's whole being became filled with the Holy Spirit. This bestowal of the Holy Spirit upon Paul was for the sake of the work which Paul was to do. It was to prepare him and strengthen him for the many things which he would have to endure as a Christian. Such fillings with the Spirit are never for the sake of self, but always for the sake

[7] Acts 22:12. Apparently the hostility of non-Christian Jews toward Christian Jews was not so prevalent in Damascus as in Jerusalem.

of service to be rendered. It was with Paul as it had been with the disciples on the day of Pentecost.

When Ananias, in carrying out his instructions, explained to Paul what Paul's lifework thereafter was to be, Paul displayed no surprise. It was none other than that which he already had heard from the lips of Christ himself.[8] But the fact that Ananias had thus come to him and had reiterated the commission which the Lord had given him (Paul, it may be, had discussed it as yet with no one), gave him the assurance for which he had been praying so earnestly. Paul knew then that his work henceforth was to be the telling of what he had seen and heard. He was to be Christ's ambassador to the thousands, Gentiles as well as Jews, who did not know Jesus as Lord and Christ.

But first there was something which Paul needed to do. Ananias made known to Paul the importance of baptism. It was not essential to Paul's salvation, for Paul already had been thoroughly converted. His sins had been washed away when, on the Damascus road, he had first called on the name of the Lord. Of that inner cleansing to which Ananias made reference,[9] the external washing of baptism could be only a public affirmation and representation. But submission to baptism was essential to Paul's obedience to Christ. Christ had commanded baptism, and Paul's acceptance of it would be evidence of his readiness to obey Christ in all things. Furthermore, Paul's baptism, since it would be performed publicly, would be his confession to one and all that he had become a follower of Christ. It would bring him into fellowship with the baptized believers in Damascus. Paul's understanding of baptism as symbolizing a resurrection—a resurrection from death in sin to new life in Christ—is not set forth in The Acts, but in the Pauline epistles.[10] After Paul had been baptized, he broke his fast, took food, and was physically strengthened. For a few days he gave himself to an enheartening fel-

8 Acts 26:16-18.

9 Acts 22:16.

10 In such passages as Rom. 6:3-4; Col. 2:12 and 3:1.

lowship with the Christians of Damascus. Fellowship with the very Christians he had set out to persecute!

## Paul Begins His Preaching of Christ (Acts 9:20-25)

But Paul was not one who could long be inactive. The words of his Lord, commissioning him, echoed in his ears; and gratitude for his salvation prompted him to give to his Lord complete and unquestioning obedience. There in Damascus, where he had planned to put an end to the Christian movement, he began his preaching of Christ. If Paul's first efforts at Christian preaching won no converts (none are reported), they at least caused widespread comment. All were amazed to learn that the persecutor had turned preacher.

It may be that this first essay at Christian preaching convinced Paul that he needed to organize his thoughts better, that he needed to consider more fully the implications of his conversion, and that he needed in particular to determine what bearing this way of salvation by grace, by which he had found peace with God, might have upon Israel's long and futile quest after righteousness through a punctilious keeping of the Mosaic law. Paul had received the Holy Spirit, but the impartation of the Holy Spirit does not make all mental effort unnecessary. It may be, therefore, that it was the desirability of readjusting his thinking, of outlining his future program, and of preparing suitable Christian sermons that led Paul to make that journey into Arabia to which he refers in Galatians 1:17.[11] In the quiet of the desert he studied the Old Testament Scriptures afresh and he communed with God.

In all, Paul spent three years in Arabia and Damascus. How much of that time was spent in the desert, we cannot tell; but since Paul was a man of active disposition, it is likely that he soon returned to Damascus and that the greater part of the three-year period was spent in that city. This is sure: when Paul returned from Arabia he had "increased the more in strength." So much had he grown in Christian character and ability that he then was able to refute all the arguments

[11] It is likely that by "Arabia" the Hauran in Transjordania is meant. That district was peopled with a mixture of Jews and Arabs.

which were advanced by the non-Christian Jews. So successful was he in showing that Jesus was the Christ that some of the discomfited Jewish leaders began to plot his death. Thus, his preaching of the gospel caused him to experience in Damascus the same deadly hostility which Peter and John had faced in Jerusalem. Paul's enemies lay in wait to slay him, but their plot became known to the believers, who quickly took steps to get Paul out of the city safely. Because all of the city gates were being watched both night and day, they waited until an hour came when, under the cover of night, they could secretly lower Paul in a basket over the wall.[12] This was but the first of many narrow escapes which Paul was to experience. Already he was discovering that it was neither easy nor safe to witness for Christ.

## Paul Goes Up to Jerusalem, Then Returns to Tarsus (Acts 9:26-31)

Once safely out of Damascus, Paul made his way back to Jerusalem. Apparently he wished to contact the apostles, to tell them personally of his conversion. It was not to receive any commission from them, for he steadfastly maintained that he had received his apostleship and commission directly from Christ himself. Perhaps he felt under obligation to preach Christ in the city where he had so sorely persecuted Christ's followers. The reception he received in Jerusalem was not one calculated to give him much encouragement. Of those who had been closest to Christ, he found in the city only Peter and James the Lord's brother.[13] The latter had become the head of the church in Jerusalem. Little or no word of Paul's labors in Damascus had reached Jerusalem, and the Christians, for the most part, feared Paul. They doubted his sincerity. At this juncture, Barnabas—the generous Levite from Cyprus—came to Paul's aid. Barnabas believed in Paul and vouched for him. All told, Paul was in Jerusalem on this occasion for fifteen days.

12 For a more detailed account of Paul's escape from Damascus, see 2 Cor. 11:32-33.
13 Gal. 1:18-19.

While in Jerusalem Paul undertook to preach Christ, speaking boldly. He sought to win to Christ some of the Hellenists (Grecian Jews). He understood them best, and thought perhaps that they would be most ready to receive the gospel. But his arguments only aroused their anger. Seeing that they planned to slay Paul, his Christian brethren hurried him out of the city. They took him down to Caesarea, on the coast, and saw him safely aboard a ship bound for Tarsus, the city of his birth.

The conversion of Paul, the chief persecutor, put an end, for a time, to the troubles of the churches. Throughout Judea, Galilee, and Samaria, the churches were strengthened in the faith, "edified." Their members walked "in the fear of the Lord, and in the comfort of the Holy Ghost." That being so, it is not surprising that the number of believers multiplied.

## CHAPTER 9

# The Early Preaching to the Gentiles

ACTS 9:32–11:18; 12:1-19

NOW a brief turning back, for Luke is desirous of keeping his account of the expansion of Christianiṭy in correct chronological order. He does not find this easy to do, for important events were happening daily, in many lives, in many places. Before continuing his account of the life and labors of Paul, he has something more to tell us concerning the apostle Peter, something which will have a bearing upon Paul's future work.

## Peter's Ministry in Lydda and Joppa (Acts 9:32-43)

When Paul, following his escape from Damascus, scene of his first preaching, had gone up to Jerusalem, he had found none of the apostles there save Peter and James the Lord's brother. It is obvious that the rest of the apostles, taking advantage of this respite from persecution, were busy spreading the gospel in various parts of Judea and Samaria. Luke would not have us think that Peter was taking no part in this work of carrying out the first stages of the Great Commission. To correct any such false impression, he proceeds to tell of Peter's ministry in Lydda and Joppa.

Lydda was a village on the Plain of Sharon. There were some Christians (saints)[1] there, probably as a result of the

---

[1] The first use of the word "saints" occurred in Acts 9:13. Note that Luke never uses this word in its present-day Roman Catholic sense. Luke is not speaking of certain ones who have died and been glorified, but of living Christians who have dedicated their lives to Christ's service.

preaching of Philip.[2] In the course of a preaching tour, Peter came down to Lydda, and there he found a man named Aeneas[3] who, being afflicted with some form of paralysis, had not been able to leave his bed for eight years. Though it is not definitely so stated, it is implied that Aeneas was a Christian. At any rate, when Peter said to him: "Aeneas, Jesus Christ maketh thee whole: arise, and make thy bed," he had faith enough to obey immediately. Strength entered into his limbs; he was healed! So impressed were his neighbors and friends— those who knew how helpless he had been—that they told everyone of the miracle. In consequence, many more people of Lydda and vicinity turned to the Lord.

It was much the same in Joppa, a coastal city not far distant. The Christians of that city sent for Peter, because Dorcas, a Christian woman beloved by all for her good works, had died. The members of her family were grief-stricken, and the church felt that it had suffered an irreparable loss. Perhaps Peter could help them. When Peter reached Joppa, he found the body of Dorcas already laid out in preparation for burial. The room was filled with mourners, among them the impoverished widows whom Dorcas had aided by her almsgiving and needlework. Peter did not immediately address the dead woman, for he felt a need to pray. Probably his prayer was not so much for power as for an understanding of the will of God. It was for God to say whether or not this dead woman should be restored to life. Only after the room had been cleared of mourners and he had prayed to the point where he felt he knew the will of God, did he address the lifeless form. Speaking in Aramaic, it was but natural that he should address her by her Aramaic name, Tabitha, rather than by her Greek name, Dorcas.[4] "Tabitha cumi," he said; that is to say, "Tabitha, arise." Dorcas opened her eyes and sat up. Peter assisted her to her feet, and, taking her by the hand, led her into the room where her Christian friends were assembled.

[2] Acts 8:40.

[3] The name Aeneas is Greek, but it was not uncommon for a Jew to have a Greek name. Had he been a Gentile, that fact would have been mentioned.

[4] Both names, Tabitha and Dorcas, mean "a gazelle."

This raising from the dead was not for Dorcas' sake only; it was for the sake of the church also. As a result of this miracle, incontrovertible in its evidential value, many more persons believed on the Lord. Peter remained in Joppa for some time, that he might give direction to the growing work there.

Do we find it hard to believe that this humble Galilean fisherman should work such miracles as these? Let us remember that Peter had walked with Christ, and that the Holy Spirit had been bestowed upon him in order, most importantly, that he might be able to do the work of the Kingdom. Let us remember also that Peter took no credit to himself for any of the things which he did. He had but offered himself as a human channel through which the risen and all-powerful Christ might operate. When he was questioned concerning the healing of the man lame from his birth, he said: "Be it known unto you all, and to all the people of Israel, that by the name of Jesus Christ of Nazareth, whom ye crucified, whom God raised from the dead, even by him doth this man stand here before you whole." [5] His word to Aeneas was, "Jesus Christ maketh thee whole." And in his *"Tabitha cumi,"* both the voice and the authority were those of Him who had said to the dead daughter of Jairus, *Talitha cumi.*[6] Truly, The Acts of the Apostles is a book of wonders, but the wonders are those wrought by the Son of God.

*Peter, in Obedience to a Vision, Preaches to Gentiles*
    *(Acts 10:1-48)*

Peter's ministry to the Jews, both in Jerusalem and on the Plain of Sharon, was good, but it did not reach far enough. It stopped short of that part of the Great Commission which says, "unto the uttermost part of the earth." But before Peter would be ready to go very far afield, he needed to be taught to overcome his Jewish prejudice against all things Gentile. The Holy Spirit already was directing matters to that end.

That Peter already had overcome some of his prejudices

[5] Acts 4:10.

[6] Luke (in Luke 8:53) gives only the Greek translation; for the actual Aramaic words, see Mark 5:41.

and was beginning to have a Christian regard for men, based
on their worth as men rather than on their race, customs, or
occupation, is indicated by the fact that during his stay in
Joppa he lodged with "one Simon a tanner." According to
the rabbis, the business of tanning, since it required the handling of dead animals, made anyone who engaged in it cere-
monially unclean. But Peter remembered, it may be, that
Jesus had taught that it was the inner spirit, never the external things, which made a man unclean; and he doubtless
remembered also that Jesus had not hesitated to break certain
of the rabbinic regulations.[7] At any rate, Peter lodged with
Simon the tanner. Simon, at least, was a Jew, not a Gentile.
Men find it easier to surrender a religious scruple than to give
up their pride of race.

One day, while he was upon the housetop praying, Peter
had a vision. It seemed to him that the heavens opened, and
out of them a great vessel was lowered. This vessel really was
such a sheet as was used for the sail of a large boat. Held
within the sheet were all manner of animals, those that were
unclean, by their proximity, rendering all the rest of the
animals unclean. Then Peter heard a heavenly voice saying:
"Rise, Peter; kill, and eat." Peter was indeed hungry, for it
was midday and the noon meal had not yet been served.
Peter's appetite prompted him to obey, but his Jewish scruples
concerning clean and unclean foods held him back. In fact,
he somewhat indignantly replied that he had never in all his
life eaten any unclean food. Whereupon the heavenly voice
declared: "What God hath cleansed, that call not thou common" (i.e., unclean). Furthermore, making the entire vision
more emphatic, this happened not once only, but three times.
While Peter still puzzled over what this vision might signify,
the Holy Spirit, ever the divine Interpreter and Teacher,[8]
made known to Peter that three men were seeking him, and
that he should not hesitate to go with them, for they, like
Peter himself, were being divinely directed.

In Caesarea, nearly thirty miles away, was a Roman cen-

[7] See Luke 11:37-41, noting especially Jesus' words: "All things are
clean unto you."
[8] John 16:13.

turion named Cornelius. This captain was a devout man; he prayed to God and he gave generously to the poor. But he was not a Jew; he was a Gentile. He was not even a proselyte. The most that could be said for him was that he was a Jehovah-worshiper and that he sought to live in accordance with high ethical standards. But that was enough to secure for him a special revelation. God answered his prayer for light by giving him a vision. In it an angel bade him send for Peter. He would find Peter in Joppa, in the home of Simon the tanner. Peter would tell him what he should do. The three men of whom the Holy Spirit had advised Peter were the messengers Cornelius had sent to invite Peter to his home. God's timing is always perfect, and it so happened that at the very moment when God had prepared Peter to receive these three men, their knock was heard upon the door.

The messengers were weary and lodging was provided for them that night. The next morning Peter set out with them for Caesarea. Wisely, he took with him "certain brethren" (six Jewish Christians), for he was going at the request of a Gentile, and he would need, most likely, to enter that Gentile's home. It would be well, he thought, to have these responsible persons present to witness all that took place. If Peter felt any reluctance to go on this errand or had any doubts as to its propriety, he did not let these things slow his steps. It had become clear to him that his vision had a significance beyond that of clean and unclean meats; it had to do also with races and persons. If God had revealed His will to Cornelius, a Gentile (i.e., had dealt with him as clean), who was he, Peter, to treat Cornelius as unclean? It clearly was God's will that he should go; and if God did not count the Gentiles as unclean, then he would suffer no defilement from entering Cornelius' house or even from eating with him.

When Peter reached Caesarea, Cornelius showed him the utmost courtesy; in fact, he would have worshiped him as a divine messenger if Peter had permitted it. Peter found that Cornelius had summoned all the members of his family and a large company of his friends—Gentiles all. First, Peter related his vision; then Cornelius related his vision. Cornelius concluded his account by saying to Peter: "We are all here present before God, to hear all things that are commanded thee of God." These Gentiles were waiting for Peter to preach to them!

Peter began his sermon by declaring: "Of a truth I perceive that God is no respecter of persons: but in every nation he that feareth him, and worketh righteousness, is accepted with him." That is to say, God is not one who is swayed by favoritism; He deals justly with all. Whereas our human inclination is to regard first a man's nationality, race, and outward appearance, and to give only secondary consideration to his character, God always looks upon the heart. That declaration by Simon Peter, marking as it does another milestone in his apprehension of the gospel, has lost none of its timeliness, and it is not unworthy of being placed alongside his profession of belief uttered at that other Caesarea (Philip's Caesarea).[9]

As for the rest of Peter's sermon, it did not differ, save in details, from sermons which he had preached on other occasions. After all, there is but one gospel; one gospel, for Jews and Gentiles alike. Peter told his hearers how Jesus had gone about doing good, how He had been crucified, and how God had raised Him from the dead. There could be no doubt about the tremendous fact of the resurrection. He and many others had been witnesses of it. The resurrection was divine proof that this Jesus was indeed the Christ, the Saviour, the One whom God had appointed to judge every man, living or dead. He concluded his sermon with an invitation which was breath-taking in its scope and generosity: "Whosoever believeth in him shall receive remission of sin."

All who heard Peter recognized his sincerity. Indeed, he but related facts which already had been widely discussed. These Gentiles acknowledged the truth of his statements; they believed on the Lord Jesus Christ. That they were genuinely converted is indicated by the startling thing which happened next. Even before Peter had completed his sermon, the Holy Spirit came upon these Gentile believers. Came upon them in the very same way as upon the Jewish believers on the day of Pentecost. There was the same spiritual exaltation,

9 At Caesarea Philippi. See Luke 9:20.

the same fortification of spirit, the same ecstatic speaking with tongues, the same praising of God. The Jewish witnesses whom Peter had brought with him were astonished, but they could not gainsay what they themselves had seen and heard. Since these Gentiles had already received the Holy Spirit,[10] evidence of God's approval, there was no reason why they should not be baptized. Accordingly, arrangements for their baptism were speedily made. These earnest Gentile believers besought Peter to remain with them as long as he could; doubtless Peter did so, spending the time in giving these converts further instruction in the Christian way.

## Peter Defends Spiritual Freedom  (Acts 11:1-18)

News of Peter's trip to Caesarea spread quickly among the "apostles and brethren" (i.e., the Christian Jews). There were some self-appointed defenders of Jewish orthodoxy among them, and these men were not slow to voice their criticism of Peter's conduct. Instead of rejoicing that so many Gentiles had been won to Christ, they berated Peter for having fraternized with Gentiles: "Thou wentest in to men uncircumcised, and didst eat with them." We wonder if Peter may not then have recalled that day when the Pharisees criticized Jesus for having eaten with publicans and sinners, and Jesus answered them, saying, "They that are whole need not a physician; but they that are sick." [11] It may be that these brethren had not learned of Peter's vision; at least, they were showing themselves unwilling to admit the full import of it.

The issue which was joined was deep seated, one which would disturb the church for many years to come. It involved more than Peter's preaching to Gentiles. The psalmists and

10 Here, contrary to the usual order, the bestowal of the Holy Spirit preceded baptism. This, no doubt, was to give evidence to Peter and his companions that God had accepted these Gentile believers. Obviously, then, baptism is essential neither to conversion nor to the reception of the Holy Spirit. Only those are suitable candidates for baptism who have already believed. The enduement with the Holy Spirit on this occasion (it has been called the Gentile Pentecost) was for the purpose of equipping these believers for Christian service.

11 Luke 5:31.

prophets had foretold a witnessing to the "nations" (Gentiles), but that witnessing, in its Old Testament context, was with a view to winning these "heathen" peoples to Judaism. It anticipated that the believers from among the Gentiles would become Jewish proselytes, that they would observe the Mosaic law, and, in particular, that the males among them would submit to the rite of circumcision, the outward sign of obedience to the Mosaic covenant. Only by becoming Jewish proselytes—so it was maintained—could Gentiles have any part in the rich heritage and divine blessings promised to the chosen people.

Christianity, at the first, was understood by many Jewish believers to be but an extension of Judaism, an added privilege bestowed upon believing Jews. The only proper procedure for a Gentile, according to the sticklers for Jewish orthodoxy, was first to become a Jew by adoption and circumcision, then to become a Christian by believing on Jesus as the promised Messiah of the Jews. But Peter had not followed this legalistic procedure. He not only had done violence to Jewish scruples by eating with Gentiles, but also had accepted these believing Gentiles as fellow Christians. He had enjoined none of the Mosaic demands upon them. This seemed to the more Pharisaic among the Jewish believers to be an unwarranted "letting down of the bars." What if there should be a great influx of these uncircumcised Gentiles? Would they not endanger the church? Would they not, indeed, endanger the whole structure of Judaism? Who could tell what foreign modes of thought or what unbecoming conduct they might introduce, if no Mosaic standards of morality were imposed upon them? The criticism of Peter's work reached such a pitch that Peter, upon his return to Jerusalem, was compelled to defend what he had done.

This incident shows how lacking in New Testament support are all of the Roman Catholic claims of papal preeminence for Peter. Here the church puts Peter on trial for a supposed breach of church discipline, and Peter, far from being able to dismiss the matter by a reference to his supreme authority, finds it necessary to explain to his brethren that in all that he had done he had but obeyed the leading of the Holy Spirit.

Peter recounted to them the vision which he had seen. He explained how his own experience had received confirmation in the Spirit's message to Cornelius. At the very moment when he was pondering the meaning of his vision, the messengers from Cornelius had arrived. The Spirit had bidden him go with them, "nothing doubting," and he had done so. On arriving in Caesarea, he had found the situation to be exactly as the messengers had reported it to him. Cornelius, the centurion, was desirous of learning how he and his household might be saved. Peter then related how he had preached the gospel to them, and how, before he had completed his sermon, the Holy Spirit had come upon them. The same Holy Spirit that had come upon themselves, Jewish believers, on the day of Pentecost. The same Holy Spirit, and in the same overpowering and unmistakable fashion. To all these matters the six Jewish brethren whom Peter had taken with him could bear witness. If God had accepted these Gentile believers, as the bestowal of the Holy Spirit clearly indicated, how could he deny them the baptism which they requested? "What was I," Peter concluded, "that I could withstand God?"

Thus, the final stage in the carrying out of the Great Commission had begun. The gospel had been preached, not to Jews only, not to Samaritans only (the Samaritans were half-Jews), but to Gentiles as well; and not to an occasional Gentile proselyte such as the Ethiopian instructed by Philip, but to a substantial group of Gentiles, none of whom were proselytes. To be sure, it was but a small beginning, but the fact that this had been done possessed significance, and the Holy Spirit had given an undeniable sign of approval upon this extension of missionary effort.

The legalists among the Christians were silenced. For the moment, they held their peace. But the controversy would break out afresh upon Paul's preaching to Gentiles. In our modern world the battle between form and spirit still goes on. Men find it hard to believe that the new covenant under which it is their privilege to live is a covenant "not of the letter, but of the spirit: for the letter killeth, but the spirit giveth life." [12]

## Peter Is Divinely Delivered from Prison (Acts 12:1-19)

In order that we may continue our study of the experiences of Peter, we shall postpone until the next chapter our consideration of Acts 11:19-30, and take up instead Acts 12:1-19, a passage which tells of Peter's arrest and subsequent deliverance from prison.

The Herod who had put to death James the brother of John, and who now ordered Peter's arrest, was Herod Agrippa I, a grandson of the Herod the Great who had ruled Judea at the time of the birth of Jesus.[13] The emperor Caligula made him ruler, first, over Galilee, then over Iturea, Trachonitis, and Abilene also. Finally, under the emperor Claudius, he ruled as king over Palestine from A.D. 41 to 44. This king sought the support of the Pharisaic party, and to gain it he displayed, probably hypocritically, a great zeal for the observance of the Mosaic law. Likely it was with a view to pleasing the Pharisees that he had put to death the apostle James. That brutal and wholly unwarranted execution was so well received by the Pharisees that Herod thereupon ordered the arrest of Peter.

It was Herod's intention to put Peter to death also, but it was the season of the passover [14] and at that time no judicial business could be carried on without doing violence to Jewish customs. Observe the regard for the letter of the law and the blindness to the innocence of the man condemned. Accordingly Herod had Peter held in prison until the feast should be concluded. Because he remembered, it may be, that Peter once had been delivered from prison,[15] he took special pains

[12] 2 Cor. 3:6.
[13] Luke 1:5.
[14] The word "Easter," occurring here in the KJV, represents a somewhat unfortunate attempt to find an English word which would show the new significance which the passover season had acquired for the Christians. It was at the time of the passover that Jesus was crucified; it was on what we now call Easter Day that He was raised from the dead.
[15] Acts 5:17-20.

to insure that this time he should be well guarded. Peter was chained to two soldiers; one to each of his wrists. Two additional soldiers were posted as guards, one at the inner door of the prison, the other at the prison's outer door. At the conclusion of each of the four watches into which the twenty-four hours were divided, four new guards would come on duty. How futile these elaborate precautions were to prove! All were made of none effect by reason of the fact that the Christians, through prayer, brought divine aid to Peter.

That they might engage together in praying that Peter's life should be spared, the Christians (a considerable number of them, at least) had assembled in the home of Mary, the mother of John Mark. This Mary apparently was a widow, but she possessed sufficient wealth to own a home large enough for it to be a place where the Christians regularly assembled for worship. If the "certain young man" mentioned in Mark 14:51-52 is to be identified with this John Mark, the author of that Second Gospel, then not impossibly it was in her upper room that Jesus and his disciples had kept the passover and that the Holy Spirit had come upon the disciples on the day of Pentecost. In that same upper room, then, the Christians now were met for prayer.

But on this very night when the Christians prayed, the night preceding the day when Herod planned to put Peter to death, one of God's ever available and ever ready helpers— an angel—clothed in ineffable light, entered Peter's cell. Who, what, are these angels? Let the writer of Hebrews answer that question: "Are they not all ministering spirits, sent forth to minister for them who shall be heirs of salvation?" [16]

The chains fall from Peter's wrists. The angel speaks quick words of command: "Arise, put on your coat, follow me." Peter obeys. He walks as an automaton might walk, for all this, he thinks, can be nothing more than a dream. He and the angel pass the soldiers guarding the inner and outer doors of the prison. Then the great iron gate, the gate into the city, swings open of itself. The angel leads Peter down the street. Then the angel, as suddenly as he had come, disappears. For a moment Peter is confused. He rubs his eyes, pinches him-

16 Heb. 1:14.

self, to be sure that he is awake. It is no dream; Peter has been
delivered from prison a second time, *divinely* delivered. Any
effort to find a human explanation of this deliverance is a
work of supererogation. Luke already has recorded the words
of Christ: "The things which are impossible with men are
possible with God." [17]

Peter hastens to the home of Mary. The Christians praying
there must be informed that their prayers have been answered. Rhoda, a young serving maid, answers his knock upon
the gate. In her excitement at hearing his voice, she fails to
unlock the gate, but runs into the house to spread the good
news. When she announces to those assembled there that
Peter has been delivered from prison, that he is outside, at the
gate—the very thing for which they had been praying—they
tell her that she is out of her wits. When she insists that she
is not mistaken, the most logical explanation that occurs to
them is that Herod already has carried out his intention of
putting Peter to death, and that this is Peter's ghost, or possibly Peter's guardian angel, in the guise of Peter himself,
come to bid them farewell. They do not have the faith to
believe that God has actually answered their prayers! We may
well believe that by this time Peter's knocking upon the gate
has become more insistent, too importunate to be any longer
ignored. They open the gate and find Peter standing there.
It *is* Peter; not his ghost, but Peter in the flesh. What rejoicing then! When Peter can quiet their excitement sufficiently,
he relates to them the manner of his deliverance, and bids
them carry word of it to James (that James who was brother
to our Lord and who had become head of the church in
Jerusalem).

That done, Peter hastens away to "another place." It is
idle to speculate as to what place that may have been. Certainly it was not Rome, as Roman Catholic tradition since the
days of Eusebius would have us believe. If Peter eventually
went to Rome, it was not until a much later time. Acts 15:7-10
shows Peter still in Jerusalem.

Herod's rage on learning of the deliverance of Peter was

[17] Luke 18:27.

great, but wholly impotent. All he could do was to order that the guards, though they had been in no wise responsible for what had taken place, should be put to death. That done and the feast of the passover being ended, a feast which had brought him to Jerusalem out of courtesy to the Jews, Herod returned to his capital, the Roman city of Caesarea.

## CHAPTER 10

# The Church with a World Vision

ACTS 11:19-30; 12:20—13:3

*B*EFORE there can be a world Christian mission, there must be a church with a world vision. The Holy Spirit had created such a church in Antioch in Syria. Before there can be any practical carrying out of such a world Christian mission, there must be a man with a world vision; a man, furthermore, who with that vision ever before him would let the Holy Spirit direct his steps. The Holy Spirit had created such a man in Paul. Paul who once had persecuted the Christians, but who had been converted, and who thereafter had devoted his life to the preaching of the gospel. It is with the story of that church in Antioch and of Paul's connection with it that we shall be concerned in this chapter.

## A Gentile Church Is Established in Antioch *(Acts 11:19-21)*

We recall that the severity of the persecution which began with the stoning of Stephen compelled many of the believers to flee Jerusalem. But these Christian refugees witnessed as they went. They were "scattered abroad," but this scattering, far from putting an end to the Christian movement, only served to spread the gospel in more remote districts which otherwise might not have heard the good news so soon. Some of the refugees traveled as far as Phenice (Phoenicia) and settled, no doubt, in the busy port cities of Tyre and Sidon. Others, who possibly had come originally from Cyprus, secured passage on boats bound for that island some two hundred miles distant. Still others made their way to Antioch in

Syria. Of all the cities in the Roman Empire, Antioch ranked third in size and importance. In general, these refugees were Christian Jews and their practice was to preach the gospel to Jews only; they called upon these Jews to believe on Jesus as their Messiah.

We know, however, that among the Christian Jews in Jerusalem there were many Hellenists. These Hellenists were Jews who had come from lands where the Greek culture was dominant; although Jews, they spoke Greek, and they were more broad-minded, less bound by Jewish custom, than were the Jews native to Palestine. Stephen had been one of these Hellenists; so also, if we may judge by their Greek names, were five of the six other brethren who, with Stephen, constituted the first board of deacons.[1] The seventh, Nicolas (better, Nicolaus), was more than a Hellenized Jew; he was actually a Greek (a Gentile) who had come from Antioch. This Greek had first become a Jewish proselyte, then a Christian believer. The Jewish ecclesiastical authorities considered these Hellenized Jews who had become Christians a more serious threat to the established order than the Palestinian Jews who had become Christians. The latter, so they believed, were more likely to be conservative in their attitude toward Jewish customs. For this reason, the persecution had fallen most heavily upon the Christian Hellenists.

Some of these Christian Hellenists came to Antioch. These men were natives of Cyprus and Cyrene, and Nicolas, since Antioch was his birthplace, quite possibly was with them. Being either Hellenists or Greeks who had become Jewish proselytes, they did not limit their preaching to Jews. They preached the Lord Jesus to any Greeks[2] who would listen, and the Lord blessed their efforts. In some striking way the Lord's "hand" (power) was manifested. A "great number" of the Greeks believed; in consequence, a church made up

[1] Acts 5:6.

[2] The KJV, it is true, has "Grecians" here, i.e., Hellenists; but the RSV more correctly, we believe, reads "Greeks." The manuscripts differ, but the whole point of the passage, and of much that follows, rests upon the fact that these Antioch Christians were not Jews (Hellenists or otherwise), but Greeks, Gentiles.

wholly, or largely, of Greeks came into being. This was the first Gentile church of which we have any record.

*Barnabas and Paul in Antioch  (Acts 11:22-26)*

Word of this Greek church was carried back to Jerusalem. The members of the Jerusalem church felt that this unprecedented development called for some investigating. If there was anything irregular about it, the irregularity ought to be corrected; if the new church was a true church, one which God recognized, then they owed to it any encouragement and assistance within their power. The man whom the Jerusalem church chose as the one to visit Antioch and bring back word concerning the situation there was Barnabas, to whom we were introduced in Acts 4:36-37. Since he had come from Cyprus (i.e., was a Hellenist), he would harbor no initial prejudice against the work of the Hellenists who had made their way to Antioch and had preached the Lord Jesus Christ there. His sympathies were broad, his character was unimpeachable. For this special task, a better man could not have been chosen.

Barnabas was made extremely happy by what he found in Antioch. He saw that the grace of God was at work there. Men were being saved. There was no one to reprimand; he needed only to exhort these Greek believers that with strong purpose they should "cleave unto the Lord." Then, because he was indeed a "good man, and full of the Holy Ghost and of faith," he did not immediately return to Jerusalem, but remained in Antioch that he might join his soul-winning efforts with theirs. In consequence, yet more souls were won to the Lord. We may well believe that all these matters were faithfully reported to the church in Jerusalem by the first messenger traveling to that city.

The church in Antioch had been founded by laymen. Now that it had grown to such size, it required a leader who could devote his entire time to promoting its interests. It needed a leader of more than average ability. That leader, to do the best work, should be able to preach in the Greek language; he should be acquainted with the Greek culture and also

with the Jewish background out of which Christianity had
come; and he should be sympathetic toward the social customs and the religious aspirations of these Gentile believers.
Where could such a man be found? But the Lord had foreseen that need, had trained a man to meet it, even before the
need for such a man had become apparent to Barnabas. That
man was Paul.

Barnabas had thought much about Paul. He recalled the
day when he had vouched for Paul's sincerity in the hearing
of the Jerusalem disciples.[3] He recalled also Paul's zealous
and courageous attempt to preach the gospel to the Greek-
speaking Jews of Jerusalem, an attempt which nearly had
cost Paul his life.[4] Paul, having been born in Tarsus and
having spent many years in that Greek city, would feel at
home in a Greek environment. He knew all that was noble
in Greek literature and philosophy. More than that, he had
lived in Jerusalem, had been thoroughly trained in all matters connected with the Jewish religion.[5] Above all, he had
been genuinely converted; he had received the Holy Spirit,
and for approximately twelve years he had been gaining experience in Christian work. Barnabas wondered if he could
enlist Paul's help. He would tell Paul of what the Holy Spirit
had wrought in Antioch; he would lay upon Paul's heart the
need and the opportunity in that city. But Paul was in Tarsus. He had been working there quietly for the past nine or
ten years. Barnabas made the considerable journey to Tarsus
to find Paul.

Barnabas did find Paul, was pleased with what he saw of
Paul's work there, and readily persuaded Paul to return with
him. For an entire year Barnabas and Paul labored together
in Antioch. They bore a faithful witness to the Lord, and
the Lord added many more believers to the Antioch church.
Barnabas and Paul gave these new believers careful instruction in the Christian way. If we may judge, this was a more
mature Paul, a more thoughtful, poised, and patient Paul,
than the Paul who had begun his preaching in Damascus and

3 Acts 9:26-27.
4 Acts 9:29-30.
5 Acts 22:3.

Jerusalem. In consequence, the results of his preaching were more enduring.

To his account of that memorable year of work, Luke adds this interesting historical note: "The disciples were called Christians first in Antioch." [6] Probably the name was first applied to the believers in derision; but it was a wholly logical designation, and those who were taunted with it, feeling gratitude for all that Christ had done for them, accepted His name as their own, even gloried in it.

### The Antioch Church Sends Aid to Judea (Acts 11:27-30)

Near the close of that year, certain prophets from Jerusalem visited Antioch; among them, one named Agabus. Who were these prophets who for a brief period appear in the life of the New Testament church? Luke tells us only what may be gathered from this passage and from Acts 21:8-13 (a passage in which Agabus reappears). But Paul, in his letters, speaks of these prophets and discusses their Spirit-bestowed gift.[7] Probably we shall come closest to the truth if we do not think of them as belonging to a special ministerial order (clerical orders, in many instances working harm to the churches, were a somewhat later development), but instead regard them as believers in whom the gift of the Holy Spirit took a special form, namely, the ability on occasion to prophesy. What Agabus foretold, he foretold "by the Spirit"; that is to say, to the extent that the Spirit revealed the future to him, and only to that extent, he could predict events still in the future.

[6] This is the first occurrence of the name "Christian" in the New Testament. It appears only here (Acts 11:26), in Acts 26:28, and in 1 Pet. 4:16.

[7] See, for example, Eph. 2:20; 4:11; and 1 Thess. 5:19-20. Incidentally, in the last named passage, there should not be a period between the two clauses, but only a semicolon or comma. He who despises prophesyings quenches the Spirit, for all true prophecies are the voice of the Spirit. In his detailed discussion of the Spirit's gifts (1 Cor. 12:28—14:40), Paul rated prophecy as a higher spiritual gift than speaking with tongues, for although both gave evidence of the Spirit's presence and power, speaking with tongues, except in rare instances, tended to take the form of ecstatic utterances addressed to God and to be meaningful only to the worshiper and God, whereas prophesying, being understood by all who heard, edified the church.

There was never any purposeless predicting, but only such revelations of the future as, in the Spirit's planning, it was well for churches or individuals to have. For this reason the predictions regularly were accompanied by warnings and exhortations. These New Testament prophets, like their Old Testament predecessors, were spokesmen for God.

In the present instance, Agabus, addressing the Antioch church and speaking by the Spirit's direction, made it known that famine conditions would soon prevail throughout the eastern Mediterranean lands. This "great dearth" was some one of the numerous famines which historians tell us occurred in Syria and Palestine during the reign of the emperor Claudius, A.D. 41-54. Probably it was the famine in A.D. 45, of which Josephus tells.

The Antioch Christians, knowing that the Jerusalem Christians had suffered sorely from persecution and would be reduced to even more acute distress by the famine, determined to send them such financial aid as they could. Here was Christian brotherhood in action. They gave "every man according to his ability," [8] and in that way raised a sizable sum of money. With this offering, Barnabas and Paul hastened to Jerusalem. This would be Barnabas' first opportunity to tell the Jerusalem church, by word of mouth, of all that had happened in Antioch. Did any of the conservative Jewish Christians in Jerusalem still doubt the sincerity of the Gentile Christians of Antioch? Did any think that these Gentile Christians who were disregarding the ceremonial requirements of the Mosaic law had no concern for moral living? If so, they had their answer in this offering which Barnabas and Paul delivered into the hands of the elders of the Jerusalem church. The offering was tangible evidence of good will, brotherhood, practical helpfulness, and readiness to accept responsibility— evidence which could not be gainsaid. The offering was more than a token of these things. Substantial aid was given in a situation where aid was greatly needed. At the same time, we may see in the raising and distribution of these relief funds

[8] This was the plan which Paul regularly recommended for financing any kind of Christian work. The plan is stated more fully by him in 1 Cor. 16:1-2.

one of Paul's early efforts to bind together in Christian fellowship Jewish and Gentile believers.

## Judgment Visited upon Herod Agrippa I (Acts 12:20-25)

It was at this time or thereabouts, perhaps while Barnabas and Paul were still in Jerusalem, that the judgment of God fell upon Herod Agrippa I. This king, it will be recalled, had put to death the apostle James, and he would have put to death the apostle Peter also, if the Lord had not delivered Peter from prison. The cities of Tyre and Sidon in some way had incurred the king's displeasure, and the action which he had taken against them had deprived them of the food supplies which previously they had received from Judea. Since it was a time of famine, these cities were in a desperate plight. They dispatched an embassy to Caesarea (Herod's capital), and finding Blastus, the king's chamberlain, they persuaded him (bribed him probably) to secure for them an audience with the king. Josephus has related in considerable detail what then occurred.[9] It was the time of the Greek games, and a great multitude were come together. Herod resplendent in royal robes, addressed the throng. Upon the conclusion of his words, those from Tyre and Sidon sought by flattery to gain the king's favor. They praised him *as a god;* they shouted, and their words were caught up by others: "It is the voice of a god, and not of a man." Here is an indication of the growing cult of emperor worship. Herod, being at least a half-Jew, should have recoiled from this blasphemy; but filled with vanity, he forgot the central teaching of the law of Moses, forgot the chief insistence of the Pharisees, and accepted this praise. He permitted the people to worship him as divine. In that moment judgment was visited upon him. An angel of God smote him. He suffered an excruciating pain in his abdomen (peritonitis?), and becoming inwardly "worm-eaten," he soon died.

Josephus represents this Herod as a king who, after his youthful profligacy, sought to live in accordance with the best traditions of the Pharisees. He states that had it not been for this fatal indiscretion, he might have gone down in history as

---

[9] Josephus, *Antiquities,* XIX, 8, 2.

one of the great rulers of the Jews. But it is difficult to believe that he was actuated by motives of so high a character.[10] The people generally—and so also Luke—saw in Herod's sudden and horrible death a judgment of God, a judgment so obvious and convincing that many were led to turn to God. Herod's persecutions having been thus brought to an end, "the word of God grew and multiplied."

Their work in Jerusalem accomplished, Barnabas and Paul returned to Antioch. They took with them a young man named John Mark.[11] Mark was the son of that Mary in whose home the Christians had met to pray for Peter's release from prison, and a cousin of Barnabas.[12] He could be of much service to Barnabas and Paul as an amanuensis and helper. We shall hear more of Mark very shortly.

## A Mission to the Gentiles Organized (Acts 13:1-3)

We have learned how there was built up in the great Greek city of Antioch a Christian church. It had not been founded by one of the apostles. Perhaps this was the first church to be fully independent of the mother church in Jerusalem. This church, because of its predominantly Gentile character, felt a concern for the salvation of all Gentiles, of whatever race they might be. Its members were capable of thinking in world terms. They were evidencing a readiness to give obedience to the Great Commission in its third and most extensive (its world-wide) aspect.

10 Klausner's defense of Herod's character and conduct in his *From Jesus to Paul* (Macmillan, 1943), p. 348, while scholarly, is far from convincing. He argues that this king did not persecute the Nazarenes for their belief that Jesus was the Messiah, but because they had violated certain ceremonial requirements which were, in his time and kingdom, the laws of the state, and because they had failed to do honor to the Temple, which had become a politico-religious institution.

11 It is possible that John Mark had these two names from birth. John is Jewish; Mark is Roman.

12 Some authorities make Mark the nephew of Barnabas. The newer translations of the text and most modern scholars make him a young cousin of Barnabas. Mary, the mother of Mark, is believed to have been either the sister or the sister-in-law of Barnabas' father. See Col. 4:10 in the KJV and in the RSV.

Associated in the leadership of this church were five Spirit-filled men. Two of them we know already: Barnabas and Paul. The others were Simeon, Lucius, and Manaen. The five are described as "prophets and teachers." We are not to suppose that some of them were prophets and that the rest were teachers, but rather that these men served the church sometimes as prophets (preachers) and sometimes as teachers. We should note how cosmopolitan this group was. Barnabas was a Greek-speaking Jew, originally from the island of Cyprus. Simeon (or Symeon) also was a Jew, but one who had taken in addition a Roman name, Niger. Niger means black, and this adjective may have been applied to him because of his dark skin. The name Lucius is Latin, but since he came from Cyrene on the north coast of Africa, a district where there were many Jews, it is possible that he also was a Hellenistic Jew. The name Manaen comes from the Jewish Menahem. He is described (see the RSV) as "a member of the court of Herod the tetrarch." Herod was an Idumean, and so also may have been this Manaen. Paul, as we know, was a Hellenistic Jew, born in Tarsus in Cilicia. The membership of the Antioch church was predominantly Greek (Gentile). Obviously the stirrings of the Spirit were not limited to members of any one race, but were independent of race.

We find these five men devoting themselves wholeheartedly to the service of God. They fasted and they prayed, indicative of a great spiritual concern. From the outcome, it is evident that their concern was for the salvation of the millions who made up the widespread Gentile world. It is reasonable to believe also that Paul long before this had seen the need for this wider preaching of the gospel and had been one of the first to lay that responsibility upon the hearts of the Antioch congregation.

Although Paul was a Jew by race and by religious heritage, the Gentile world was, in a special way, his world. He had come from Tarsus, a great Greek city, and the part which he was to take in the winning of the Gentiles had been made known to him at the time of his conversion.

At this point it may be well to take account of the "call"

which Paul had received, noting in particular the missionary (Gentile) aspect of it. Following Paul's conversion, the Lord in sending Ananias to restore Paul's sight, said to him concerning Paul: "Go thy way: for he is a chosen vessel unto me, to bear my name before the Gentiles, and kings, and the children of Israel." [13] Paul was not to neglect his responsibility to the children of Israel, but significantly the Gentiles were mentioned first. Ananias, of course, made known to Paul what the Lord had said concerning him and his future work. We have an acknowledgment of this in Paul's own words. Telling of Ananias' visit to him, he reported that Ananias said to him: "The God of our fathers hath chosen thee . . . for thou shalt be his witness unto all men of what thou hast seen and heard."[14] Not a preaching to Jews only, but a witnessing "unto all men"! Finally, from the third account of Paul's conversion, we learn that Ananias but reminded Paul of what the Lord already had said to him. Paul states that the Lord had addressed his thus: "I have appeared unto thee for this purpose, to make thee a minister and a witness both of these things which thou hast seen, and of those things in the which I will appear unto thee; delivering thee from the people, and from the Gentiles, unto whom now I send thee, to open their eyes, and to turn them from darkness to light, and from the power of Satan unto God, that they may receive forgiveness of sins, and inheritance among them which are sanctified by faith that is in me." [15]

Nor did it stop there. When Paul was in Jerusalem the first time after his conversion (that brief fifteen day visit following his escape from Damascus), he was no doubt much discouraged by the unwillingness of the Jews to hear his message. While worshiping in the Temple the Lord appeared to him in a vision and bade him leave Jerusalem at once. In part, this was because his life was in danger; but, beyond that, it was because the Lord had other work for him to do. The Lord said to Paul: "Depart: for I will send thee far hence unto the Gen-

13 Acts 9:15.
14 Acts 22:14-15.
15 Acts 26:16-18.

tiles."[16] The time had now come when all these unforgetable experiences, these divine calls to special service, were to come to fulfillment.

What the Holy Spirit said to the men of the Antioch church who, in prayer and fasting, had sought divine guidance, was: "Separate me Barnabas and Saul for the work whereunto I have called them." The will of the Spirit was made known by them to the congregation. It amounted to this: that the church, foregoing the services of their two most influential leaders, should set them apart to carry out a mission to Gentiles in more distant regions; and, in sending out these two foreign missionaries, should undertake their support spiritually, by praying for them, and materially, by their gifts.

The church did not take action lightly, but fasted and prayed, as their leaders had done, that they might be sure that they were being directed to take this momentous step by the Holy Spirit. Assurance came. The church thereupon "set apart" Barnabas and Paul; commissioned them, that is, for this special service. In sign of this, they "laid their hands on them." This done, the church—with what hopes and with what anxieties, we may not know—bade them farewell and sent them on their way. The missionary spirit and the missionary program, of course, had been implicit in the gospel from the very beginning. It had been made explicit in the Great Commission. Here the missionary enterprise achieved an organized form: men specially commissioned for the task, a church accepting responsibility for their support. Born in prayer, Spirit-directed, it yet will accomplish the evangelization of the world.

[16] Acts 22:17-21. There appears no sufficient reason for holding, as do some commentators, that this vision came to Paul during the days when he was in Jerusalem delivering the offering for famine relief that had been sent by the Antioch church.

## CHAPTER 11

# The First Mission to the Gentiles

*I*N ALL the centuries since the resurrection of Jesus Christ, has there ever been a day more freighted with promise for the future than that spring day in A.D. 47 when Barnabas and Paul, having been solemnly commissioned by the Antioch church, set forth upon that first mission to the Gentiles? Their departure for the island of Cyprus marked the beginning of all the organized missionary efforts which the Christian churches have put forth—efforts which, under the blessing of God, have given the light of Christ to millions who dwelt in darkness.

To be sure, it was a modest beginning; so small a start, in fact, that to many persons the going of Barnabas and Paul must have seemed, if not foolhardy, certainly inconsequential. Two messengers of Christ sent out to win the millions in the Gentile lands included within the far-flung Roman Empire! But other messengers would follow in their train.

Look well, then, at Barnabas and Paul as they restlessly pace the deck of the merchant ship which, taking full advantage of the prevailing easterly wind, quickly bears them out to sea. They are the forerunners of all that noble company of missionaries, men and women, who have endured privation and loneliness, and who have counted not even the laying down of their lives too great a price to pay for the privilege of being ambassadors of Jesus Christ. And the little band of Christians on the wharf, waving farewell, then falling upon their knees to pray—it is the first of all the Christian congregations which, by their prayers and gifts, have supported the missionaries in their work.

### Barnabas and Paul Sent to the Island of Cyprus (Acts 13:4-5)

Luke's statement calls for notice: "So they, being sent forth by the Holy Ghost, departed unto Seleucia; and from thence they sailed to Cyprus." If the Holy Spirit had not sent them forth, their going would have been to no purpose. "Except the Lord build the house, they labour in vain that build it." [1] On this score there was no uncertainty in the minds of Barnabas and Paul. To the best of their human ability, they were endeavoring to carry out the Great Commission which Christ had given His followers. Furthermore, their vision of a needy Gentile world and their sense of having been called to this special service had received confirmation in the church's concern (a Spirit-awakened concern) for the salvation of the Gentiles. Barnabas and Paul were not self-appointed missionaries; a Spirit-directed church, after fasting and prayer, had sent them out. Observe that only a verse before, Luke had written: "they [i.e., the church] sent them away." There is no contradiction between Luke's "they sent them away" and his "they, being sent forth by the Holy Ghost." Both statements are true. The Holy Spirit can work through a congregation which prays equally as well as through an individual who prays.

So these missionaries, these "sent-forth men" (for that is what the word "missionary" means), together with their young assistant John Mark, had gone down to Seleucia, Antioch's seaport, located at the mouth of the Orontes River. From thence they had sailed for Salamis, the most important as well as the most easterly port on the southern shore of the island of Cyprus. From this point on, we shall need to refer constantly to the map, for the significance of the missionary achievements of which we shall learn must be measured not alone in terms of years of Christian service, but also in terms of miles traveled, of hazardous voyages by sea and wearisome journeys by land. We shall have no adequate comprehension

[1] Ps. 127:1.

of the character of Paul or of his missionary companions, if we fail to take account of the persistence with which they pushed on, despite poor means of transportation, from land to land in their zeal to spread the gospel.

The choice of Cyprus as the scene for the beginning of their missionary labors was a wise one. There already had been some preaching of Christ on that very sizable island, for some Cyprians who had taken up their abode in Jerusalem had become Christians, and when driven out of Jerusalem by the persecutions there, they had returned to their ancestral homes.[2] Furthermore, Cyprian Christians had had a part in the founding of the Antioch church.[3] These natives of Cyprus may have urged that the island offered a field ripe for evangelization, inasmuch as such preaching as had been done there had been addressed to the Jews, whereas the greater part of the island's thickly settled population was Gentile. Cyprus, it will be recalled, was Barnabas' home. He knew the country well, and no doubt he had relatives and friends there who could be of assistance to him and his companions in their missionary labors. Besides, Cyprus was not far distant, and boats bound for Cyprus sailed frequently during the spring and summer months.

The voyage to Cyprus was uneventful and quickly made. Salamis, where the missionaries landed, was the commercial center of the island. Its population consisted mostly of Greeks and Phoenicians, but there were many Jews there also. Barnabas and Paul began their preaching in one of the synagogues. Paul had been given a ministry to the Gentiles, but he was not unmindful of the fact that he had a responsibility to those of his own race. So long as the synagogues were open to him, he made use of them. The Jews whom he met in the synagogues and the Gentile proselytes who worshiped with them—one would expect—would be more easily won to Christ than Gentiles who knew nothing of the Scriptures and faith of the Jews. But this did not always prove to be the case. The missionaries doubtless spent some little time in Salamis; then they began to journey on foot westward across the island,

2 Acts 8:4; 11:19.
3 Acts 11:19-20.

preaching in each town and village through which they passed.

## The Conversion of Sergius Paulus (Acts 13:6-12)

At Paphos, in the western part of the island, Barnabas and Paul won a significant Christian victory. Paphos was the capital of Cyprus and the residence of its Roman ruler, the proconsul Sergius Paulus.[4] Luke's account reflects credit upon this governor's character, for it represents him as a man of inquiring and discerning mind. When Sergius Paulus learned of the preaching of Barnabas and Paul, he asked to be more fully informed concerning the things they taught.

In the court of the proconsul there was an unscrupulous Jew, named Bar-jesus. How much significance we should attach to this name is not clear. He may indeed have been the son of some Joshua (Hebrew) or Jesus (Greek), for "bar" means "son." But inasmuch as Joshua (Jesus) means "saviour," it may be that he had adopted this name to further his claim of possessing supernatural powers. He was also known as Elymas, a name of uncertain derivation which Luke says had the same meaning as "*magus*," i.e., a magician. This "false prophet" and "sorcerer," by means of some really very simple tricks, had long preyed upon the credulity and superstition of the people, and it may be that he had gained some influence over Sergius Paulus. Elymas not only contradicted publicly the true statements which were made by Paul, but also sought to dissuade Sergius Paulus from giving any heed to them. He knew that once the proconsul learned the truth, his own profitable, but dishonest, business of sorcery would be brought to an end.

There in Paphos, on this very first missionary journey, the issue was joined—the clear-cut issue between truth and falsehood, between light and darkness, between life and death, between Christ and the black arts which infested the ancient

---

[4] W. M. Ramsay, in his volume *St. Paul the Traveller and the Roman Citizen,* tells of the finding in Cyprus of a Greek inscription which impressively confirms the historical accuracy of Luke's statement that Sergius Paulus was "deputy" (proconsul) of Cyprus at this time.

world and which missionaries encounter on many fields even to this day. It is not surprising, therefore, that the Spirit moved Paul to rebuke this sorcerer in the severest fashion.

We can readily discern wherein Elymas deserved this condemnation. Far from being a "son of a saviour," he was a "child of the devil." He was the enemy of everything that was true. Being a Jew, he was well aware of the Old Testament prohibition of sorcery in all its forms.[5] By his false prophecies he parodied the works of the Holy Spirit and made doubly difficult the task of God's true prophets.

Elymas was stricken with blindness. One must become blind to the things of this world before he can see the things that are spiritual. Chrysostom's comment is: "By the sign whereby he [Paul] had himself been won he desired to win the sorcerer." Elymas, who had made others blind, now himself became blind; he who had led others astray, now himself needed to be led by the hand. But the judgment was mingled with mercy. The blindness was to be but for a season. When Sergius Paulus beheld this well deserved judgment come upon the sorcerer, he realized that Barnabas and Paul were representatives of the true God, and he straightway believed on Christ.

This incident, standing as it does near the beginning of organized missionary effort, possesses more significance than may at first appear. A notoriously wicked man had been overthrown, and a distinguished and influential Roman had been won to Christ. Sergius Paulus, now that he had been liberated from his superstitious fears, could find a new purpose and happiness in life; more than that, he in turn could pass that same blessing on to others. But in a larger sense, this scene is a parable enacted for the instruction of all later generations. God's Word, when fearlessly and truthfully proclaimed, brings judgment upon evil-doers, brings salvation to those who will believe it. Spells and incantations, witchcraft and sorcery, dishonesty and ill will, cannot withstand the power of God. The victory always is with the true and loving and forgiving Christ. What happened at Paphos is typical of the entire history of Christian missions.

5 Lev. 20:27; Deut. 18:10-11.

Before concluding our consideration of these events, we must notice what Luke writes in the ninth verse of this thirteenth chapter: "Then Saul, (who also is called Paul,) . . . ." Luke is serving notice upon the reader that hereafter he will employ the name Paul, rather than Saul. The suggestion that Paul adopted the name Paul at this time out of deference to Sergius Paulus, the proconsul, seems out of keeping with the independent spirit of the apostle. The probability is that he had been given both names at birth: Saul being his Jewish name, and Paul (Paulus, in Latin and Greek) his Roman name. When he was in Jerusalem, it was but natural that he should be known by his Jewish name; now that he was among Gentiles and was encountering Greeks and Romans, he wisely employed his Roman name and made the most of his Roman citizenship. The name Saul does not occur again, except in those passages in which Paul is relating the manner of his conversion; in them he states that the Lord addressed him by his Jewish name.

## By Sea and Land to Antioch in Pisidia (Acts 13:13-41)

When Paul had finished his work in Paphos, he did not return to Antioch in Syria, the city from which he had set forth, but he (adventurous soul that he was) journeyed on to the mainland of Asia Minor. In due course, he and his companions reached Perga in the coastal district of Pamphylia.

What happened at Perga is not entirely clear. Many think that in that low-lying district, with its marshes and mosquitoes, Paul became ill with a malarial fever. This may have been why he decided not to remain in Perga, but to go inland to the town of Antioch in Pisidia,[6] where he would find a healthier climate due to its higher altitude. But this would require a journey into the interior that would be both difficult and dangerous. It would necessitate climbing the Taurus

[6] This Antioch was one of sixteen towns named in honor of Antiochus, general in the army of Philip of Macedon. It lay within the Roman province of Galatia, and was about one hundred miles from Perga, where the missionaries had landed.

mountains and passing through a district infested with bandits. There likely was some debate as to the wisdom of pushing on to Antioch in Pisidia. At any rate, the young John Mark at this time left their company and returned to Jerusalem. Why he did so is not stated. Perhaps it was because this missionary journey was proving longer than he had bargained for. More about John Mark when we come to the consideration of Acts 15:37-38.

On reaching Antioch in Pisidia, Paul quickly made his way to the Jewish synagogue. It was there that he proposed to begin his preaching. It is worthy of note, in passing, that Paul, rather than Barnabas, is now directing the missionary tour.[7] When the rulers of the synagogue indicated that Paul might speak, he rose to his feet and delivered the sermon which is recorded in vss. 16-41.

Since this is the first of Paul's sermons of which we possess an account, it will be worth our while to consider it. It was addressed to the Jews who were present in the synagogue and to the proselytes (Gentiles who had embraced the Jewish faith) assembled with them. It rehearsed the stirring history of the Jewish race, a tactful approach to his hearers and one well calculated to awaken in them a sense of their solemn accountability to God. In content it resembled closely the sermon Peter preached on the day of Pentecost[8] and also the sermon Stephen preached before the Sanhedrin.[9] It showed by the Scriptures that Jesus who had been crucified was the Christ of God, and that it was by Him and Him only that they could have forgiveness of sins.

Because Paul's sermon was based upon the Scriptures, his hearers could not contradict it without convicting themselves. They seem, on this occasion, not to have been offended by his plain speech, but rather to have been impressed by it. For the moment, it appeared that he might be successful in winning them to Christ.

7 Observe that in Acts 12:25 and 13:2 it is "Barnabas and Saul"; whereas in Acts 13:43 and 13:46 it is "Paul and Barnabas."
8 Acts 2:14-40.
9 Acts 7:2-56.

*Paul Turns to the Gentiles* (*Acts 13:42-52*)

The Gentiles in particular heard Paul's words with joy. They rejoiced that there was for them, and for all men, a way of salvation, and that this way did not demand that they become Jews by adoption, or require them to keep the burdensome Jewish ceremonial regulations. They requested Paul to speak again upon the following sabbath; they even followed him down the street, beseeching him to tell them more concerning this way of life. Paul answered their eager questions. He bade them "to continue in the grace of God"; that is, to continue their inquiries and prayers, if they could not yet believe on Christ, and to remain steadfast in their loyalty to Christ, if they already had accepted Him as Saviour and Lord.

Word of Paul's preaching spread rapidly throughout the city. Those who had been converted told others of their experience. Paul and Barnabas themselves labored diligently. Possibly they called from house to house. The result was that on the next sabbath the synagogue was thronged. It seemed that the whole city had come together to hear the Word of God.

But by this time the Jewish leaders were beginning to be envious of the success Paul was having in his work among the Gentiles. When Paul preached, they disputed the things he said. The Jewish elders were disturbed principally because Paul was telling the Gentiles that all that really mattered was belief in Christ and obedience to Him. He did not tell his converts that they must submit themselves to the Jewish ceremonial requirements. Might not this new freedom in Christ undermine their Jewish culture and religion? What then would become of their inheritance and special privileges?

Paul and Barnabas were not overawed by this show of opposition. Paul replied, in effect: "We have preached the gospel to you, as it was right that we should do[10]; but since you

[10] Note Paul's words in Rom. 10:1: "Brethren, my heart's desire and prayer to God for Israel is, that they might be saved." He did not lack appreciation of what it meant to be a Jew (Rom. 3:1-2; 11:1), but he saw the essential matter was not outward conformity, but inner spirit; and that Gentiles, by believing on Christ, might become true children of Abraham and enter into the promises made to him and to his seed (Rom. 2:28-29).

reject it, and by your rejection show yourselves unworthy of eternal life, we turn from you to those who will gladly receive it—to the Gentiles." [11]

Because of this decision and Paul's continued preaching to the Gentiles, many of them found salvation. Luke's statement is: "As many as were ordained to eternal life believed." Salvation may be viewed from either the divine or the human side. Had not these men been ordained to salvation, they could not have been saved (the Godward side); had they not desired salvation, they would not have been saved (the human side). Paul did not say (in vs. 46) that God had declared the unbelieving Jews to be unworthy of everlasting life; that is to say, God had not made their salvation impossible. What Paul said was that these unbelieving Jews had judged themselves unworthy of everlasting life. In other words, they had rejected eternal life and in so doing had condemned themselves.

The Jews of Antioch determined to rid themselves of Paul and Barnabas. They enlisted the help of certain influential women and certain of the city officials, and stirred up such a persecution that the two missionaries, to save their lives, were compelled to leave the city. They did not flee ignominiously, however; they merely transferred their activities to the next town—Iconium. We read that Paul and Barnabas, in leaving Antioch, "shook off the dust of their feet against them." This was a symbolic action which was well understood and which meant that the people of that place henceforth would be left to go their own way.[12]

There is yet another significant statement here to claim our attention. Luke reports that as Paul and Barnabas were departing amid the jeers of the populace and enduring—it may well be—a pelting with stones, they were "filled with joy, and with the Holy Ghost." Filled with joy because they had been counted worthy to suffer for Christ's sake! When the Holy

[11] This is not an announcement that they would never again preach to Jews, but rather that in Antioch they would preach thereafter, not in the synagogue, but to the Gentile populace. This became their established missionary policy. In whatever city they labored, when the Jews refused their message they turned to the Gentiles.

[12] Cf. Matt. 10:14.

Spirit is in one's heart, the whole of life is transformed. Even persecution can be endured, can be counted an occasion for joy.

### Paul and Barnabas at Iconium  (Acts 14:1-7)

In journeying eastward from Antioch in Pisidia to Iconium, Paul and Barnabas walked along one of Rome's well built and justly famous military roads. The distance by road was nearly ninety miles. Today, a small Turkish town, its name short-ened to Konia, marks the site of ancient Iconium.

Paul's experience in Iconium was but a duplication of what he had experienced in Antioch. He and Barnabas went first to the synagogue. There they found some who listened eagerly to their message. A number, some of them Jews and some of them Gentiles, believed. But the unbelieving Jews, by spread-ing some libellous report, turned many of the Gentiles against Paul and Barnabas. The upshot was that a mob made plans to waylay Paul and Barnabas and to stone them. But the missionaries learned of the mob and of the mob's intention to kill them. Paul and Barnabas were not lacking in courage, but they could see nothing to be gained by playing into the hands of the mob. For the sake of the work which they had set out to do, a work which was but little more than begun, they quickly got out of Iconium and made their way to Lystra. Lystra, a Roman colony, was located eighteen miles to the south, and was connected with Iconium by that same Roman road which they had followed. Observe that the missionaries were not retreating. Because danger threatened, they pushed farther into the Gentile world!

### At Lystra, Paul Is Stoned  (Acts 14:8-20)

It is not stated that Paul visited the synagogue in Lystra. Perhaps there was none. The population of Lystra consisted mostly of Lycaonians. Though these natives had their own language, most of them could understand Paul when he ad-dressed them in Greek. If there was a synagogue, Paul may have avoided it because he did not wish to precipitate in Lystra such a conflict with his Jewish brethren as had oc-curred in Iconium. Paul's arrival in Lystra, however, was soon known and everywhere excitedly discussed. The excitement was due not so much to Paul's preaching as to an act of mercy.

Paul, patterning his life after his Master's, was never too busy to turn aside to give to the poor and needy any help that lay within his power. Among those who heard Paul preach was a man who had been lame from birth. This man listened attentively to the gospel, and Paul presently perceived in his attitude a growing faith in Christ. Paul was able to heal him. The divine power which had flowed through Paul to visit blindness upon Bar-jesus, here operated to make this cripple well. Now witness the efficacy of a demonstrated religion. (Christianity proves itself by its fruits.) When the people saw this man walking and leaping for joy, they were filled with astonishment. The entire city was aroused.

The people of Lystra were worshipers of Zeus and the other Greek gods, and a temple to Zeus stood near the gate to their city. On seeing that the cripple had been healed, the only explanation that they could think of was that two of the gods had assumed the form of men and had come down into their midst to work this miracle.[13] Barnabas, because of his tall stature and dignified bearing, they thought might be Zeus (Latin, Jupiter) ; Paul, being short of stature and the spokesman for the pair, they thought might be Hermes (Latin, Mercurius; English, Mercury) , the wing-footed messenger of the gods. Because the people were speaking in their own Lycaonian tongue, Paul did not understand what they were saying; neither did he perceive what they were planning to do. But when the priest from the temple of Zeus appeared, bringing festive garlands and oxen in readiness for a sacrificial offering, their purpose became clear. They were preparing to worship Paul and Barnabas as gods!

Paul and Barnabas were both astonished and filled with horror. They could not be a party to any such sacrilege. They did not toy with the idea of being worshiped as divine, and

[13] The idea that the gods sometimes took the shape of men and mingled with men was common in antiquity. The Roman poet Ovid (B.C. 43—A.D. 18) , in his *Metamorphoses,* tells how Jupiter and Mercury once visited the earth and were received as guests by Baucis and Philemon. It is a striking fact that the locale of this legend is laid in Phrygia, not far from where Paul then was.

they did not find pleasure in the fact that divine worship had been offered to them, as Herod Agrippa had done, with such fatal consequences, at Caesarea. Instead, they resisted the proposal with all the energy of which they were capable. Running among the people, they shouted: "We are but men like yourselves." To dramatize the anguish which they felt because they had been mistaken for gods, they tore their clothing.[14]

Paul, when he was able to make himself heard, explained that the whole purpose of his coming had been to show them the vanity of worshiping pagan divinities which had no real existence. They should turn to the one God who actually had being, the God who had created heaven and earth and all things in them. Remembering that the majority of the Lycaonians were farmers, Paul exhorted them to turn to the true God who had given them "rain from heaven, and fruitful seasons," filling their hearts with "food and gladness." With such words, Paul and Barnabas quieted the excitement and persuaded the people to give up their plan of worshiping them as gods.

All might yet have ended well if certain unbelieving Jews from Antioch in Pisidia and from Iconium, the places where Paul and Barnabas had recently been, had not followed them to Lystra. By spreading some malicious report, they succeeded in turning the people against the missionaries. How changeable the emotions of these Lycaonians![15] They who only a short time before had been prepared to worship Paul, now began to stone him. How Barnabas escaped this stoning, we are not told. Beneath the cruel pelting of the jagged rocks Paul fell to the ground, sank into unconsciousness. The people, feeling sure that Paul was dead, dragged his body outside the city and left it beside the road. Some hours later, when the mob had dispersed and only a few believers lingered sorrowfully near by, Paul regained consciousness. This return to

14 Barnabas here (vs. 14) is mentioned before Paul, but this is to be expected inasmuch as the Lycaonians had recognized Barnabas as Zeus, the chief god. We may be sure that Paul was the speaker of the words recorded in vss. 15-17.

15 Later, Paul will write to these fickle-minded, temperamental folk: "O foolish Galatians, who hath bewitched you . . ." (Gal. 3:1).

consciousness, though remarkable, is not described as a miracle. Luke is careful not to claim a miracle where none occurred. It was, however, a remarkable manifestation of Paul's indomitable purpose, of his Spirit-strengthened will to "carry on." Bruised, bloody, and weak though he was, Paul went back into the city to find Barnabas. The next day, he and Barnabas set out for Derbe.

## From Derbe, Back to Antioch in Syria (Acts 14:21-28)

Of Paul's work in Derbe (modern Zoska), located on the eastern boundary of the province of Galatia, we have only a brief account. Apparently he suffered no persecution there, and his preaching called forth a good response. Many of his hearers became disciples (i.e., learners).

Paul was now confronted with a difficult decision. He was but a short distance from the Cilician Gates. By the military road which ran through that famous mountain pass, it was only one hundred and sixty miles to Tarsus, his home. If he went by way of Tarsus, he would be traveling the most direct route to Antioch in Syria, the city from which he had set forth. More than a year had passed since he had left that city, and it was high time that he should report to the church there all that he had done as their missionary representative. But Paul felt that he could not yet leave Galatia. The converts he had won needed to be established in the faith. Accordingly, instead of passing through the Cilician Gates, he and Barnabas turned back to walk once more the road over which they had come. What devotion to duty, what courage, that was! They went back to Lystra, where Paul had been stoned and left for dead; back to Iconium where he had narrowly escaped being stoned; back to Antioch in Pisidia where, by his preaching of freedom in Christ, he had incurred the enmity of the Jewish leaders.

In each of these cities, Paul and Barnabas sought out those who had believed on Christ. Some of these believers likely had already experienced some persecution. The apostles encouraged them, explaining that entrance into God's kingdom necessarily was attended by "tribulation." Paul could say this because he still bore upon his body the scars left by the stoning. Churches were organized, and certain of their oldest and most responsible members ("elders") were appointed[16] to direct their activities. Then, when the last good-bys had been said, they set out for the coast. By this time the snows had left the passes of the Taurus Mountains, and with no special difficulty other than the weary climbing they crossed the range and came down to Perga. Paul now had a brief opportunity to preach the gospel in that city, and he made the most of it. On learning however that there was at Attalia a ship which was soon to sail for Antioch in Syria, he and Barnabas hastened to that near-by seaport.

This ship, passing by the island of Cyprus, bore them safely to Seleucia, port for Antioch of Syria. They were back at last with the church which had sent them out as missionaries. How much they had to tell! But mark this well: they told, not what they had done, but rather, what "God had done with them." There was no dramatic recital of their hairbreadth escapes, but rather a joyous reporting to the church that God had opened a door by which Gentiles might enter into the kingdom. On the mission fields to which they had gone, it had been demonstrated repeatedly that salvation was not dependent upon being born a Jew, or becoming a Jew by adoption, neither was it dependent upon the observance of any ceremonial requirement. The door which had been opened was the door of faith. There was salvation for everyone, whether Jew or Gentile, who would believe on Christ. As witness to this truth were the Gentile Christians now in Derbe, Lystra, Iconium, Antioch in Pisidia, Perga, and Paphos, Gentile believers whom God Himself had saved.

Paul and Barnabas had been gone from Antioch in Syria nearly two years. They had traveled, by boat and on foot, more than fourteen hundred miles. They had endured many hardships. They were entitled to a period of rest and refreshment, of body and of spirit.

16 The Greek word translated "appointed" meant originally to vote by a show of the hand. It does not, therefore, rule out the idea of a democratic election of these elders. The apostles saw to it that the voting was done in fair and orderly fashion, and only after earnest prayer and fasting.

## CHAPTER 12

# The Jerusalem Conference

## Acts 15:1—16:10

*P*AUL and Barnabas had not long been back in Antioch in Syria before they found themselves in the very center of a heated theological controversy. This controversy which sorely distressed Paul's spirit was not of his making. It was precipitated by the arrival in Antioch of a group of Judean (Jewish) Christians who attached great importance to the Mosaic law. These men challenged the things which Paul preached and criticized his way of dealing with Gentiles. They said it was not enough for a Gentile to believe on Christ. Before a Gentile could be saved, so they argued, he needed to submit to the rite of circumcision, the sign in the flesh of obedience to Moses' law. Paul had not required circumcision of his Gentile converts. Though these men may not have been an official delegation, they voiced the convictions of a large number of influential Jewish Christians whom we may call Judaizers.

## The Controversy with the Judaizers (Acts 15:1-5)

Paul could not remain silent when the validity of the missionary work which he had done was being called in question. He knew that his work had been directed by the Holy Spirit and that it had received God's blessing. He knew also that if men zealous for the law were to require circumcision of every male Gentile convert, the missionary's task would be made immeasurably harder, for the Gentiles looked upon that rite with repugnance. They regarded it as a mutilation of the flesh. The Gentile churches, having found life in Christ apart from the observance of the Mosaic law, would never be willing to submit themselves to it. Any insistence that they should do so would serve only to destroy their fellowship with the Jewish churches. Paul, therefore, debated the issue with the Judaizers.

The Judaizers maintained that Christianity was really a movement within the Jewish faith. To them Christianity meant only that a new chapter had been added to the long history of Judaism. They did not deny that God would save the Gentiles; the Scriptures plainly declared that he would do so. The question, they said, was as to what a Gentile had to do in order to be saved. They held that he needed first of all to identify himself with the Jewish race, for it was to that race that the promise had been made.

Paul maintained that although Christianity, viewed historically, had come out of the Jewish religion, it was intended for all races and nations. A man could become a Christian, he said, without becoming a Jew. One became a Christian by believing on Christ, not by keeping the Mosaic law. With the coming of Christ, a way of life had been revealed that was free from the legalism which the Jews had found to be ineffectual for righteousness and also an intolerable burden. Keep in mind, as you read, that this was not a controversy between believers and unbelievers, but between Christian believers who differed in their views concerning the way of salvation.

During the "long time"[1] when Paul was in Antioch in Syria following his first missionary journey, certain events occurred which Luke does not relate. We learn of them in the second chapter of Paul's letter to the Galatians. It may be that Luke did not know of these happenings, for they were of a somewhat private nature. More likely, he considered them foreign to his purpose in writing. They are introduced in this narrative only because they throw some light upon later developments.

From Galatians 2 we learn that when the controversy with the Judaizers was still in its early stages, Paul, together with Barnabas and Titus, made a brief visit to Jerusalem. There

[1] Acts 14:28.

Paul conferred "privately" with James, Peter, and John.[2] He left Jerusalem believing that he would no longer be hindered in his work among the Gentiles by the Judaizers. When Peter came down to Antioch he at first mingled freely with the Gentiles. But upon the arrival of some men who represented (or, at least, claimed that they represented) James, the chief elder of the Jerusalem church, both Peter and Barnabas began to feel that possibly they had gone too far in the matter of having fellowship with Gentiles. Much to Paul's indignation, they began to give their support to the Judaizers.[3] It was shortly thereafter that Paul wrote his impassioned letter, Galatians, to the Gentile churches he had established on his missionary journey. He had learned that the Judaizers were making inroads upon them, and he was determined to do all in his power to keep the Judaizers from depriving them of their freedom in Christ.[4]

Luke, as has been said, is silent on these matters. He considered it sufficient to tell what happened when the conflict with the Judaizers came more into the open. Of the conference in Jerusalem, called to settle the controversy, he gives full account.

## The Jerusalem Conference (Acts 15:6-29)

When it became evident that no progress was being made in settling this vexing and divisive issue, the Antioch church arranged for Paul and Barnabas, together with some others, to lay the whole matter before the wisest and most honored of all the Christians, namely, the apostles and the elders of the church in Jerusalem. They would be able to give wise counsel. Paul and Barnabas accordingly set out for Jerusalem. It is characteristic of the enthusiastic spirit of Paul that, when passing through Phoenicia and Samaria on his way up to Jerusalem, he told all the brethren whom he encountered what he had done on his missionary journey. The news that many

2 Gal. 2:2,9.
3 Gal. 2:11-14.
4 Gal. 4:17; 6:12-13.

Gentiles had been converted, Luke says, gave these brethren great joy.

On reaching Jerusalem, Paul related to the church there how the Holy Spirit had honored his work among the Gentiles. As he doubtless had anticipated, there were some Christians on hand who were members of the Pharisaic party. These legalists (Judaizers) stoutly defended their position, saying that a Gentile, to be saved, needed to keep the laws of Moses.

Arrangements were quickly made for a formal hearing at which the apostles and the elders would be present. At that hearing, after there had been considerable general discussion, the apostle Peter expressed his judgment. We may be sure that Peter's words were listened to with respect and keen interest. Peter related what his experience had been. Cleansing of heart, he said, came by faith. Whether the believer was a Jew or Gentile did not enter into the matter. He said he could not see why anyone should want Gentile believers to submit to all the Mosaic ceremonial requirements, for those requirements were a burden which the Jews themselves had never been able to bear. Jews and Gentiles had their salvation in the same way, not through works of the law, but through the grace of the Lord Jesus Christ.

Then Paul and Barnabas were given an opportunity to speak. Undoubtedly they told of their work in Antioch of Syria and in Galatia; undoubtedly also they made it clear that the Holy Spirit had filled the hearts of the Gentile believers in precisely the same manner that He had filled the hearts of the Jewish converts. They surely told how loyal to Christ the Gentile believers were, how courageously and patiently they endured persecution, and how they abounded in all good works. Quite likely they reminded the company of how the Antioch church, in the year of famine, had sent an offering for the relief of the poor in Jerusalem.[5]

When all who wished to speak had been heard, James,[6] the

5 Acts 11:27-30.

6 The James here mentioned is not the apostle James, but that James who was one of the Lord's brothers. See Matt. 13:55; Gal. 1:19; 2:9. That he should have become the head of the Jerusalem church and have

head of the Jerusalem church and the chairman of the conference, summed up the judgment of the majority. He declared that what Peter [7] had said was in complete agreement with the Scriptures. In support of this statement, he gave a free quotation of Amos 9:11-12 as found in the Septuagint (the Greek version of the Hebrew Old Testament). No one, he said, should disturb the Gentile believers in their faith in Christ or impose legalistic burdens upon them. However, he did recommend that the Gentile Christians, in order to avoid giving offense to the Jews,[8] should not eat the meat of animals that had been strangled and should not drink blood (practices connected with the worship of idols). Beyond that, he called upon the Gentile converts to keep themselves free from the sexual immorality that was so prevalent among the pagan Gentiles. These were the only demands that the conference saw fit to make upon the Gentile Christians. The decision of the conference was put in writing, and two friendly and trustworthy messengers, Judas [9] and Silas,[10] were appointed to deliver the letter to the church in Antioch.

The decision of the conference, though moderate and conciliatory, fully vindicated Paul's position, and it opened the way for an even wider and more successful preaching of the gospel to the Gentiles. The restrictions laid down by the conference (i.e., careful avoidance of idolatrous practices and of immorality) were entirely reasonable, and the observance of

been the chairman of this conference is a telling argument against the Roman Catholic claim that Peter was the first pope.

[7] In referring to Simon Peter, James employs the name Simeon (or Symeon), which is the ancient Hebrew form of Simon.

[8] Vs. 21 states why these practices were to be avoided by the Gentile Christians. In every city there were Jewish teachers of the Mosaic law, and the Jews, from long instruction, were sensitive—and rightly so—on the matter of idolatry. Christian charity dictated that these Jews should not be offended needlessly. The reasons for the prohibition of immorality are obvious.

[9] Judas, "surnamed Barsabas" (vs. 22). Since Barsabas means "son of Sabas," it is likely that he was the brother of Joseph "called Barsabas" (Acts 1:23).

[10] Silas is a contracted form of the name Silvanus. In this longer form it appears frequently in the epistles (cf. 2 Cor. 1:19; 1 Thess. 1:1; 2 Thess. 1:1; 1 Pet. 5:12).

them would do no violence to any man's conscience. The Gentiles could observe these simple rules to their own profit and also for the sake of harmony within the Christian churches.

Let no one think that this debate concerning circumcision and the Jewish dietary laws, because held so long ago, is without significance today. The fifteenth chapter of The Acts speaks directly to us and on many vital matters. The Jerusalem conference endorsed what Paul had written to the Galatian churches; namely, that salvation, both in the case of a Jew and in the case of a Gentile, came through faith in Jesus Christ and not through works (i.e., not through a meticulous observance of the Mosaic laws). The regeneration of the believer is wrought by the Holy Spirit. Having received the Spirit in his heart, the believer need not then return to his observance of the law as the means of perfecting his character, for the Spirit, if obeyed, will lead him in the way of righteousness.[11] This was then, this is still, the way of salvation.

Because the Jerusalem conference recognized the way of salvation to be of this character (that is to say, saw that salvation is independent of the individual's race, nationality, and social status), the decision of the conference may be termed, without exaggeration, the Christian's Bill of Rights. It also proclaimed the supranational character of Christianity. It breached all the walls of partition, the barriers between races, between masters and slaves, between rich and poor, between the educated and the illiterate. It opened a door by which all might enter into that life of spiritual abundance which God intended for all mankind.

Let us observe also that these churches had found a way of dealing with their differences of opinion. They had found a way which was fair and eminently Christian. In public conference, after thorough discussion, after consulting the Scriptures, and after earnest prayer, they accepted the judgment of the majority as the decision of the total group. To be sure, this did not put an immediate end to the activities of the Judaizers, but it laid down a broad platform on which freedom-loving Gentile believers and legal-minded Jewish be-

11 Gal. 3:2-3.

lievers could meet as brethren in Christ. It made possible a
Jewish-Gentile co-operation in the task of evangelizing the
world. After all these centuries during which the churches
have experimented with many different procedures, they have
found no way of resolving their controversies so successful as
this democratic way.

Finally, the Jerusalem conference indicates to us a principle
which must be observed when interpreting the Scriptures. In
reading of the conference, it is probable that our sympathies
have been wholly with Paul. That is but natural in view of
the fact that we are Gentiles, and that we might never have
heard the gospel if Paul had not been given a free hand to
carry on his missionary work in Gentile lands. If we were
Jews, we might see it somewhat differently. They understood
that it was to their race that the promises had been given. The
Judaizers among them were learned men. They could quote
Scripture in support of their position. They did not feel that
Jesus had set aside the Mosaic law, but rather had reaffirmed
it. Circumcision was a divinely given rite, and God had declared to Abraham that it was to be observed forever. The
conversion of the Gentiles was prophesied in the Scriptures,
but so also was the superiority of the Jews. Dr. Charles S.
Detweiler has written: "What the council of Jerusalem had to
decide was how to reconcile the liberty of the gospel with the
authority of the Scriptures. The argument that prevailed was
the recounting of what God had done first through Peter in
the case of Cornelius and then through Barnabas and Paul
among the heathen nations. God is the ultimate interpreter
of His Word. The teaching of God's Word must be discovered
in the light of God's acts in history. The deciding factor in
the arguments advanced at that first general council of the
church was that 'God, who knoweth the heart, bare them witness, giving them the Holy Spirit, even as he did unto us; and
he made no distinction between us and them, cleansing their
hearts by faith.' " [12]

This principle, furthermore, has an application to present-

[12] From "The Acts: A Major Missionary Document for Today," by
Charles S. Detweiler. Published in *Adult Class* for April-June, 1941.
Copyright, The Judson Press.

day missionary policy. The home churches must not be too quick to impose their own rules and regulations upon the new native churches which come into existence as a result of their missionary efforts. These younger churches, in so far as they are truly the creation of the Holy Spirit, possess the Holy Spirit in the same manner as do the older churches, and sometimes in larger measure. Not only must they be permitted to work out a pattern of Christian life which, instead of being alien to their native culture, is truly indigenous to it, but also be left free to follow whatever divine leading the Holy Spirit, working in their midst, may give them. It is axiomatic that the missionary has been most successful when he does not need to hold on to his place of privilege in the government of the younger churches, but because he has adequately trained a consecrated native leadership, is able confidently to commit the direction of the work into native hands.

### A Second Missionary Journey Planned (Acts 15:30-40)

Paul and Barnabas, whom the conference had recognized as men who had hazarded their lives in the cause of Christ, returned with light hearts to Antioch. Accompanying them were Judas and Silas, bearers of the official letter setting forth the decision of the conference. Paul thereafter would carry a copy of that document with him on all his missionary journeys. The reading of the letter to the assembled congregation of the Antioch church gave those Gentile Christians great encouragement. Judas and Silas, "being prophets also," preached to the church and exhorted it to continue its missionary work.

Paul had now given thirteen years of his life to Christian service. He had journeyed widely, he had labored diligently, he had endured much persecution. A smaller man would have said: "I have done my part; let someone else now take up the task." Not so, Paul. So long as he had strength, so long as breath remained in his body, he was determined to bear witness to Christ.

Being possessed of such a spirit, it is not surprising that shortly after the Jerusalem conference his mind became occupied with plans for another missionary journey. He felt a responsibility for the welfare of the churches which he had established in the province of Galatia. He desired to visit them in order that he might learn how they fared. But his thoughts went beyond that province. He had preached the gospel in some important cities, but he knew that there were many other great cities—great cities which had not yet heard of Christ. Paul's first missionary journey had been long and dangerous; his second missionary journey was destined to prove even longer and more dangerous.

Unfortunately, trouble arose at the very start—a disagreement between Paul and his good companion Barnabas. They had traveled many miles together, they had stood shoulder to shoulder when facing danger, but now they could not agree upon the plan to be followed. The disagreement was over John Mark, who had gone with them as an attendant on their first journey, but who had turned back—we do not know exactly why[13]—when Paul had determined to go into Galatia. Barnabas, who was cousin to the young John Mark, favored taking him with them on this second journey. Paul would not hear of it. He did not propose to endanger the success of the expedition by taking along a man who at a crucial moment might run away. Barnabas believed either that his cousin had been unfairly judged, or else that he had now learned his lesson and should be given another chance to prove his loyalty.

In a sense, Paul and Barnabas both were right: Paul in his recognition that this missionary tour would call for courage and steadfastness, Barnabas in his willingness to give John Mark a second chance. Anyway, Paul and Barnabas did not permit this difference of judgment to wreck their friendship or to put a stop to the missionary program. It was agreed that

13 It has generally been assumed that John Mark deserted Paul and Barnabas because of the dangers being encountered, but John Mark is nowhere directly charged with cowardice. He may have turned back because he had only agreed to go to Cyprus, or because the journey was consuming more time than had been anticipated. Like numerous other Jerusalem Christians, he may have had some questions concerning Paul's free way of dealing with Gentile converts. In the absence of specific information, and in the light of the character which he later displayed, especially his connection with Simon Peter and his writing of the Second Gospel, we should not be too quick to condemn his conduct.

Barnabas should take John Mark with him, and that the pair should do missionary work on the island of Cyprus. Paul chose Silas as his new missionary partner. This was a wise selection, for Silas—it will be recalled—had been one of the bearers of the letter stating the decision of the Jerusalem conference. He wholeheartedly approved Paul's manner of dealing with Gentiles. He had been one of the "chief men among the brethren" of Jerusalem, and he was a prophet (i.e., a preacher). Being a Jew, he could aid Paul in disarming Jewish prejudice; being, like Paul, a Roman citizen,[14] he could travel freely in Gentile lands and meet Gentiles on equal terms. Silas measured up fully to Paul's expectations.

Vs. 34 in the KJV, which states that Silas had remained in Antioch following his completion of the task assigned him by the Jerusalem conference, is believed to be a gloss. Because the words do not occur in the best New Testament manuscripts, they have been omitted from the RSV. But whether Silas had remained in Antioch or returned to Antioch at Paul's invitation, he indicated his readiness for missionary service.

With the departure of Barnabas for the island of Cyprus, that generous man who had befriended Paul and who had shared with him the hardships and dangers of the first missionary journey appears no more in the New Testament story. There are only a few references to him in Paul's epistles. Galatians 2:1, 9, 13 was written before the events we have been considering. The reference in Colossians 4:10 is quite incidental. In 1 Corinthians 9:6, Paul speaks of Barnabas as a fellow-worker. His susceptibility to the arguments of the Judaizers and his insistence on taking John Mark with him, both appear to have been forgiven and forgotten by Paul. We may well believe that under the Spirit's direction he rendered valuable Christian service in Cyprus, perhaps in Egypt also, before meeting the martyr's death which tradition says befell him.

Similarly, there are only a few references in the epistles to the later activities of John Mark. In addition to Colossians 4:10, we have Philemon 24, in which Paul speaks of him as

14 This is indicated in Acts 16:37.

one of his "fellowlabourers." Most interesting of all is 2 Timothy 4:11, in which Paul, imprisoned and lonely, urges Timothy to find Mark and to bring him to Rome, "for," writes
Paul, "he is very useful in serving me" (RSV) .

*Through Syria, Cilicia, and Galatia to Troas*
    *(Acts 15: 41—16:8)*

After the Antioch congregation had offered earnest prayers
on his behalf, Paul, accompanied by Silas, set forth upon his
second missionary journey into Gentile lands. This time he
did not sail for Cyprus, as perhaps had been his original intention. Because Barnabas and Mark had gone to that island,
he and Silas traveled by land. First of all, they journeyed
through Syria and eastern Cilicia. Ten years before, Paul had
planted churches in that region. These Gentile churches had
been sorely disturbed by the Judaizers, and they now hear with
joy Paul's account of the Jerusalem conference. Again and
again Silas would be called upon to read the letter stating the
decision of that conference; namely, that the Jewish ceremonial requirements were not to be imposed upon Gentile
believers.

The two missionaries, continuing their way westward, came
eventually to Tarsus, Paul's birthplace. How long Paul tarried
there "confirming the churches," we do not know. Probably
it was not for any great length of time, for he felt a graver
concern for the newer churches in Galatia. Persecution had
forced him out of the Galatian cities before his work in them
had been fully done. To the west of Tarsus were the Taurus
mountains. It will be recalled that when Paul and Barnabas
were returning from their first missionary journey they had
approached this range from the west; but at that time, instead
of following the road through the historic pass (the Cilician
Gates) , they had turned back in order that they might visit
again the Galatian cities where they had preached. They then
had made their way southward, crossing the range at another
point, and eventually had reached the port of Perga. This
time Paul, journeying westward, passed through the Cilician
Gates and by that route came down to the cities of southern
Galatia.

At Lystra, it was Paul's pleasure to greet a young man named Timotheus (Timothy), whom he had led to Christ at the time of his first visit to that city. Paul rejoiced to see how the lad had grown, how he had grown spiritually as well as in physical stature. Timothy was well spoken of throughout the region. Paul, being very fond of him, desired to have him with him. He could be Paul's attendant in much the same way that John Mark had been. His parents offered no objection, and arrangements were made for Timothy to accompany Paul and Silas.

Timothy was the son of a Jewish mother (Eunice). His father, however, was a Greek. Because of this fact, Timothy, although he had been well trained in the Scriptures,[15] had never been circumcised. Before taking Timothy with him, Paul arranged that he should be. By the decree of the Jerusalem conference, this could not be required of Gentiles. But Timothy was part Jewish. This willingness on Timothy's part to undergo the rite out of consideration for the strong feelings of the Jews, made him a more acceptable minister to Jews and a more useful member of the missionary team. To the limit of his strength Paul would defend the freedom of the Gentiles, but he sought to avoid giving needless offense to his Jewish brethren. As for Paul's other work in Galatia, we are told merely that the churches were "established in the faith, and increased in number daily."

We come now to an unusual experience in the apostle's life, an experience which we may be sure caused him great perplexity and distress of spirit. Having finished his visiting of the churches in Galatia and Phrygia, it was his intention to push westward and to preach the gospel in the great cities of the Roman province of Asia. Ephesus, in particular, held out a challenging opportunity. But Paul was "forbidden of the Holy Ghost to preach the word in Asia." Apparently it was no divine vision which checked the apostle, but some human condition or circumstance of which we are not told.

Paul then undertook to go northward into Bithynia. If the prevalence of malaria to the south and west (a disease to which Paul was susceptible and from which he suffered much)

[15] 2 Tim. 1:5; 3:14-15.

made a journey in those directions inadvisable, he would escape it in the higher elevation and cooler climate to be found in the northern provinces. But again some circumstance blocked the way. Perhaps these less thickly settled regions did not offer him the evangelistic opportunity that he sought. The record states merely that "the Spirit suffered them not." Paul would find these frustrations, these thwartings of his plans, difficult to understand. He would search his heart to see if he had displeased God; he would ask God if there were anything within himself that made him unworthy of the privilege of preaching the gospel in those districts. Only later did he discover that these baffling experiences had all been part of the gracious providence of God.

Yes, it all had been the work of the Holy Spirit. By shutting one door after another, the Spirit had kept Paul from going in the wrong direction. Paul had to learn that the Spirit sometimes restrains instead of urges on. Paul did not let his mistakes discourage him or put a stop to his trying. He turned toward the northwest, the only direction left open to him, and came down to the coast city of Troas. Unknown to Paul, the Holy Spirit all the while had been leading him toward the discovery of his greatest missionary opportunity.

## Paul Called into Macedonia (Acts 16:9-10)

Troas was an important city on the shores of the Aegean Sea. It had been built a few miles to the south of the ruins of a far more ancient city, the city we know as Troy, celebrated in Greek legend and history.

While at Troas, Paul had a vision, one of the most important of his entire life. In it he saw a man of Macedonia who implored him, saying, "Come over into Macedonia, and help us." Macedonia, take note, was not a part of Asia, but of Europe! Then Paul understood why the Holy Spirit had blocked off every other road and had brought him down to the coast. The great cities of Europe were waiting for the gospel. Paul responded to that call. Without hesitation he and his missionary companions boarded a ship. They left Asia Minor behind them and sailed for Europe—for Philippi, in the province of

Macedonia. It would be difficult for us to overemphasize the significance of this step. Whereas some conservative Jewish believers had looked askance at Paul's preaching to Gentiles, here he was, after having crossed the whole of Asia Minor, approaching Gentile Europe. He was journeying toward the great cities of the Greek world, toward Athens and Corinth!

We have reason to believe that Luke, the author of the Third Gospel and of The Acts, joined Paul at Troas. Note the word "we" in Acts 16:10. Luke was an eyewitness of many of the events which followed. His account of these events, therefore, is more vivid and detailed than is his account of events of which he learned from others. It is interesting to speculate as to how much he may have had to do with Paul's decision to carry the gospel to Europe. Some scholars believe that Luke was a Macedonian and that his account of the cities of Macedonia and of their need of the gospel may have influenced Paul to make this momentous decision. However it was accomplished, Paul saw in the course of events the leading of the Holy Spirit. He entered Europe.

## CHAPTER 13

# The Gospel in the Cities of Europe

## Acts 16:11–18:11

THE present-day trend of population from the open country to the great cities is by no means a new phenomenon.
In ancient times, even as today, the cities with their milling
crowds, with their temples and amusements, with their mar-
kets and universities and halls of government, held a power-
ful allure. The cities represented a concentration of power,
wealth, and influence. They set the fashions. They dominated
—politically, socially, and religiously—the surrounding regions.

Paul was a city man. He had been born in Tarsus, "no
mean city." [1] He had spent most of his life in great cities. He
felt at home in the midst of a city's teeming life. But there
was a deeper reason why Paul felt drawn to the cities. He saw
their strategic importance for the kingdom of God. He directed
his missionary efforts chiefly toward the winning of the cities,
for he believed that the cities, despite their paganism and
moral corruption, could be made centers which would radiate
a Christian influence upon all the rural communities near
them. Perhaps this explains why Paul, who first set foot on
European soil at Neapolis (i.e., New Town), now called
Kavalla, did not tarry at that small port, but pushed on at
once to the much larger city of Philippi, nine miles inland.

### Paul Preaches in Philippi; Lydia Is Converted (Acts 16:11-15)

Philippi (founded in the fourth century B.C. by Philip of
Macedon and bearing his name) was the chief city of that
[1] Acts 21:39.

129

district. It boasted a highly prized distinction. Antony and Octavian, following their victory over Brutus and Cassius in the battle of Philippi, 42 B.C., had declared the city a Roman colony. Its citizens, therefore, were counted as citizens of Rome; they had all the political rights of Romans, and they managed their own civic affairs by means of a city government set up in accordance with the Roman pattern.

Paul's first step on reaching Philippi would be to ascertain if there was a synagogue there in which he might preach to the Jews and to the proselytes who met with them. He found none. It is possible that Jehovah was counted a foreign deity and that the worship of foreign deities was forbidden within the city limits; or it may be that the Jews of Philippi were too few in number to build a synagogue either within the city limits or beyond them. Accordingly, on the sabbath day, Paul went outside the city and walked along the river bank.[2] He anticipated, and rightly so, that he would find there some prayer-place; for the Jews, when they had no synagogue, were accustomed to worship out of doors and preferably (why is not known) beside a running stream.[3] It so happened that on that sabbath only a few women assembled for prayer. Religious devotion appears to have been at a low ebb. But Paul, even though he had but few hearers, did not disdain his opportunity to preach. Neither did he disdain his hearers on the score that they were women. The rabbis, it must be admitted, entertained a low opinion of the intelligence and capabilities of women. Paul knew, however, that Christ had given a new and higher status to womankind, even as He had to Gentiles. Women figure prominently throughout the entire gospel story and have been active in spreading the gospel ever since. Paul seated himself, as was the custom of Jewish teachers, and in a respectful manner talked with these women concerning Christ.[4]

[2] The name of this river is variously given. Appian gives it as Gangas or Gangites; Herodotus as Angites.

[3] Tertullian, writing a century and a half later, mentions "prayers on the shore" as a characteristic of the Jews. Consider, in this connection, Ps. 137:1.

[4] Actually, this was not the very first witnessing to Christ on the continent of Europe. We know that there were Christians in Rome at a very early date. Some of them (soldiers, merchants, and slaves, it may

Among those who heard Paul speak that day was a woman of some prominence in Philippi. Her name was Lydia. She was not a Jew, but a Gentile proselyte ("God-fearer"). She had come to Philippi from the city of Thyatira in the province of Asia, a city famous for the purple dyed goods which were manufactured there. Apparently she was a widow, for she made her living by selling dyed garments which she imported from Thyatira. Apparently also she had enjoyed some success in this business venture, for she owned a home sufficiently large to make it possible for her, following her conversion, to offer lodging to Paul and the other members of his missionary party.

Paul had not spoken long before the Lord opened Lydia's heart to receive and heed his words. Mark how carefully God had ordered all things. The Holy Spirit had brought Paul to Philippi to preach the gospel; the Holy Spirit, at the same time, had prepared the heart of Lydia to receive the gospel. This opening of Lydia's heart to the gospel foretokened the opening of the entire continent of Europe. The genuineness of Lydia's conversion was attested, not only by the warmth of her hospitality to Paul and his companions, but also by her zeal in acquainting all the members of her household with Christ. The statement that the members of her household also were baptized cannot justly be cited as evidence that infant baptism was practiced. By "household" we are to understand her servants and attendants. If Lydia had been a woman with a family, her husband and her children would have been mentioned in some specific way, and she would have been a housewife rather than a business woman.

The conversion of Lydia marked the beginning of a fruitful ministry in Philippi. Soon there were enough Christians to make possible the organization of a church. Ten years later, when Paul was a prisoner in Rome, he sent a letter to this church. We call it the epistle to the Philippians. It shows how dear this church—the first he had founded on European soil—was to his heart. Although the letter contains some para-
be) had made the long journey from Palestine to Rome. But Paul's work in Philippi marked the beginning (although a very humble one) of organized missionary effort aimed at winning Europe to Christ.

graphs of correction and reproof, it is in the main an expression of the apostle's thankfulness. The church had sent him help in his hour of need; it had displayed a Christlike liberality in all good causes. This letter contains more expressions of gratitude and affection than any other letter that Paul wrote.

*Paul and Silas Are Imprisoned and Delivered (Acts 16:16-40)*

Trouble, however, followed hard upon the heels of this initial success in Philippi. Certain unscrupulous men in that city owned a slave girl who was possessed by an evil spirit. They exploited her madness, giving out that she possessed supernatural power as a diviner and fortuneteller. Now, even as the evil spirits which Christ confronted truthfully acknowledged him to be the Lord, so did the evil spirit within this girl. She followed Paul and his companions wherever they went, and she cried out constantly that they were servants of "the most high God" and had come to show "the way of salvation." This was true, but when Paul was endeavoring to preach, her shrill and frequent cries created a serious distraction. Besides, the gospel had better accrediting than that afforded by the testimony of an evil spirit. Accordingly Paul, speaking in the name and power of Jesus Christ, bade the evil spirit to come out of the girl.[5] Immediately her frenzy ceased; it gave place to a quiet and trustful devotion to Christ. The masters of this girl were quick to perceive that with the evil spirit gone out of her, their lucrative business of divination was gone also. They vented their wrath upon Paul and Silas. Seizing them, they dragged them into the market place where the city rulers (*archons*) held court. How often the apostles were persecuted, not because they had done evil, but because they had done good!

When the masters of the slave girl gained a hearing before the magistrates (*strategoi*), they did not report their real grievance, but charged Paul and Silas with having preached in their city a forbidden religion ("These men, being Jews,

[5] Compare Jesus' rebuke of the evil spirits who testified to Him: Mark 1:25; Luke 4:41.

do exceedingly trouble our city, and teach customs, which are not lawful for us to receive, neither to observe, being Romans"). This was, to the minds of the magistrates (Rome-appointed military judges), a serious offense. Eager to uphold the authority of Rome and swayed by the clamor of the crowd, the magistrates tore the clothes from the backs of Paul and Silas and commanded the lictors to beat them with rods.[6] When they had received "many stripes," they were delivered into the custody of the jailer, who was charged to guard them with special care. He accordingly confined them in the inner prison (dark, unventilated, and probably underground), and, as an extra precaution, he made their feet fast in the stocks.

Next, those immortal songs at midnight. What are we to make of them? Not that the apostles experienced no pain, for their backs were still bloody, their feet held cruelly in the stocks. Not that the apostles were capable of a stoicism which enabled them to deny the existence of pain, but that they possessed a spiritual resource, a consciousness of the indwelling Christ, comforting, sustaining, encouraging, giving assurance of victory even in the midst of human suffering. What wonder that the other prisoners, hearing Paul and Silas praying and singing their way through those dark hours, marveled!

Then, with dramatic suddenness, the earthquake. It shook the prison to its foundations, broke down every door, unlocked every fetter, opened every stock, set every prisoner free. All attempts to find a rationalistic explanation fall short of the facts which Luke has related so circumstantially. Paul and Silas were divinely delivered from prison, even as Peter had been delivered from the Jerusalem prison. We can readily understand the dismay of the jailer. In addition to experiencing a very natural fear of the supernatural, he knew that he would be held personally accountable for the escape of all his prisoners. So distressed was he that he would have taken his own life, if Paul had not restrained him. Paul assured him that not one of his prisoners had fled. When the jailer had secured a light, he came into the dungeon where Paul and Silas still were and prostrated himself before them. His ques-

[6] In 2 Cor. 11:25 Paul mentions three occasions on which he was beaten with rods. This was one of them.

tion was one which distracted souls are ever asking: "Sirs, what must I do to be saved?" He was not thinking merely of what he might do to escape the wrath of the magistrates; he desired to know if there was any way by which he might be delivered from the wrath of that "most high God" whose messengers he had treated so despitefully.

Paul's answer was brief, to the point, sufficient: "Believe on the Lord Jesus Christ, and thou shalt be saved. . . ." "And thy house," for what was the way of salvation for him was the way of salvation for all. How long they talked there in the ruined jail, we are not told. Probably the jailer soon took Paul and Silas into his own quarters, where he washed and treated their wounds, then listened while Paul explained more fully what it meant to believe on Jesus Christ. When the other members of the jailer's household joined him in confessing faith in Christ, Paul baptized at once all of these new believers. Then, when they had returned to the jailer's quarters, the jailer set food before Paul and Silas. He would show his gratitude to these two who had transformed his hour of fear and perplexity into an hour of fellowship and rejoicing.

The next morning the magistrates, who apparently had no clear knowledge of all that had taken place that night, sent word by the police (*lictors*) that the jailer should release Paul and Silas. Perhaps the magistrates thought that their prisoners had been punished sufficiently; perhaps they had begun to wonder if they might not have acted too hastily in arresting them. They were the more perturbed when Paul and Silas, instead of leaving town at once, sent back word that they did not intend to be run out of Philippi in any such ignominious fashion. They were Roman citizens, they said; they had been subjected to mob violence, they had been deprived of a fair trial, and they had been flogged publicly and imprisoned. Let the magistrates acknowledge their mistake by coming to the prison and, in the eyes of all the people, bringing them forth and setting them free. The magistrates, now much alarmed lest they be called to account for having so mistreated Roman citizens, made public apology and besought Paul and Silas, for their own safety and for the peace of the city, to leave Philippi. Paul and Silas first made their way to the home of Lydia. They found Luke and Timothy there and informed them of all that had taken place. It was agreed that Luke and Timothy should remain in Philippi for a time to give encouragement and supervision to the Christian work which had been begun there, while Paul and Silas, when they had gathered up their personal belongings, should push on to the next cities.

## Paul and Silas in Thessalonica (Acts 17:1-9)

The two missionaries then made their way southwestward along one of Rome's busiest and most famous roads, the *Via Egnatia*. After thirty-three miles of travel they reached Amphipolis; thirty miles farther on they came to Apollonia. Apparently their reason for not tarrying in either of these cities was that neither of them contained any large number of Jews. Another thirty miles along the *Via Egnatia* brought Paul and Silas to Thessalonica, the largest city in Macedonia.

Thessalonica (the modern city is called Salonika and is still of some size and importance) was founded about 315 B.C. by Cassander, who named it in honor of his wife Thessalonica, a half-sister of Alexander the Great. This city contained a considerable Jewish population. Paul sought out the synagogue, and on three successive sabbaths he preached to the congregation that Jesus, crucified and risen from the dead, was the Messiah prophesied in their Scriptures. Some of the Jews believed on Jesus; the number of Greek God-fearers who turned to Christ was even greater. Among the latter were some of the leading women of the city.

The principal Jewish authorities, not willing themselves to believe on Jesus and envying Paul his success in winning so many Greeks, rounded up certain tough characters who made the market place their hangout and incited them by one means or another to violence against the missionaries. This mob, growing in size with each passing minute, spread terror throughout the city. Descending upon the house of Jason, who hospitably had opened his home to Paul and Silas, the mob demanded that he deliver the apostles into their hands. For-

tunately, Paul and Silas were not in the house at the time.
The mob thereupon turned upon Jason, and although that
good man had committed no offense, they brought him and
certain other believers before the rulers (*politarchs*[7]) of the
city.

The charge brought against Paul and Silas was twofold. It
alleged that they were disturbers of the peace ("These that
have turned the world upside down are come hither also")
and that they were political revolutionaries in that they violated Caesar's decree (probably his decree forbidding the introduction into Roman cities of the worship of foreign deities)
and also preached that "there is another king, one Jesus."
This was a charge which the politarchs could not ignore. In
asserting that Paul and Silas were turning the world upside
down, the mobsters paid the apostles more of a compliment
than they intended. Their topsy-turvy world, with "right forever on the scaffold, wrong forever on the throne," needed
nothing so much as to be turned right side up. Paul and Silas
were not troublemakers except in the sense that any true
preaching of the gospel disturbs our human complacency. The
word of God, "sharper than any two-edged sword," divides
men into two classes by compelling them to take a stand *for*
Christ or *against* Christ.[8] In that sense, and in that sense only,
did Christ say: "Think not that I am come to send peace on
earth: I came not to send peace, but a sword." [9] Certainly,
Christ was in no sense a contender for Caesar's throne. Had
He not said plainly to Pilate, "My kingdom is not of this
world"? [10]

The politarchs, on hearing this charge, chose to follow what
seemed to them the simplest and most expedient course. They

[7] Luke, ever the accurate historian, uses his terms with care. The
word "politarchs" is not found elsewhere in Greek literature. In vindication of Luke's use of this unusual word are several inscriptions which
have been found at Thessalonica. One which is now on display in the
British Museum begins with the words: "In the time of the politarchs.
. . ." So far as our present knowledge goes, Thessalonica was the only
city to be ruled by politarchs.

[8] Heb. 4:12.

[9] Matt. 10:34.

[10] John 18:36.

put Jason and the other brethren under bond to keep the peace and released them. Paul and Silas, seeing that they could not preach any longer in Thessalonica without endangering the lives of the Christians there, made plans to leave the city at once.[11]

*Paul and Silas in Beroea (Acts 17:10-14)*

That night Paul and Silas, with the help of their Christian brethren, slipped out of Thessalonica and made their way to Beroea. This was a quiet village in an agricultural district a little off the main road. Paul found the Jews there more ready to listen to his explanation of the Scriptures than any he had encountered elsewhere. They not only listened to his teaching, but of their own initiative searched the Scriptures to see whether or not the things which he asserted were true. Many of these earnest, Scripture-loving Jews believed, and also a number of Greeks, both men and women.

But not even in Beroea was Paul to be allowed to work in peace. When the irate Jews of Thessalonica heard that Paul was preaching in Beroea, they came down to that town, and, as in their own city, they succeeded in turning many of the people against him. But Paul, despite these disheartening experiences, never once thought of abandoning his mission or of turning back. It was agreed that Paul should go on to Athens. Silas, against whom the populace was not so incensed as against Paul, was to remain for a time in Beroea to look after the work which had begun so auspiciously. Timothy, who had now joined Paul and Silas, was to remain in Beroea as Silas' helper.

11 Luke's account of Paul's work in Thessalonica is much abbreviated. One might suppose from it that Paul stayed there but little more than three weeks. The reason is that Luke was not with Paul in Thessalonica, consequently his account is not so detailed as it is when he is describing events of which he was an eyewitness. From Paul's letters to the Thessalonians, we judge that following the first three sabbaths (after which, no doubt, the synagogue was closed to him) he continued his work, with increasing success, for several months. Pauls letters to the Thessalonians deal with problems which arose in the life of the church he established there.

*Paul Preaches in the City of Athens (Acts 17:15-34)*

The brethren who were looking after Paul's safety helped him reach the sea coast,[13] and they remained with him until he came to Athens. Paul, mightily challenged by all that he saw in that city of glorious history, sent back word by the returning brethren that Silas and Timothy should come to his assistance at the earliest possible moment.

In Athens, as in no other city, was centered all the culture of the ancient world. True, the most creative period in Athens' history had long since passed, but her streets and her hilltops were still adorned with the beautiful temples, monuments, and statues conceived and executed by Phidias in the latter half of the fifth century B.C. In Athens also philosophers, despite an increasing shallowness of thought, still found delight in scholarly argumentation. We may be sure that Paul, with his wide acquaintance with the Greek culture, was deeply moved when he beheld the Acropolis, crowned with the Parthenon, and bearing on its less precipitous slopes scores of other temples and public buildings. But what he, as a Jew, found especially distressing, was the fact that all this worldly culture and wisdom had been dedicated, not to the one true God who had created all and who ruled over all, but to a multitude of pagan gods and goddesses, who were not gods at all and who had no existence apart from the idols which were supposed to represent them.

Stirred by this idolatry, and without waiting for the arrival of Silas and Timothy, Paul began his preaching. His first sermons were in the synagogue. As always, he desired that his fellow Jews should have the first opportunity to believe the gospel. Then, either because the Jews would no longer permit him to make use of their building or because he desired to secure for his message a larger hearing, he transferred his preaching to the busy market place (*agora*) .[14]

[13] Paul found at Methone or Pydna a ship which took him as far as the Piraeus, the port five miles distant from Athens. That the journey was made by sea, rather than by land, is indicated by the reading of the text adopted by the RSV.

[14] The agora, situated some distance northwest of the Acropolis, covered a wide area. It contained many temples and public buildings.

Paul's preaching, as always, concerned Jesus and the resurrection. Most of the Epicurean and Stoic philosophers who heard Paul dismissed him as a harmless babbler. They were not sufficiently interested to give close heed to what he said. Others, however, took a more serious view of the matter. It occurred to them that he might be undertaking to introduce into their city the worship of strange and forbidden gods. Freedom of religious discussion was permitted, but the introduction of new religions from the East was not tolerated. These Athenians, therefore, took Paul before the Areopagus,[15] the court which at that time had jurisdiction in political and religious matters. Paul, it would appear, was not so much put under arrest as summoned to appear before this court, in order that it might determine whether or not there were grounds to justify his arrest.

Paul's speech before the Areopagus, reported by Luke in welcome detail, is one which reflects credit upon Paul both as a scholar and as a Christian preacher. He spoke with dignity and in a courteous and studious fashion well calculated to win the philosophically minded Athenians. First of all, he commended them for their deep interest in all religious matters,[16] as evidenced by their many altars. One that he had observed had upon it the inscription "To an Unknown God." [17] As for the charge that he preached strange gods, he said that he had done no more than to give fuller knowledge of that God which the builders of that altar had sought to know and honor. That was the true God, the God who had created heaven and earth,

Archeologists have uncovered a considerable part of it, and its political and religious significance, as well as its commercial importance, has been disclosed.

[15] Areopagus is the name of a hill immediately northwest of the Acropolis. It had a height of approximately 377 feet, as compared with the superior height of 512 feet enjoyed by the Acropolis. Areopagus may be translated "Hill of Ares," Ares being the Greek name of the war god whom the Romans called Mars. Hence vs. 22 in the KJV has "Mars' hill." The court which had this hill for its meeting place was called by the same name, the Areopagus. In vs. 34, Dionysius, a member of this court, is called "the Areopagite."

[16] The words "too superstitious," which occur in vs. 22 in the KJV, are an unfortunate translation. Paul would not wish to offend his hearers in his opening sentence. Read, with the RSV, "very religious."

and who had given to men life, and breath, and all things. This omnipotent God had made of one every nation of men (a fact to which modern biological findings give abundant testimony). Although too great to be confined in any humanly built temple or to be represented by any humanly erected idol, God was near at hand to all who would sincerely seek him. In support of these statements (since these Athenians would attach no weight to quotations from the Old Testament), Paul cited quotations from some of their own poets. Epimenides, in his *Minos,* had written, "For in him we live, and move, and have our being"; and both Aratus and Cleanthes, philosophic poets, had written, "For we are also his offspring." Paul then pressed home the point up to which he had been leading; namely, that it was the will of this God that all men should repent. They needed to do so, because they were all to be put on trial before that Man whom God had ordained to be the Judge of every man. That is to say, all would be judged by Jesus Christ, whose divinity and authority had been conclusively shown in the fact that God had raised Him from the dead. (A direct and personal application, if ever a sermon had one!)

Up to this point, Paul had been given a respectful hearing. His mention of a resurrection from the dead, however, set some of his auditors to mocking. They had listened long enough to this foolishness! Others, with a greater show of courtesy, said that they would hear Paul again at some later and less busy time. A chance they were never to have! The court adjourned without taking any action. Paul was at liberty, but the scornful laughter of these quick-witted Athenians had made it difficult for him to do any further work in their city.

Paul seems to have been greatly cast down by this defeat. Some writers hold (basing their statements on 1 Corinthians

17 There is no article in the original, and the inscription may be translated either "To the Unknown God" or "To an Unknown God." We now know, from a study of the writings of Philostratus (who quotes Apollonius) and of Pausanias, that altars so dedicated were not uncommon. There are said to have been many of them in Athens. As yet, none of them has been found in the ruins of Athens, but such an altar was uncovered in Pergamum in the year 1909.

2:1-2) that Paul concluded that he had depended too much upon his knowledge of philosophy and poetry, too much upon his skill in debate, and not enough upon prayer and the effectiveness of a simple, but Spirit-inspired, recital of the gospel story. But it hardly behooves any of us to say that there was ever a time in the apostle's ministry when it was not his supreme purpose to magnify "Jesus Christ, and him crucified." When one considers the circumstances under which Paul spoke in Athens, when one bears in mind that he was addressing men who were more interested in dialectics than in a knowledge of God, and when one remembers that his address was never really finished, it is difficult to see wherein he could have spoken more impressively. Furthermore, Paul's words were not wholly in vain. Although no church was established in Athens, a man named Dionysius (he was a member of the Areopagus), a woman named Damaris, and several others were won to Christ.

## Paul's Ministry in the City of Corinth (Acts 18:1-11)

Whereas Athens was the intellectual center of Greece, the city of Corinth to which he went next was the commercial center. Completely destroyed by the Romans in 146 B.C., the city grew rapidly in population when it was refounded one hundred years later by Julius Caesar. Augustus made Corinth the capital of Achaia. The commercial importance of Corinth arose out of the city's fortunate location upon the isthmus connecting central Greece with the Peloponnesus. To Cenchreae, Corinth's eastern port, came ships laden with merchandise from the provinces of Asia and Syria. Their cargoes, by a short haul of only four miles across the isthmus, could then be loaded upon ships which, westward-bound, would take them to Italy or to lands even more remote. Some smaller ships, in order to avoid the two hundred miles of stormy sea encircling the Peloponnesus, were placed on rollers and pulled to the other side of the isthmus. This shipping, buying and selling, and the inevitable customs, all meant profit for thrifty merchants. But this increase of wealth had been accompanied by an increase of vice and materialism. Corinth's population, as one would expect, was cosmopolitan. On her streets, Romans—government officials and soldiers—rubbed shoulders with merchants, sailors, and slaves from many lands. The Isthmian Games, featuring all kinds of athletic contests, were attended by vast throngs from near and far. Corinth's temples, erected to Aphrodite, profited through the activities of their thousands of priestess-prostitutes. Immorality of the most debased sort was encountered on every hand.

Such a city offered no easy field for a preacher of the gospel, but Paul, sensing the importance of the city, girded himself for one of the greatest efforts of his life. The campaign would be a long one, and of necessity he must find a permanent dwelling place. He encountered a Jew named Aquila who was a tentmaker. Tentmaking was the trade which Paul had learned in his youth. Aquila, though born in Pontus (in northern Asia Minor), had but recently come to Corinth from Rome. His wife Priscilla (Prisca), if we may judge by her name, was a Roman lady of high birth. They had been compelled to leave Rome, due to an edict issued by the Emperor Claudius Caesar in A.D. 49 expelling all Jews from the Eternal City.[18] Aquila and his wife offered Paul lodging, and Paul, so as not to be a burden upon them during his prolonged stay in Corinth, assisted Aquila in his work of tentmaking.[19]

Paul, as usual, began his preaching in the synagogue.[20] By so doing, he hoped to win the Jews and such Greeks as worshiped in the synagogue with them. While Paul was busily

[18] Suetonius, in a statement which is none too clear, relates that Claudius issued this edict because the Jews in Rome had "made a great tumult because of Chrestus." Chrestus, likely, is a perversion of the name Christus or Christ. It is possible, therefore, that there had been some conflict between the orthodox Jews and those who had accepted Jesus Christ.

[19] This was not the first time that Paul had thus furnished his own support. We know from 1 Thess. 2:9 that Paul had worked at his trade while in Thessalonica.

[20] In 1898 there was found in Corinth a stone which once formed the lintel over a doorway. Inscribed upon it in Greek letters are the words, "Synagogue of the Hebrews." It is believed that this inscription was carved sometime between 100 B.C. and A.D. 200. It is possible, therefore, that this stone, now preserved in the museum in Corinth, is from the ruins of the very synagogue in which Paul preached.

engaged in this ministry, he was greatly cheered in spirit by the arrival in Corinth of his good friends and faithful helpers, Silas and Timothy. We can imagine how eagerly Paul inquired of them how the work progressed in Thessalonica and Beroea.

But Paul's preaching that the Christ had come in the person of Jesus was rejected, as so often before, by the majority of the Jews. The synagogue was closed to him, and once again he was forced to turn to the Gentiles. One God-fearing Gentile, Titus (better, Titius) Justus, however, had believed. This good man, seeing that Paul was in need of a place in which to preach and teach, offered the use of his house. It was conveniently located; in fact, next door to the synagogue. Another of Paul's Jewish converts was no less a personage than Crispus, the ruler of the synagogue. Crispus not only believed on Christ, but led the members of his household to believe on Him. Thus, Paul's preaching in the synagogue had been far from fruitless.

Out of the heathen population of Corinth, Paul eventually won a sufficiently large number of converts to make possible the organizing of a church. We shall not appreciate how great an achievement this was unless we keep in mind the character of the city of Corinth. From Paul's letters to this church (letters written some three years later), we learn what some of the problems he had to contend with were. That there were periods of discouragement, we may be sure; that there were times when Paul's life was in danger, we may be equally sure. But the Lord had not forgotten his faithful missionary. One night the Lord appeared to Paul in a vision. The gracious words which Paul heard from the lips of his Lord were well calculated to dispel his despondency and to give him courage in the face of danger: "Be not afraid, but speak, and hold not thy peace: for I am with thee, and no man shall set on thee: for I have much people in this city." "Much people"? What did the Lord mean? Apparently this, that there were many more people in Corinth who would believe, if only Paul would continue his preaching there. His work in Corinth was not yet done. As for the danger, had he not been given the greatest of all assurances? The Lord Himself had said: "I am with thee."

With this encouragement, Paul settled down in Corinth. He

devoted himself, not only to evangelism, but also to teaching. He instructed his converts both with respect to Christ and with respect to the Christian way of life. While engaged in these tasks, Paul found time to write two letters (1 and 2 Thessalonians) to the church which he had organized in Thessalonica. A year and six months sped by.

## CHAPTER 14

# The Labors of Paul in Ephesus

ACTS 18:12–19:41

*P*AUL'S missionary labors in the commercially prosperous but morally corrupt city of Corinth, when viewed as a whole, display a pattern with which we are fast becoming familiar: first, he preaches to the Jews in the synagogue; second, when they reject the gospel, he turns to the Gentiles; third, his successful work among the Gentiles arouses the envy and opposition of the anti-Christian Jews; and, fourth, these Jews bring about his arrest, but he is delivered. That Paul's work in Corinth followed this pattern will become apparent when we have given consideration to the events connected with the close of his stay in that city.

*Paul Is Brought Before Gallio (Acts 18:12-17)*

It was while Gallio was proconsul of Achaia (the province of Achaia then included all of southern Greece) that the Jewish opposition to Paul's work came to a sudden head. The hostile Jews laid hold on Paul and brought him for trial before the proconsul, who was (to give his name in full) Lucius Junius Annaeus Gallio. He was the elder brother of Seneca, one of the most famous of all Latin authors, and the uncle of the poet Lucan; more than that, he was something of a scholar in his own right. If Seneca's words concerning his brother may be taken at their face value, Gallio was gentle, frugal, courteous, tactful, truthful, modest, and amiable. He had but recently come to Corinth as proconsul.[1]

[1] Near the close of the last century, there was found at Delphi an inscribed tablet on which the name of Gallio appears. It both confirms

It is possible that the Jews mistook Gallio's gentleness for weakness, and thought that with a little pressure they could induce him to carry out their will. In their haste they did not carefully formulate their charge against Paul. Whereas the Jews of Thessalonica, very shrewdly, had charged Paul with violating the decrees of Caesar, these Corinthian Jews merely charged Paul with a proselyting which was contrary to the laws of Moses. Paul was about to speak in his own defense (he would gladly have borne witness to Christ in the hearing of this distinguished Roman), but Gallio gave him no opportunity. Because no infraction of Roman law had been alleged, Gallio took the position that the affair was no concern of his. The Jewish leaders were responsible for the handling of such controversies as might arise in connection with their manner of worship. Besides, he resented the noisy and unceremonious way in which the Jews had crowded into his presence. He ordered the lictors to clear the courtroom.

The Jewish mob, seeing that it had failed to accomplish its purpose, turned its spite upon Sosthenes.[2] This man, following the conversion of Crispus, had become the ruler of their synagogue. He, no doubt, had urged that Paul should be taken before Gallio. They had heeded his counsel, and in consequence had been made to appear ridiculous in the eyes of the law. In their anger and disappointment, they caught hold

Luke's statement that he was proconsul in Corinth and gives the date of his proconsulship, namely, A.D. 51 to 52. Since Gallio had come to Corinth only a little while before Paul's trial, it becomes evident that the apostle reached Corinth in A.D. 50 and that he left that city in A.D. 52. The dates for the other events in the life of Paul are arrived at by figuring either forward or backward from this fully established date, A.D. 51. The chronologies for the life of Paul which were worked out before the discovery of this inscription, and its publication in 1905, are apt to be several years in error.

2 The KJV (Acts 18:17) has, "Then all the Greeks took Sosthenes. . . ." But the word "Greeks" does not occur in the manuscripts, and the RSV gives the correct translation: "And they all seized Sosthenes. . . ." That is to say, the Jewish mob seized him. If it is this same Sosthenes who is mentioned in 1 Cor. 1:1, we must believe that presently he followed the example of Crispus, his predecessor as ruler of the synagogue, in becoming a Christian. However, the identification must remain uncertain, because the name was of common occurrence.

of him and beat him severely. Gallio did nothing to stop this violence. Perhaps he thought that Sosthenes, having brought a false accusation against Paul, was receiving at the hands of the mob a rough kind of justice. Feigning either indifference to what went on or else preoccupation with the next case, he let the crowd do as it was minded. Whereas Gallio has often been castigated as a conspicuous example of religious indifference, the probability is that Luke, at this point in his narrative, was most concerned to show that this distinguished Roman governor and judge had declared Paul to be innocent of any violation of Roman law.

## Paul Returns to Antioch  (Acts 18:18-22)

Although this conflict with the Jews increased their animosity toward Paul, it did not make it necessary for him to leave Corinth immediately. As a matter of fact, Paul remained in Corinth "many days longer" (RSV). But nearly three years had passed since that spring day in A.D. 49 when he had reported to the church in Syrian Antioch the decision of the Council held in Jerusalem. That church had sent him out on his first missionary journey, and also on this, his second missionary journey, which already had proved longer both in point of time and in number of miles traveled. Paul felt that it was high time that he reported back to it, and also to the church in Jerusalem.

Paul's good friends, Aquila and Priscilla, decided to accompany Paul as far as Ephesus. Aquila, it will be recalled, was a native of Pontus, and it may be that he had it in mind, when opportunity offered, to make his way back to that province. Nothing is said of Silas and Timothy, but we have reason to believe that they also accompanied Paul.[3] Although they are by no means unimportant figures in the story of the spread of Christianity, it is noteworthy that from this point on in Luke's narrative, they, and all others like them, drop into the background, whereas the figure of Paul, indefatigable in his missionary labors, becomes steadily more imposing.

3 We know that Timothy attended Paul on his next (third) missionary journey, and the probability is that Silas did so also.

The little company of Christians walked together down to
Cenchreae, Corinth's eastern port. There they found a ship
which would carry them to Ephesus in the province of Asia.
Luke remarks that Paul, who was never unmindful of the fact
that he was a Jew and who was determined not to fall behind
his fellow Jews in any matter of personal devotion, had some
time previously taken upon himself a Nazirite vow.[4] During
the period of time in which the Nazirite was bound by his
vow, he permitted his hair to grow. The fulfillment of the vow
usually had its culmination in a visit to the Temple in Jerusalem. At that time the hair was cut and sacrificial offerings
were presented. Because Paul had now fulfilled his vow and
because it would be yet some weeks before he reached Jerusalem, Paul had his hair cut before he left Cenchreae. This
practice was permitted in the case of those who were located
at a great distance from Jerusalem. The offering, however,
would not be made until Jerusalem was reached.

Of the return voyage, Luke reports only that when they had
reached the great city of Ephesus, Paul tarried there only
briefly. Before saying farewell to Priscilla and Aquila, however, he visited the synagogue in Ephesus and debated with
the Jews whom he found there. Perhaps the fact that Paul had
recently carried out a Nazirite vow disposed these Jews to
listen to what he had to say concerning Christ. At any rate,
they asked him to remain with them for a longer period. Paul
felt that he must hurry on to Jerusalem. But their interest in
the gospel, and, indeed, all that he had seen in Ephesus, convinced him that he should return to that important city for a
protracted work at the earliest opportunity. It will be recalled that on his westward journey the Holy Spirit had not
permitted him to preach in Ephesus; now the entire province
of Asia, including the city of Ephesus (of which we shall have
more to say presently), offered a challenging opportunity.

From Ephesus, Paul traveled by ship to Caesarea, the
Roman-built port from which one went up to Jerusalem. On
this occasion, Paul's visit to Jerusalem was of brief duration.
No doubt he visited the Temple to give final discharge to his
Nazirite vow; no doubt also he saw those of the disciples who

4 Num. 6:1-21.

chanced to be in the city at that time. Then, having given his Christian greetings to the Jerusalem church, he hurried down to Antioch in Syria, that he might give to the church which had sent him forth an account of all that had happened since that day when he and Silas had set forth upon what we now call his second missionary journey. In the course of it he had preached the gospel in some of the greatest cities of Europe. In several of them, he had succeeded in establishing strong churches.

### Paul Sets Out for Ephesus (Acts 18:23)

Luke gives no account of the circumstances attending the start of Paul's next (his third) missionary journey. He takes it for granted that the reader will understand that Paul, having dedicated his life to missionary service, will continue in that work to the very end of his days. Within the limits of a single verse, Luke relates that the apostle, after he had spent "some time" with the church in Antioch, set forth once more. Again he journeyed westward, following the now familiar highways, until he came to Galatia and Phrygia. He visited again the churches which he had established in those districts. He greeted those whom he personally had led to Christ, and such other believers as they, in his absence, had won to the Lord. When he had strengthened all of them in the faith, he pushed on westward.

Ephesus, toward which Paul directed his steps, was one of the three great cities of the eastern Mediterranean region; only Antioch in Syria and Alexandria in Egypt could compete with it for supremacy. Its commercial and political importance grew out of its location with respect to the great trade routes of that day. True, it was located three miles from the sea, but the Cayster River, beside which it had been built, was at that time navigable for seagoing ships. All account of the beginnings of the city are lost in antiquity. We know, however, that the earliest inhabitants were of Asiatic stock. In the seventh century B.C. Greek colonists arrived at this site, and the Hellenistic period of the city's history began. Ephesus, therefore, was already an ancient city when Paul visited it.

For a full century archeological research has been carried on at the site of this famous Greek metropolis, and the impressive ruins which have been uncovered fully support all that the ancient historians wrote concerning the city's size, importance, and beautiful buildings. Its principal street, about thirty-five feet wide and nearly one half mile long, ran from the city's river gate to the great theater which had been built in the hollow of a hill. This colonnaded thoroughfare was lined with impressive structures—a great library, temples, gymnasia, and baths. The city's huge market place also was colonnaded and surrounded by the shops of merchants. The most imposing and artistic monument in Ephesus, however, was the temple of Artemis.[5]

This temple (called the *Artemision*), because of its size, beauty, and wealth, was accounted one of the seven wonders of the ancient world. It did not stand within the city proper, but could be seen a little more than a mile to the northeast. How long worship had been conducted on that spot is not known. We do know, however, that the temple which Paul saw was already four centuries old, and that it had replaced an earlier, and also famous, temple that had been destroyed by fire. Alexander the Great, who visited Ephesus in 334 B.C., saw the unfinished temple and made a munificent gift toward its completion. The temple proper (340 feet long and 160 feet wide) stood upon an elevated platform of even larger dimensions. Its one hundred marble columns rose nearly sixty feet into the air. Its roof was of gleaming white marble tiles. The entire building was adorned with impressive sculptures, colorful paintings, and gold ornamentation. Because of the temple's strength and sanctity, the citizens of Ephesus deposited in it for safekeeping their wealth and treasures. The temple, therefore, did a thriving banking business, and represented

[5] The goddess Artemis, so it seems, began as a Lydian deity, with a character akin to Phoenicia's Astarte; i.e., as a fertility goddess, which, in a measure, accounts for the orgiastic rites by which she was worshiped. This goddess, whom the Greeks called Artemis, was identified by the Romans with their goddess Diana. The shout of the populace in Acts 19:34 is rendered, in the KJV, "Great is Diana of the Ephesians"; the more literal and correct translation, as given in the RSV, is "Great is Artemis of the Ephesians."

the financial life, as well as the religious life, of Ephesus. We can readily understand from these facts the pride which the Ephesians took in their temple and the readiness with which they caught up the cry, "Great is Artemis of the Ephesians."

*Paul Meets Followers of John the Baptist (Acts 18:24–19:7)*

While Paul was making his way through Galatia and Phrygia en route to Ephesus, there arrived in that city a man of more than ordinary accomplishments. His name was Apollos. He was a Jew, a native of Alexandria, and a disciple of John the Baptist. Some of the disciples whom John had made (there were many of them scattered among the Jews) still held to the belief that John himself was the Messiah; others had not yet learned that the Messiah of whom John told had already come in the person of Jesus of Nazareth. The latter appears to have been the case with Apollos. He was well informed concerning the Scriptures, he knew the prophecies concerning the Messiah, and he could explain those prophecies in an inspiring fashion. But Apollos had no personal knowledge of Jesus Christ as Lord and Saviour. When Priscilla [6] and Aquila heard him speak in the synagogue, they were impressed by his sincerity and eloquence. Accordingly, they proceeded at once to instruct him in those matters wherein his knowledge fell short. They seem to have experienced no difficulty in winning him to Jesus Christ. This personal work done by Priscilla and Aquila proved to be a highly significant Christian conquest, for Apollos became a foremost preacher of the gospel.

When Apollos, following his conversion, expressed a desire to visit Achaia that he might bear witness to Jesus Christ there, the little company of Christians in Ephesus gave him all possible encouragement and assistance. They furnished him with a letter of commendation to the Christians in Corinth. On reaching that city, Apollos preached to the Jews there.

[6] The RSV corrects the KJV of Acts 18:26 by naming Priscilla before Aquila. In four of the six occurrences of these names in the New Testament, Priscilla is mentioned first. The reason for this is not clear. It has been suggested that she was born a Jewess, whereas her husband had not been born a Jew. More likely she was given this greater prominence because of her greater zeal as a Christian.

With much skill and effectiveness, he showed them by the Scriptures that the Christ had come in the person of Jesus.[7]

Paul, on arriving in Ephesus, learned of Apollos' zeal and rejoiced to know of it. But although Apollos had already left Ephesus, there were other followers of John the Baptist still to be found in that city. Paul contacted a dozen of them. These men, it appears, had repented of their sins; and they had received John's baptism as a ceremonial sign indicative of their desire to be prepared in heart and life for the coming of the Lord in judgment. And there their knowledge and experience, like the knowledge and experience of Apollos, had stopped short. Not knowing that Jesus Christ already had come in the flesh, they had not come into fellowship with Him. Their baptism showing forth repentance and anticipation, though possessing significance so far as it went, had been a Jewish rather than a Christian baptism. Paul, however, was not so much concerned with the manner of their baptism as with their deficient Christian experience. Accordingly, he instructed them concerning Jesus Christ, and, at their request, baptized them in the name of Christ. He then laid his hands upon them. When he did so, they were filled with the Holy Spirit. They became spiritually uplifted, indescribably happy, and inwardly strengthened. Thus empowered, they began at once to bear testimony to Christ. They spoke with tongues and prophesied.

*Paul's Ministry, First in the Synagogue, Then in the Hall of Tyrannus (Acts 19:8-20)*

As was his custom, Paul began his ministry in Ephesus by preaching in the synagogue—the same synagogue, no doubt, which Priscilla and Aquila attended, and in which they had heard Apollos expound the Scriptures. The Jews, at first, listened with interest to Paul's teachings. For three months they permitted him to speak without hindrance. But by the end of that period it became apparent to the synagogue leaders that Paul preached a gospel of redemption which, if logically

[7] For indications of Apollos' fruitful ministry in Corinth, see 1 Cor. 1:12; 3:5-6, 22; 4:6; 16:12.

acted upon, would carry them far beyond the views and practices long held sacred by Judaism. There was, accordingly, a
sharp division of opinion. In the end, Paul was forced to seek
another preaching place.

Paul thereupon transferred his activities to the lecture hall
of a philosopher-teacher named Tyrannus. It would be pleas-
ant to believe that Tyrannus had become a Christian, but
there is nothing to support the view. Probably Paul merely
rented these quarters for use during those hours of the day
when Tyrannus himself did not have need of them. Ordinarily the Ephesians did the heavy work of the day in the cool
of the morning; they then rested from 11 a. m. to 4 p. m. But
those were the very hours (so some of the ancient manuscripts
declare) when Paul did his teaching! This makes it appear
that Paul used Tyrannus' lecture hall after that Greek teacher
had finished his work for the day. When we consider that Paul
supported himself by working at his trade[8] and that he spent
his evenings conducting religious services in the homes of the
Christians or in calling from door to door,[9] we can see how
crowded his days were and what heavy demands they made
upon his strength.

The preaching and teaching in the hall of Tyrannus was
continued for two years, with the result that the word of the
Lord was heard not only by Jews and Greeks within the city,
but also by many throughout the province of Asia. Luke has
not recounted for us all of Paul's experiences in Ephesus. They
must have been rich and varied, for Paul labored in Ephesus
longer than in any other city. The three years he spent there[10]
proved to be the most profitable and, at the same time, the
most perilous of his entire life. In a letter written from Ephesus (1 Corinthians) he mentions in the same breath "a wide
door for effective work" (RSV) and his "many adversaries," [11]

8 This is indicated in the words "These hands have ministered unto
my necessities" (Acts 20:34).

9 See Paul's statement that he had taught "from house to house"
(Acts 20:20).

10 That Paul's total ministry in Ephesus was of this duration is shown
by Acts 20:31.

11 1 Cor. 16:9.

He speaks also of having "fought with beasts at Ephesus." [12]
This, apparently, was the apostle's vivid way of describing the
rage and savagery of the mobs which threatened his life. It
appears that at one time he was imprisoned and under sentence of death.[13] For his safety, Priscilla and Aquila risked
their own lives.[14]

It may have been because Paul had to undergo such severe
trials while in Ephesus that God gave him at that time the
power of the Holy Spirit in so unusual a measure. By reason
of the Holy Spirit, Paul was enabled to do marvelous things.
Put more correctly, Paul became the human instrument
through which God wrought these "special miracles." Such is
the curative power of faith that some who believed on Christ
received healing of body as well as forgiveness of sins; others
who had been troubled by evil spirits, on believing, were delivered from that torment. That handkerchiefs or aprons which
Paul had handled sometimes were taken to those sufferers
whom the apostle could not visit personally, seems to have
been a means of making it easier for them to exercise that
faith which is essential to health of body and of spirit. That
Luke, the physician, has nothing more than this to say concerning these miracles may be considered an indication of his
ability to see all things in true perspective. Amazing though
the miracles were, they were only such concomitants as might
be expected in connection with the Spirit-empowered spreading of the gospel.

But there were others, however, who specially marked
Paul's power over the evil spirits and coveted that power for
themselves. Among them were the seven sons of a certain
Jewish high priest named Sceva. These seven sons had become
itinerant Jewish exorcists; they made their living by pro-
nouncing (for a charge) magic spells which, so they claimed,
would drive away evil spirits. They knew that they possessed
no such power as they had beheld in Paul. Accordingly, they
watched Paul closely and sought to imitate his manner of
dealing with the demon possessed. But when they essayed to

[12] 1 Cor. 15:32.
[13] 2 Cor. 1:8-10; 11:23. Note also "my fellowprisoners" in Rom. 16:7.
[14] Rom. 16:3-4.

put into practice what they had seen, and made use of the name of Jesus as though it were a magic formula, they met with a surprise. The evil spirit in the man whom they had addressed moved that man to answer them: "Jesus I know, and Paul I know; but who are ye?" Thereupon the man, with demoniacal fury, leaped upon these exorcists and fought them so furiously that they were compelled to flee from the house. When this fact became noised abroad, many more persons (both Jews and Greeks) believed on the Lord Jesus.

It is significant that when the Ephesians learned the truth about God, they lost their superstitious fears. Many of these fears had been fostered by unscrupulous magicians who profited by them. Christianity is a religion of truth; it leaves no room for hocus-pocus. There is as much difference between a Christian prayer and the mumbo-jumbo of a magic formula as there is between light and darkness, between heaven and hell.[15]

Accordingly, the Ephesians, when they had come to believe on Christ, had no further use for the magic charms, the curious words, and the repetitious formulas which they had purchased from the magicians. They therefore brought together their books of magic and made a bonfire of them in the sight of all the people. The worthless books they burned had cost them fifty thousand pieces of silver (estimated to be the equivalent of $10,000)! This act, of course, aroused the opposition of those whose business was the making and selling of such books of magic. They saw their profits dwindling; they saw their influence waning. If the preaching of the gospel were continued, if more and more people were delivered by it from

15 Papyri which have been found have given us many of these ancient magic formulas. One of them, of a Jewish character, after invoking the spirit of Abraham, of Isaac, of Jacob, of Jesus Christ, and of the Holy Spirit, continues: "I adjure thee, O demon, whoever thou art, by the God Sabarbarbathioth, Sabarbarbathiuth Sabarbarbathioneth Sabarbarbaphai. Come forth, O demon, whoever thou art, and depart from so-and-so at once, at once, now. . . ." The long, resounding words make no sense, but undoubtedly were impressive. Furthermore, unauthorized persons, hearing them only once, would not be able to recall them sufficiently well to pronounce them correctly. If they wanted to work the charm themselves, they would have to pay for a written copy of it.

their superstitious fears, their trade in magic would come to
an end. It is not surprising, therefore, that these unscrupulous
magicians turned against Paul.

## The Riot of the Silversmiths (Acts 19:21-41)

If Paul's preaching of the love and truth of Christ aroused
those who made their living by professing a knowledge of
magic, his preaching against idolatry provoked even greater
anger on the part of the silversmiths of Ephesus, whose chief
business was the manufacture of images and shrines of the
goddess Artemis. The resulting uproar and mob violence, as
we shall presently see, very nearly cost Paul his life.

Now that Christianity had been firmly established in Ephesus (as demonstrated convincingly by the large number of
converts who had burned their books of magic, and also by
the zeal of those converts in carrying the gospel into all sec-
tions of the province of Asia), Paul began to consider what
his next steps should be. He felt led of the Holy Spirit [16] to
visit the churches in Macedonia and Achaia, and when he had
received their offerings to carry the money up to Jerusalem.
We see that Paul was still concerned to bind together the Gentile churches and the Jewish churches in a fellowship of love
and service. When that mission had been accomplished, he
cherished the hope of journeying even to Rome and of preaching the gospel there.

Paul rightly judged that this was the Spirit's plan for his
life, but he had no intimation of the strange and difficult way
by which that plan would be carried out. The Spirit had set
the long-range goal, but the apostle had to plan each day's
work as best he could. In order that no time might be lost,
Paul dispatched two of his helpers, Timothy and Erastus, to
go ahead of him. While they were encouraging the churches of
Europe to have their benevolent gifts in readiness for Paul to
carry up to Jerusalem,[17] Paul himself would have opportunity

[16] The reading of vs. 21 in the KJV ("Paul purposed in the spirit")
would let one believe that the plan was of Paul's own devising. The
RSV ("Paul resolved in the Spirit") shows that the plan had been
worked out under the prompting of the Holy Spirit.

[17] Concerning this "collection for the saints," see 1 Cor. 16:1-2 and
2 Cor. 8:1–9:15.

to give attention to a few last duties in Ephesus. While Paul
was still in Ephesus and thus engaged, the riot occurred.

Demetrius, who appears to have been the leader of the
guild of silversmiths,[18] instigated the commotion. These craftsmen had enjoyed a thriving business in the manufacture and
sale of images of Artemis. Those who visited the temple of
Artemis bought these images as souvenirs. If they came from
a distance, they could take a miniature shrine of Artemis home
with them and by means of it continue their worship of the
goddess. Some of the images, undoubtedly, were of silver and
displayed beautiful workmanship; most of the images which
have been unearthed by the archeologists, however, are cheaply
and crudely made of terra cotta. The original image of which
these were a representation is described as a "sacred stone
that fell from the sky," [19] which gives rise to the supposition
that it may have been, at the first, nothing more than a me-
teorite. That the Ephesians should have worshiped such a
black stone is an indication of the ignorance and superstition
which prevailed. This stone came to be regarded as the image
of the fertility goddess Artemis, widely worshiped throughout
the East. The representation of the Ephesian Artemis which
appears on ancient coins shows her as many breasted, symbolizing the fruitful and nurturing powers of nature. Her
figure, standing upright and tapering downward, looks not
unlike a mummy in its stiff wrappings. Her body is covered
with figures of mystical animals, and on the pedestal on which
she stands are engraved signs or letters.

Demetrius aroused his fellow craftsmen by pointing out to
them that the preaching of the Way, as carried on by Paul
and the other Christians, was leading many persons to abandon the worship of Artemis. It was being asserted that images
made with human hands were not gods at all. He appealed to

18 Dr. B. W. Robinson, in his excellent *Life of Paul* (University of
Chicago Press, 1928), states that the Roman Empire was more modern
in many ways than is usually realized. Inscriptions and papyri, he says,
tell not only of labor unions, but also of trusts or corporations, and even
of the imperial regulation of prices by public proclamation. Ephesian
inscriptions mention two brotherhoods: that of the workers in wool and
that of the surveyors. Undoubtedly there were many more.

19 See Acts 19:35 in the RSV.

his hearers to give expression to their loyalty to Artemis. To this religious motive he added a patriotic one. It would be a disgrace to their great city and to themselves as citizens if their city's chief glory (the temple of Artemis) were allowed to decline. In more subtle fashion, he let them see that this would mean money out of their pockets. Already the sale of images was falling off. This interference with their business had gone on long enough!

"Great is Artemis of the Ephesians!" In a moment the air was filled with this rallying cry. Hundreds caught it up. Other hundreds, though they did not know what all the commotion was about, were unwilling to be thought lacking in devotion to Artemis. They too caught up the cry, "Great is Artemis of the Ephesians!"

The mob, roaring through the city in their search for Paul, spread confusion everywhere. Fortunately they failed to find him; but discovering Gaius and Aristarchus, two Macedonians who were known to have accompanied Paul on his travels, they dragged these two men into the great open-air theater, being minded to make public examples of them.

The ruins of the theater where these events took place may still be seen. It once had an impressive facade. The semicircular tiers of seats, supported by the sloping hillside, are said to have accommodated 50,000 people. Although the theater underwent extensive repairs following Paul's day, it is reasonable to believe that this restoration followed the lines of the original theater. Because of its size and accessibility, it was the scene of many public gatherings.

When Paul learned that the mob had seized Gaius and Aristarchus, he undertook, without thought for his own safety, to go to their defense. But his good friends restrained him. At the same moment, some of the city's police arrived. They had been sent by the Asiarchs (representatives of Caesar and rulers over Asia, including Ephesus, its chief city), some of whom were kindly disposed toward Paul. They joined with Paul's brethren in pointing out that he would be making a needless and futile sacrifice of his life if he persisted in his intention of going to the theater at that time. Perhaps the Asiarchs knew that Paul was a Roman citizen and desired to afford him this protection.

In the theater, in the meantime, a Jew named Alexander had been endeavoring to make himself heard. The Jews, knowing that they, as well as the Christians, might suffer at the hands of the mob, had asked him to explain their position. But the crowd, perceiving that Alexander was a Jew and knowing that the Jews opposed all worship of idols, would not listen to him. Instead, they shouted all the more loudly, "Great is Artemis of the Ephesians!" For fully two hours the tumult continued. Not until the town clerk of Ephesus entered the theater did the crowd quiet down. This city official (his position would correspond to that of a present-day mayor) reminded the throng that all the world knew of Ephesus and its glory. Had it not been chosen as the keeper and guardian of the image of Artemis? There was nothing to be gained, therefore, by their loud shouting. Of more moment was the fact that, since it had not been shown that Gaius and Aristarchus had committed any sacrilege or blasphemy, they themselves were in danger of being charged with having incited a riot and violence. If any of those present had a legitimate cause for complaint, they would find the established courts open to them.

Gaius and Aristarchus were saved. At the command of the town clerk, the crowd that had filled the theater quickly dispersed. If any of the silversmiths plotted further violence against Paul, they did it secretly and not in the hearing of the town clerk or of the Asiarchs. It was evident, however, that it would be both unwise and unsafe for Paul to delay any longer his visit to Macedonia and Achaia. Note, in passing, that Luke, while acknowledging that Paul was involved in this disturbance, makes it clear that the Roman authorities found nothing blameworthy in his conduct. They had not restrained him in any way, but rather had protected him.

CHAPTER 15

# The Journey Up to Jerusalem

*P*AUL perceived that the situation in Ephesus was too explosive to permit him to carry on further work there. True, the Roman authorities had taken no action against him (indeed, they had given him some measure of protection), and Gaius and Aristarchus had been released; but mob violence might flare up again at any moment. Because this hostility was directed chiefly against himself, and because his continued presence in Ephesus might subject his Christian brethren to persecution, he decided to depart. The work in Ephesus, he believed, was now well enough established for his faithful helpers to carry it on in his absence. Clearly the time had come for him to set forth upon that journey to Europe which he had planned some months before.

The Acts gives only a very brief account of this journey; and it gives no direct statement as to the reasons for it. From Paul's epistles, however, we learn that the apostle desired that the Gentile churches of Europe should complete as quickly as possible the fund they were raising for the relief of the impoverished Jewish Christians of Jerusalem. This benevolence, he hoped, would be the means of cementing that fellowship which he had long sought to establish between the young Gentile churches and the older Jewish churches. Furthermore, Paul's letters to the Corinthians reveal the great concern which he felt over conditions which existed in their church. These conditions, he feared, might require his personal attention.

160

*Back to Macedonia and Greece  (Acts 20:1-5)*

It must suffice to say, then, that when Paul had bidden fare-well to the Christians of Ephesus, he journeyed by sea to Macedonia. We may be sure that he visited the churches in Philippi, Thessalonica, and Beroea—churches which he had established on his first journey into Europe. We may be sure also that the brethren were glad to see his face once again. This was no hurried visit, for we are told that it was not until after he "had gone over those parts, and had given them much exhortation," that he left Macedonia and journeyed southward into Greece. This "going over" of those parts doubtless included that ministry in Illyricum, to which reference is made in Romans 15:19.

Paul then went down into Greece, where he abode three months. The greater part of the time was spent in Corinth.[1] Happily, the worst disorders in the Corinthian church had been corrected before the apostle's arrival. Consequently, his stay in Corinth did not prove so trying as he had feared might be the case. During that winter in Corinth, he found time to write his letter to the Romans, the most profound of all his epistles.

Paul's plan for further missionary work, so it appears, was as follows. He would first see that the sums of money raised by the churches reached Jerusalem safely. Then he would set forth for Rome, that he might have the privilege of preaching the unsearchable riches of Christ in the Imperial City. There-after (the Lord willing), he might push on to Spain, at the westernmost end of the Mediterranean. Had not his Lord given commandment that the gospel should be carried "unto the uttermost part of the earth"? The distance from Corinth to Jerusalem, to Rome, and to Spain would be at least four thousand miles. If he were then to return to his home in Tarsus, or to Antioch in Syria, or to Jerusalem, he would need to travel three thousand miles more. Considering the slow

---

[1] 2 Cor. 12:14 and 13:1 imply that at some time during his stay in Ephesus, Paul had made a quick visit to Corinth. This, then, would not be the second, but the third time that Paul had visited Corinth.

and hazardous character of travel in those days, we see at once how great a task the apostle had set for himself.

Lest anyone should think that he was reaping some personal profit from these offerings made by the churches, Paul had arranged that in each case the offering should be taken by the church before his arrival on the scene. He had arranged also that each church should send its contribution to Jerusalem by a messenger of its own choosing.[2] Vs. 4 lists those who were Paul's travel companions at this time. Three of them were from the Macedonian churches which he had recently visited; namely, Sopater, son of Pyrrhus, from Beroea, and Aristarchus and Secundus, from Thessalonica. Gaius and Timothy were from Derbe and Lystra, respectively, in Galatia. Tychicus and Trophimus were from the province of Asia, and probably from the city of Ephesus. Aristarchus and Gaius had been with Paul during his stay in Ephesus, and had suffered cruel treatment there at the hands of the mob. Some of these men, possibly all of them, were bearers of offerings from the churches in the districts from which they came. References scattered throughout the Pauline epistles indicate, in one way or another, that all of the churches which Paul had founded had part in this benevolent project. The possible exception were the churches on the island of Cyprus, churches which Paul had relinquished to the supervision of Barnabas.

When Paul and these men were about to sail from Corinth for Troas, en route to Jerusalem, word reached them that some fanatical Jews making the pilgrimage to Jerusalem, and traveling by the same ship, had formed a plot to take Paul's life. It was decided that Paul's companions should make the trip as planned, giving no indication that Paul was not with them; and that Paul, for safety's sake, should travel by another route. His companions would wait at Troas until he caught up with them. Paul, taking the circuitous overland route, was under necessity of retracing his steps to Macedonia. This journey on foot along the much-traveled *Via Egnatia* was tiring; it was also the cause of much delay. Paul had got no farther than Philippi when the Passover season arrived.

2 See 1 Cor. 16:1-3.

*From Philippi to Troas (Acts 20:6-12)*

It is worthy of note that in Acts 20:5, where we would
expect the name "Paul" (or at least the pronoun "him"), we
find the plural pronoun "us." In Acts 20:6, 13, 15; 21:1; etc.,
we have the pronoun "we." Obviously, Paul found at Philippi
his good friend Luke. Obviously, also, Luke arranged to accompany Paul on this journey to Jerusalem. He was able,
therefore, to give an eyewitness account of many of the subsequent events. The narrative, as one would expect, gains
immeasurably in richness of detail. No doubt Luke, in writing
this portion of The Acts, was able to draw upon his own
travel diary and notes in the same manner that he had done
when recounting events which had occurred during his earlier
travels with Paul (i.e., Acts 16:10-18).

At Philippi, Paul found a ship bound for Troas. Since he
had successfully eluded his enemies, there was no longer need
for him to continue his journey on foot. Accordingly, he and
Luke booked passage upon this ship. The ship, however, must
have encountered severe headwinds, for the sail to Troas, which
ordinarily took no more than forty-eight hours (cf. Acts 16:11-
12), required a full five days. At Troas, Paul rejoined his
companions. A week slipped by before they could arrange
passage which would advance them on their journey. Paul put
the time to good use, however, for he visited and encouraged
the Christians in that city.

Apparently, these Christians in Troas were organized as a
church. We read that on the first day of the week (the Lord's
Day, as distinguished from the Jewish sabbath), they came
together to break bread. The expression "break bread," in
this context, almost certainly refers to an observance of the
Lord's Supper. This was the last night that Paul could be
with them. Accordingly, the testimonies and prayers were
long and earnest; so also was Paul's sermon. Midnight came,
and the service was not yet concluded. The lateness of the
hour, the crowded condition of the room, and the heat and
poor ventilation,[3]  proved too much for one member of the

---

[3] Luke writes: "There were many lights in the upper chamber, where
we were gathered" (Acts 20:8 RSV). Note that the RSV has "we" where

congregation. A young man named Eutychus, who had been sitting upon a third-story window-sill, had dropped off to sleep. To the dismay of all who were present, he fell out of the window to the ground. No doubt, one of the first to examine the young man was Luke, the physician. The young man gave every indication of being dead. Paul, however, did not despair of Eutychus' life. He first bent over the lad, then embraced him; no doubt praying as he did so that the Lord might restore him to life.[4] Presently he was happy to announce that life had returned to the lad's body. Everyone felt greatly relieved when the lad showed no ill effects from his fall, and with this added reason for thanksgiving they returned to the upper room and proceeded with their observance of the Lord's Supper.

*From Troas to Miletus (Acts 20:13-38)*

It was daybreak when Paul bade farewell to these earnest Christians, and still later when he departed from Troas. Luke and Paul's other companions had already sailed for Assos. Paul himself had elected to walk to Assos, which was about twenty miles distant. Because the ship had to round Cape Lectum, Paul, by following the direct Roman road across the cape, reached Assos as soon, or very nearly as soon, as the ship did. Paul frequently traveled by sea, for often the sea offered him the only practical way of getting where he wanted to go; but he nowhere displays such a love for the sea as Luke does.[5] The Greek love of the sea was foreign to the Jew.

Paul went aboard at Assos, and the little ship continued on

the KJV has "they." The best manuscripts confirm what we would have surmised from the context; namely, that Luke was present.

[4] Compare the manner in which the prophet Elisha prostrated himself upon the lifeless body of the son of the Shunammite woman (2 Kings 4:32-35). Compare also Peter's raising of Dorcas to life (Acts 9:36-42). Our Lord Jesus Christ had raised from the dead Lazarus, the daughter of Jairus, and others. Through the Spirit of Christ dwelling in him, the apostle Paul was able to draw upon that same life-giving power.

[5] Luke takes delight in recounting the details of his sea voyages. He names each port of call and gives the sailing time. As an example of this, see Acts 20:15.

its course from island to island. The next day's sail brought the ship to the harbor of Mitylene on the island of Lesbos. The next night the ship dropped anchor in the strait between the mainland and the island of Chios. The following day the ship touched at Samos,[6] and one more day's sail brought it to Miletus. In the time of Paul, that port, though exceeded in importance by Ephesus, nevertheless was a busy place.

We may be sure that it was with deep regret that Paul had sailed past Ephesus, where he had labored so long and so successfully. There were many Christians there whom he would have liked to visit, but he felt that a side trip to Ephesus would consume more time than he could afford. It was his desire to reach Jerusalem before the day of Pentecost. That day, commemorating the bestowal of the Holy Spirit, would be an appropriate time to present the offering of the Gentile churches. Was not the offering an evidence of the Holy Spirit's working in the lives of the Gentile Christians?

Paul had not been able to visit Ephesus, but on learning that his ship was to remain at Miletus for several days more, he sent word to the Ephesian church that he desired a conference with its leaders. The elders of that church (there appears to have been a considerable number of them) hurried to Miletus. When they were come together, Paul addressed them. Paul's "address to the Ephesian elders," as it has come to be called, was an earnest and deeply moving exhortation.

Paul began by reminding them of his faithfulness in the gospel ministry while in their city. Despite many difficulties and dangers, he had given them instruction both publicly in their church and privately in their homes; before both Jews and Greeks he had held up the necessity of repentance toward God and faith in Jesus Christ. Then the apostle informed the elders of something of which he had long been aware, but which we, reading Luke's narrative, may not have perceived, for this is Luke's first explicit mention of it. Paul announced

6 The words "and tarried at Trogyllium," which appear in the KJV probably are a gloss; and, for want of sufficient textual support, they have been omitted from the RSV. They present no difficulty, however, for it is a known fact that many ships making this coastwise journey did anchor off Cape Trogyllium.

that he felt under a divine compulsion to go up to Jerusalem at this time. The Holy Spirit was bidding him go, and his own spirit (his own understanding of what was demanded by the Christian program) confirmed the Spirit's promptings.

At the same time that the Spirit bade him go, the Spirit gave him warning that bonds and afflictions awaited him. Paul would have expected this, anyway, for had it not always been so? Had not his faithfulness to the gospel invariably aroused the wrath of ungodly men? Had not his enemies made one plot after another against his life? Now he was going up to Jerusalem, where Jewish fanaticism was at its height. He knew that in all human probability his life would be cut off, but the prospect of death did not deter him. His supreme concern was that in his life, however long or short it might prove to be, he should show himself in all things obedient to the commission which the Lord had given him—the commission to make known everywhere the good news concerning God's grace. Then he said that which he must have found very hard to say: that they, his good brethren from Ephesus, should not expect in this life ever to look upon his face again.

Several matters may here be noted. First, Paul's journey up to Jerusalem was in that same spirit of complete dedication which had characterized his Lord's last journey up to that city. Recall that Jesus had "stedfastly set his face to go to Jerusalem," [7] and that He had made the journey knowing full well that at its end a cross awaited Him.[8] Second, we can understand now, as we did not earlier, the reason for that all-night church service at Troas. It had been Paul's farewell to the Christians of Troas, as this was his farewell to these Ephesians; and there were many things that he desired them to remember. Third, it has been asked if Paul was not mistaken in declaring that he would never see these Ephesians again. Certainly at this time he had no expectation of ever seeing them again; and certainly there is nothing here to indicate that he, in accordance with the generally accepted tradition, revisited Ephesus some eight or nine years later. The question is a very difficult one and cannot be answered on the strength

7 Luke 9:51.
8 Luke 18:31-34.

of this single passage. If Luke had known, at the time of writing Luke-Acts, of a ministry in Asia Minor following Paul's release from his first Roman imprisonment, it seems likely that he would have given some hint of that knowledge here. The passage, as it stands, constitutes a strong argument for an early date for the writing of Luke-Acts.

It was a most solemn charge, therefore, that Paul laid upon these Ephesian elders. He reminded them that the Holy Spirit had made them overseers,[9] and that they, as such, should show themselves faithful shepherds over the Lord's flock. Inasmuch as their appointment as overseers was not of men only, but had received the confirmation of the Holy Spirit, their responsibility before God "to feed the church of the Lord"[10] was doubly great. Paul knew, from his experience in Galatia, Corinth, and elsewhere, that after his departure unscrupulous men would seek to draw away the flock. Some of these men, arising perhaps out of their own midst, would be teachers of false doctrines; others would be selfish seekers after power over their brethren. Let them, therefore, as faithful shepherds, display the same watchfulness over the flock that he himself had displayed night and day when with them. At the same time that they were keeping watch over their fellows, they were to display even greater zeal in keeping watch over their own conduct, lest inadvertently they themselves should be the means of leading others astray.

In conclusion, Paul commended them all to God. For such strength as they would need, he bade them draw upon the resources of the gospel, especially upon the word of God's

9 The Greek word here (vs. 28) is *episkopous*, which the KJV translates "overseers"; elsewhere "bishops." The RSV has "guardians." Observe in this passage that the term is applied, not to two or three outstanding members of the Ephesian church, but to the entire company of its elders. There were not three orders in the apostolic church (i.e., bishops, elders, and deacons) as some have claimed, but only two (i.e., elders, whose functions were those of overseers, and deacons). The special meaning which the term "bishop" came to have in the Roman Catholic Church, and the high place which the bishop later came to have in that hierarchy, make it both undesirable and unwarranted to introduce the term "bishop" here (as Roman Catholic translations do), or indeed anywhere in the New Testament.

10 Acts 20:28, RSV.

grace, which, if heeded, would build them up and give them an inheritance among all of God's consecrated ones. Once again Paul reminded them of his own example. Only a man whose conduct has been exemplary would dare to speak so personally. He charged them to aid the weak and to give generously to the support of the needy, remembering the saying of Jesus their Lord: "It is more blessed to give than to receive."[11]

When the last emotion-filled word of instruction had been spoken, Paul knelt down and joined with them in prayer. The elders were deeply moved, and they were greatly saddened by the thought that they were never to see him again. Accordingly, they found it hard to let him go. But the hour of parting had come. The night was well-nigh spent, and Paul's ship was to sail at dawn. So they accompanied him to the dock and saw him aboard. The last good-by was not called out until Paul's ship, having drifted off shore with the tide, opened its sails to catch the breeze that wakened with the day.

### From Miletus to Tyre  (Acts 21:1-6)

Once again Paul was on his way, and if we are to follow his journey understandingly we must refer frequently to the map. With the wind steadily astern, the ship had no difficulty in maintaining a straight course to the island of Cos, which was reached that evening. The next day's run brought the ship to the harbor of Rhodes, at the northern extremity of the island of that same name. Observe that the ship had then turned the southwestern corner of Asia Minor, and that its next course would be eastward along Asia Minor's southern coast.

At last they reached Patara, their ship's destination.[12] Strabo characterized Patara as "a great city with a harbor and many

11 Although this utterance of Jesus does not occur in any of our four canonical gospels, there is no reason to question its authenticity. It may have been a saying (*logion*) which had come down to Paul and his hearers by oral tradition.

12 A few of the ancient manuscripts, after the word "Patara," add the words "and Myra." If that reading should be adopted, it would merely indicate that the ship continued on to the port of Myra, no great distance beyond Patara.

temples." The temples were to the god Apollo. At Patara, Paul was pleased to find a much larger and faster ship which was soon to sail for Palestine. He and his companions took passage on it. This ship, with no fear of the high seas, took the direct course. It boldly sailed southeastward toward the port of Tyre in Phoenicia. After a quick and uneventful run, the travelers sighted, off the port side and very low on the horizon, the hills of Cyprus, the island where Paul had begun his missionary labors. Another day's sail, and their eager eyes caught sight of breakers dashing against a double rock rising out of the sea. They were within sight of the immemorially old port of Tyre.

According to Herodotus, the city of Tyre was founded in 2750 B.C. It was built originally partly upon the mainland and partly upon the rocky island that stood about three-quarters of a mile off shore. Its citizens, by turning this island into a citadel and retreating to it in times of danger, had been able to withstand many sieges. Alexander the Great, however, was not to be thus thwarted. By means of a remarkable engineering feat—the building of a rock causeway from the mainland to the island—he captured it; then visited a terrible vengeance upon those who had dared to withstand him. In the course of the years the sand which washed against this causeway considerably widened it, with the result that what had been an island became the outermost point of a peninsula. In Paul's day a busy road, with buildings on both sides, ran the length of the peninsula. Because of this causeway, Tyre came to have two harbors: the Sidonian port to the north; the Egyptian port to the south. Of ancient Tyre, once so prosperous, only a few sea-washed ruins are to be seen today. Terrible fulfillment of Ezekiel's prophecy of its doom (Ezek. 27)!

Did Paul, as the ship dropped anchor, let his mind dwell upon Tyre's ancient greatness, a greatness then still discernible, but fading? And did he call to mind the fact that his Lord once had withdrawn into "the borders of Tyre and Sidon," but that His presence there had become known? [13] Nazareth was no more than thirty miles distant.

13 Mark 7:24.

The ship, so it appears, was to proceed on to Ptolemais, some thirty miles farther down the coast, but it needed first to unload its cargo at Tyre. This would require a week. Paul, accordingly, determined to put the time to good use. He sought out such Christians as were to be found in Tyre, and discovered a considerable number of them. When they learned that Paul planned to go up to Jerusalem, they "through the Spirit" sought to dissuade him from that purpose. They knew how strong the feeling against Paul was, and they feared that when Jerusalem became filled with pilgrims come up for the celebration of the feast of Pentecost, that feeling might be fanned to fanatical fury. Paul was grateful to these Christians of Tyre for their warning and solicitude, but he felt that he must put the cause of Christ ahead of his personal safety. The entire Christian congregation, the women and children as well as the men, accompanied Paul and his companions to the waterfront, and there, kneeling on the beach, the farewell prayer was offered. We wonder what impression this made upon the sailors, the stevedores, and the ship captains who witnessed it!

## On to Ptolemais, Caesarea, and Jerusalem (Acts 21:7-16)

Soon the ship was at Ptolemais. It was by that name that the town was called during Macedonian and Roman times. During early Old Testament times it had been known as Accho[14]; today it is the town of Acre. It is situated to the north of Mt. Carmel, upon the wide bay formed by that promontory. At one time the most important port along that coast, its trade had fallen off with the building of Caesarea, seat of the Roman government. Its location at the lower end of the valley leading up to the Plain of Esdraelon had made it a gateway to the interior of Palestine. Invading armies have sought to take advantage of that fact, with the result that the walls of Acre bear the scars of battles from the days of the Egyptian Thotmes III (1400 B.C.) down to recent times. Only one day was spent in Ptolemais, for all were becoming eager to reach Jerusalem.

[14] Judges 1:31.

The next day, Paul and his companions proceeded (apparently they journeyed on foot) to Caesarea. There they sought out the home of Philip; that Philip who, lest he be confused with the Philip who was one of the Twelve, came to be characterized as "the evangelist." An appropriate designation it was, as we learned from our study of Acts 8:5-13, 26-40. This deacon [15] had found more to do than "serve tables"! He had witnessed for Christ in the predominantly Gentile city of Caesarea. No doubt the church in Caesarea met in his house. Furthermore, though an ardent evangelist, he had not neglected his own household.[16] He had given careful Christian training to his four young daughters, who are said to have possessed the spirit of prophecy. Though our text is silent on the matter, it is probable that these Spirit-filled girls warned Paul against going up to Jerusalem.

Paul remained with Philip (as courtesy demanded when visiting so distinguished a Christian leader) for "some days" (RSV).[17] At any rate, during those days while Paul was still in Philip's home, the prophet Agabus came down to Caesarea from Judea. This was that prophet Agabus who at Antioch, years before, had prophesied the coming of a time of famine.[18] We wonder if Philip's daughters may not have sent for him in order that their words to Paul (words which he showed no signs of heeding) might have the support of an older and more widely recognized prophetic voice.

Agabus employed the attention-catching practice of the Old Testament prophets; he dramatized his message to Paul. While all watched curiously to see what he would do, he removed Paul's girdle and with it bound himself hand and foot. "So," he declared, "the Jews will bind the owner of this girdle and deliver him into the hands of the Gentiles." "Deliver him," that is to say, "into the custody of the Roman authorities." All who were present then begged Paul to abandon his plan; even Luke and the messengers from the Gentile churches

---

[15] Acts 6:1-6.
[16] 1 Tim. 3:12.
[17] The "many days" of the KJV gives a wrong impression of the length of Paul's stay in Caesarea.
[18] Acts 11:27-28.

begged him to give it up. No doubt, they suggested that he remain in Caesarea while they, being not so well known in Jerusalem, were delivering the church offerings.

Paul was moved by their tears, but he implored them to cease trying to dissuade him from his purpose.[19] He reminded them that he had committed his life completely to God,[20] and that he was prepared, not only for imprisonment, but also for death if need be, at Jerusalem, for "the name of the Lord Jesus." At last, these solicitous friends saw that Paul's call to go up to Jerusalem was a call from the Lord himself. They ceased then their efforts to deter him, and voiced the prayer which was in Paul's own heart, namely, "The will of the Lord be done." Perhaps they remembered how Jesus had rebuked Simon Peter when that disciple, out of an understandable love for his Master, had presumed to tell Jesus that he should abandon his plan of going up to Jerusalem to die.[21]

Their visit with Philip being finished, "we" (so the KJV quaintly translates) "took up our carriages, and went up to Jerusalem." "Carriages," in the time of King James, meant things to be carried; that is to say, they picked up the baggage they were carrying with them, and set forth.[22] They could travel more leisurely now, for they were so near Jerusalem that they could easily reach the city before Pentecost. It was after the Passover when they had got away from Philippi in Macedonia. They had made the long journey to Jerusalem in Judea in less than seven weeks.

The journey from Caesarea to Jerusalem, however, was mostly an up-hill climb, and would require two days. But they had for company on this last stage of their journey some of their Christian friends from Caesarea. These good folks brought them that evening to the home of a certain Mnason,

19 "What mean ye to weep and to break mine heart" is equivalent to "Why do ye, by your tears, try to make me weaken in my purpose?"

20 Compare Paul's words in Rom. 12:1. Paul had committed his life completely to God as a "living sacrifice." In going up to Jerusalem, he was but doing what he had repeatedly besought others to do; namely, to give to God unhesitating obedience and full service.

21 Matt. 16:21-23.

22 The RSV, with more simplicity and directness, translates: "we made ready and went up to Jerusalem."

where they hoped they might spend the night. It is said of Mnason that he was "an early disciple." This long-time Christian was glad to provide the lodging which the party needed.

What were Paul's emotions when the walls of Jerusalem at last came into view? Four years or more had passed since he had last visited the city.[23] Did his mind now fill with dark forebodings? Or did he feel within his spirit a divinely given strength and peace, designed to prepare him for whatever the future might hold? Knowing Paul, we may be sure that, whatever his thoughts, his steps did not falter.

[23] Paul's last visit to Jerusalem had been a very brief one. It is implied in the words, "he went up and greeted the church" (Acts 18:22, RSV).

## CHAPTER 16

# The Arrest and Imprisonment

O JERUSALEM, Jerusalem, which killest the prophets, and stonest them that are sent unto thee. . . ." Can it be that the years have taught thee nothing? When the Lord of Love came unto thee, thou didst hurry Him outside thy walls and hang Him upon a tree. And now, behold, another walks thy streets—one in whom the Lord's spirit dwells—and thou dost plot his death!

## Paul Meets with James and the Elders of the Jerusalem Church (Acts 21:17-25)

The Christian brethren in Jerusalem received Paul kindly, but their gladness on seeing him again (as we shall presently discover) was mixed with concern for his safety while in their city. They hastily made arrangements whereby on the very next day Paul should appear before James and the elders of the Jerusalem church. Paul was grateful for this opportunity, for there had been moments when he had feared that his well-meant efforts might not be acceptable to that body.[1] After Paul had greeted the elders, he related to them in detail the things which "God had wrought among the Gentiles"; all the praise belonged to God, he explained, because he himself had been but the human instrument through which the Spirit of God had operated. Although it is not so stated, he doubtless, upon the conclusion of his account, introduced the messengers from the Gentile churches and they presented the offerings

[1] Rom. 15:30-31.

174

which they had brought. The elders rejoiced at hearing that the gospel had made such progress, and thanked God for it. We may be sure, also, that they were grateful for the offerings from the Gentile churches, for many of the Jerusalem brethren, in consequence of their becoming Christians, had been deprived of their ordinary means of livelihood and had been persecuted in numerous other ways.

But Paul's presence in Jerusalem presented these elders with a problem, a problem so grave that they made no effort to conceal it. Their first words to Paul following their acceptance of the offerings were in the nature of a reminder. There were among the Christians, they said, two factions. One group was wholly sympathetic toward all that Paul had done among the Gentiles; the other group, the Judaizers, felt that he had gone too far in telling the Gentiles that it was not necessary for them to keep the law in order to become Christians. After all that Paul had suffered at the hands of the Judaizers, this was scarcely news to him. Paul—let it be said to his credit—had not disparaged the law; he knew that it had its proper function, and he had honored it. What he had insisted upon was that it was faith in Christ, not the observance of the law, which was essential to salvation. He had not required circumcision of his Gentile converts, for he did not consider it essential to their salvation. He had seen the genuineness of the conversion of uncircumcised Gentiles attested by the bestowal upon them of the Holy Spirit.

Furthermore, Paul had never taught that the Jews should abandon their practice of circumcision; it was the mark of their race, a religious rite which was meaningful to them, and which it was their privilege to observe. But the Judaizers, failing to perceive Paul's fine distinction between what is necessary and what, though not necessary, is a high religious privilege, had concluded that Paul, by his liberal teachings, was undermining the whole structure of the law; that is to say, the whole Judaic-Mosaic foundation on which Christianity, as they conceived it, had been built.

These Judaizers had opposed Paul in many of the cities where he had preached. They were especially numerous in Jerusalem. The elders acknowledged that Paul's preaching and practice had been misunderstood and misrepresented, but nevertheless the hostility against Paul existed, it was extreme and violent, and had to be reckoned with. Nor had they forgotten the working agreement which had been approved by the Jerusalem Conference. They had no thought of abrogating it; indeed, they reaffirmed it (vs. 25). But for the sake of better understanding and the avoidance of strife, they did make a request of Paul. They asked him to show to these Judaizers by an act of worship in the Temple that he still possessed his early love for the sacred things of the law.

There were four members of their church, devout men, who as an act of devotion had taken upon themselves a Nazirite vow. Being poor men they were finding it difficult to raise the sum of money demanded of them by the priests, who alone could release them from their vow. Would Paul become the patron and sponsor for these worthy men? Would he join with them in their Nazirite vow, and pay, on his own behalf and theirs, the Temple fees in connection with the completion and discharge of the vow? What the elders asked of Paul was not an uncommon thing. It was something which wealthy persons frequently did as an act of piety. As for the Nazirite vow, they recalled that Paul some years before had made such a vow voluntarily.[2] By doing this now, Paul might—so the elders maintained—clear away many misapprehensions and conciliate the Judaizers.

Some commentators, following the lead of John Calvin, have declared that Paul, in agreeing to this proposal, made a compromise with his convictions. But had not Paul said of himself: "For though I be free from all men, yet have I made myself servant unto all, that I might gain the more. And unto the Jews I became as a Jew, that I might gain the Jews . . . to them that are without law, as without law . . . that I might gain them that are without law."[3] Let it be kept in mind that this which Paul did was a purely voluntary act of devotion, an act of devotion which he was glad to perform. The rite in which he participated was not one which either the Jews or the Judaizing Christians counted essential to salvation. It did

[2] Acts 18:18.
[3] 1 Cor. 9:19-21.

not contradict Paul's thesis that salvation was by faith in Christ, not by works of the law. We ought rather to commend Paul for his acquiescence. How far he was willing to go, strong-principled man that he was, for the sake of holding together the Jewish and the Gentile branches of Christ's church!

It has also been asserted that the plan, whether involving compromise or not, was ill advised. It proved, some say, a complete failure. True, it was never carried to completion. But to call it a failure is to argue from silence. We are not told what effect Paul's willingness to do this had upon the Judaizers. This, at least, is clear: Paul's arrest and imprisonment—as it turned out—was brought about, not by the Judaizers, but by non-Christian Jews who regarded Paul as a proselyter and who resented the fact that he had been so successful in winning followers to the Nazarene.

*In the Temple, Paul Is Mobbed and Arrested (Acts 21:26-40)*

Suffice it to say, then, that Paul joined himself with these four poor brethren. He took their Nazirite vow upon himself. He went up to the Temple, and in accordance with the ceremonial requirements purified himself together with them. Then he made arrangements with the Temple priests as to the time when the ceremonies should be performed which would mark the termination of the period covered by their vow.

When the seven-day period had almost ended,[4] certain Jews from Asia (from the city of Ephesus, probably) came upon Paul in the Temple. They recognized him immediately. These men had not forgotten all that had happened to the Jewish population of Ephesus at the time of the riot of the silversmiths. Paul, they held, had been responsible for that disturbance and for its unhappy consequences. Only a few days before, they had seen Paul walking the streets of Jerusalem with

---

[4] It is not clear whether this seven-day period was the total duration of the vow, or the duration of the concluding ceremonies, during which (so some have suggested) Paul and the four men would remain continuously in the Temple.

Trophimus,[5] an Ephesian like themselves, but a Gentile, not a Jew. They now beheld Paul in the Temple, in company with four men; and, making their wish the father to their thought, they came to the wholly unwarranted conclusion that Paul had taken Trophimus, the Gentile, into the inner court of the Temple. To their minds, as Jews, a greater profanation of the Temple could not be imagined.

Gentiles, of course, were permitted access to the outer court of the Temple; indeed, that area was called the Court of the Gentiles. But the inner precincts of the Temple were open to Jews only. On the balustrade which surrounded this holier part of the Temple were a number of stone slabs with plainly carved inscriptions which gave warning that "foreigners" (i.e., Gentiles) were to go no farther. One of these stones was found in Jerusalem in 1871. It is a limestone block, 23 inches high, 34 inches long, and 15 inches thick; and it may now be seen in an Istanbul museum. The deeply cut inscription has been translated as follows:

> "No foreigner may enter within the railing or boundary line of the sanctuary. Whoever is caught is himself responsible for the consequences, which are death."

More recently, a portion of another of these warning stones has been unearthed. It bears a similar inscription.

Being a Jew, Paul had every right to be within the holier part of the Temple. But these Jews from Asia, seeing him there, set up a great shout in which they summoned all loyal Jews to come to their assistance. Pointing out Paul, they declared that wherever he went he turned people against the Jews. He had spoken, they said, against the law and against the Temple; and now, to climax all, he had committed sacrilege by taking Gentiles into the holy place. Jews from the city joined with those already in the Temple, and in no time at all a mob had gathered. The mob, seizing Paul, dragged him out of the Temple. The Temple was scarcely an appropriate place for putting a man to death, even though the Temple law specifically prescribed that penalty upon offenders! In

5 On Trophimus, see Acts 20:4.

the meantime, the Levites, working feverishly, began to shut the Temple doors, lest the Temple become contaminated from the presence in it of a dead body.

At very nearly the same time, word that all Jerusalem was in an uproar was carried by the Roman guards to their military commander, the tribune Claudius Lysias. That Roman acted with commendable promptness and vigor. Perhaps he was all the more on the alert because a rebellion against Rome had broken out only a short time before. The rebellion had been put down by the procurator Felix (so Josephus tells us), but the leader of it, a Jew from Egypt who was spoken of as "the Egyptian," was reported to have escaped. Lysias thought it quite possible that this disturbance was a recurrence of that uprising. Calling to some of his centurions to follow him with their soldiers, he ran down from his quarters in the Tower of Antonia and pushed his way into the thick of the mob. Upon the arrival of the soldiers, the mob left off their beating of Paul. So far as the tribune could make out, Paul was the cause of the disturbance; at least, he was in the very center of it. Accordingly, he commanded his soldiers to arrest Paul, and to bind him, as befitted so dangerous a prisoner, with two chains. But when Lysias demanded of the mob who the man was that he had taken prisoner, and what he had done, there was so much confusion—some shouting one thing and others shouting another—he gave up the effort, and directed that Paul should be taken into the castle [6] for questioning.

The members of the mob saw that they must act quickly or they would lose their victim, and they were loath to forego the excitement and satisfaction they would find in putting Paul to death. Thinking that they might snatch Paul away from the soldiers, they pushed after him so violently that the

[6] The Castle of Antonia, as rebuilt by Herod the Great and renamed in honor of Mark Antony, stood at the northwest corner of the Temple area. Handsomely furnished within, it was the residence of the Roman procurator on those occasions when he found it convenient to be in Jerusalem rather than in Caesarea. It stood upon a high precipice, and its four towers, each rising seventy-five or one hundred feet, made it a well-nigh impregnable fortress. A cohort of Roman soldiers was quartered there, principally that they might keep order within the city of Jerusalem.

soldiers had almost to carry Paul as they made their way up the stairs leading into the tower. In the midst of all this tumult (for the mob was shouting, "Away with him!"), Paul managed to gain the attention of the tribune. "May I speak unto thee?" he asked. The courteous character of this request surprised the tribune; he was equally surprised to hear his prisoner address him in Greek. "Then you are not the Egyptian who but recently led into the wilderness that band of four thousand assassins?"

To this question, Paul responded with a quiet dignity which was all the more impressive by reason of its contrast to the frenzy of the mob. "I am a Jew" (not an Egyptian), Paul answered; "and" (far from being a fanatical assassin) "I am a citizen of Tarsus, in Cilicia, which is—as you know—an important and honored city" (this being the force of Paul's understatement). "Permit me, I beseech you, to speak to the people."

It was worth a try, the tribune thought. Perhaps his prisoner could quiet the commotion. At least, his words would reveal what the commotion was all about. He granted the permission requested, and Paul raised his hand in a gesture indicating that he desired to be heard. Seeing the gesture, the crowd gradually became silent.

## Paul Speaks from the Tower Stairs (Acts 22:1-28)

Paul, who had addressed the tribune in Greek, now wisely spoke in Hebrew (more accurately, in the Palestinian Aramaic). That was the tongue in which he would be most readily understood by his hearers; and by using it, he identified himself to them as a fellow Jew.

Paul's address in his own defense, made under these difficult circumstances and without any advance preparation, was both logical and persuasive. It was the kind of speech that can be made only by one who, being upright in character, has nothing to conceal; and who, in other dangerous situations, had often defended his conduct against similar charges. It was, in the main, a recital of the principal happenings in his life. The implied question throughout was: "How could I

have done otherwise, if I was to show myself obedient unto
God?"

He recounted, first, how he, born in Tarsus, had been
brought up as a Jew in their city, Jerusalem; how he had
studied the law under the greatest of their teachers, Gamaliel;
and how he had come to have such a consuming zeal for the
law that he had taken the lead in persecuting the Christians.
He not only had persecuted them in Jerusalem, but he also
had set out for Damascus that he might do the same there.
The elders and the high priest would have to acknowledge
the truth of his statements.

He then related how he had come to believe on Jesus Christ.
While he was making the journey to Damascus, the Lord
had appeared unto him. It had been an overpowering experience, one that had left him shaken and blind; at the same
time, it had been a revealing experience. From that moment
(and what other course had been open to him?) he had given
to the Lord unquestioning obedience. It was a devout Jew
named Ananias, one who was highly esteemed by all the Jews
of Damascus (Christian Jews and non-Christian Jews alike),
who had restored his sight, who had baptized him in the
name of the Lord, and who had informed him that God had
chosen him to be a witness to all men of the things which he
had heard and seen. It is likely that the account of this experience, this supernal and character-changing experience
which meant so much to Paul, made little impression upon
his hearers. But at least, they listened; they endured even his
specific mention (in vs. 8) of the hated and anathematized
name of Jesus!

Paul continued his account. When he had returned to Jerusalem and was praying in the Temple—the very Temple where
they then were standing—the Lord had appeared to him again.
The Lord had ordered him to leave the city at once. Its people, the Lord had said, will not receive your witness. Paul
declared that he had demurred, that he had even argued the
matter with the Lord. It had seemed to him that the people
of Jerusalem, knowing that he had persecuted the followers
of the Way, and knowing also that he had participated in the
stoning of Stephen, might be favorably disposed to listen to

what he would say to them. But the Lord had overruled his suggestion, and had ordered him, even more peremptorily, to depart. He had been commissioned, so the Lord told him, to bear his witness to the Gentiles. They would be more ready and glad to receive his words, it was implied, than would the dwellers in Jerusalem.

The crowd, which had listened quietly up to this point, now broke into an uproar. Gentiles! That was it: Gentiles usurping their Jewish privileges, taking possession of their Jewish heritage! "Away with such a fellow!" they shouted. "He ought not be allowed to live!" With that, they waved their garments, threw dust into the air, and in every way possible sought to show their contempt for Paul. Upon this new outburst, the tribune ordered that Paul should be taken within the barracks. He would have him "examined by scourging." What a euphemism! What he proposed was to beat the truth out of Paul, however brutal the business might be. It is possible that the tribune had not understood Paul's Hebrew, or that understanding it, he had not been able to figure out what was the point at issue between Paul and his Jewish brethren.

And so, to the whipping post! Strip off Paul's clothing that the lash may cut deep into his flesh! Pull the straps tight, so that he shall not be able to dodge a single blow! And all of this, because Paul had sought to worship God in the manner, and in the place, which God had appointed!

But Paul, though physically helpless in the hands of the soldiers, did not lose his presence of mind. Addressing the centurion who was directing the arrangements for the scourging, he said: "Is it lawful for you to scourge one who is a Roman citizen? And, in addition, one who has not been convicted of any crime?" At a shouted word from the centurion, the preparations for the scourging ceased. Seeking out the tribune, the centurion said: "You had best be careful, sir, for this prisoner claims that he is a citizen of Rome." Such ignominious punishments as scourging and crucifixion were forbidden in the case of those persons, relatively few, who possessed Roman citizenship.[7]

[7] Tarsus, Paul's birthplace, was a free city (an *urbs libera*). As such, though situated within a Roman province, it enjoyed the privilege of

The tribune hurried to the scene. He was having trouble enough, he thought, without being charged with having illegally flogged a Roman citizen. But before he put an end to the proceedings, he wanted to assure himself that Paul was really a Roman. "Tell me," he said, "are you a citizen of Rome?" Paul answered that he was. "I paid a great sum for my citizenship," the tribune responded. Behind the tribune's proud words was a not-too-kind insinuation: "How could such a person as you are ever have raised enough money to buy his citizenship?" Paul answered simply, "I was born a Roman citizen."

## Paul Is Brought Before the Sanhedrin  (Acts 22:29–23:10)

Paul had escaped the scourging (the "horrible flagellum"), but he was still a prisoner. Being fully prepared for martyrdom, if that was God's will for him, it is very possible that Paul spent the night with more peace of mind than did Claudius Lysias. That tribune had many reasons for concern. Would he be called to account for his treatment of Paul? Who ever would have supposed that this Jew was also a Roman? And now, how should he dispose of Paul? Release him with a word of apology? That, it will be recalled, was the way out which had been chosen by the magistrates of Philippi under somewhat similar circumstances. Paul, it appeared, was guilty of no infraction of Roman law. But to release him was to put him again in the hands of the bloodthirsty mob. Paul, being a

---

self-government. But Tarsus was not a *colonia* or *municipium*. Paul's birth in Tarsus, therefore, did not make him, *ipso facto*, a Roman citizen. Since he states that he was *born* a Roman citizen, he must have received his citizenship from his father or grandfather. There were three ways by which this citizenship may have been acquired: by manumission, as a reward of merit bestowed by the emperor, or by purchase. Paul implied that the citizenship which he had inherited had been conferred, not bought. Paul's citizenship in Tarsus would have no significance outside that city; his Roman citizenship, however, would be recognized everywhere throughout the empire. It exempted him from such degrading punishments as scourging and crucifixion and it entitled him to trial before the emperor in Rome, if he were charged with a capital offense. Paul's Roman citizenship stood him in good stead on this occasion, and also later, as we shall learn.

Roman, deserved some protection. Then it occurred to the tribune that Paul's offense, whatever it was, had to do with the religion and customs of the Jews. That was a matter for the Sanhedrin to handle. He could throw the responsibility upon that body! That very night the tribune sent word to "the chief priests and all their council" that in the morning he would bring his prisoner before them for trial.

When the Sanhedrin had assembled and had granted Paul permission to speak, Paul began by saying (we summarize his words): "Brethren, my conscience is clear with respect to everything that I have done." [8] The high priest Ananias[9] saw in this remark, or professed to see in it, great presumption. He commanded those standing near Paul to strike him on the mouth. It was not for the prisoner, but for the Sanhedrin, to say whether or not he was guilty before God! Through cut lips Paul made reply: "God shall strike you, you whitewashed wall! [10] How is it that you who pose as one judging according to the law, do yourself violate the law in condemning and punishing me before you have heard my case?"

How are we to understand this sharp word? It sounds unbecoming on the lips of one who so repeatedly had besought others always to display forbearance and love. Had the apos-

[8] The surprising abruptness and brevity of Paul's speech may have been due to the apostle's intention and frame of mind. Whereas it was customary to address the Sanhedrin with the words, "Rulers of the people and elders of Israel," Paul had for that body only a curt, "Brethren." He was not willing to recognize that hypocritical council as the God-appointed rulers of Israel.

[9] Ananias, son of Nedebaeus, was high priest A.D. 47-59. During his high priesthood he once was suspended and taken to Rome for trial. It was charged, and truthfully, that during a feud between Galileans and Samaritans he had incited the Galileans to exact bloody reprisals for the losses they had sustained. The emperor Claudius, for political reasons, acquitted him; and he returned to Jerusalem to continue in the high office, which (Josephus states) he disgraced by his rapacity and violence. In A.D. 59 he was deposed. Ten years later, because of his pro-Roman sympathies, he was murdered by the nationalist party among the Jews. Thus he came to a violent death, as Paul had prophesied.

[10] The expression "whitewashed wall" denoted hypocrisy. Recall that Jesus had so denounced the scribes and Pharisees (Matt. 23:27). They had experienced no change of character.

tle, goaded beyond endurance, at last lost his patience? That
would not be surprising, for we know of what strong emotions
the spirit of Paul was compounded. Inasmuch as Paul never
claimed perfection of character, but only that he was striving
for it, why should we count it a strange thing if on this occasion his conduct fell short of the example left him by his
Lord, who, when He suffered, threatened not; and who, when
He was reviled, reviled not again? [11]

Or should we understand that in Paul's opinion the Sanhedrin, having shut its eyes to the innocence of Jesus and having
given no heed to the witnessing of Peter and John when they
had been brought before it, was now lost in its sins, hardened
in its iniquity, and gone beyond all hope of repentance? After
all, may there not be a time when even the divine love ceases
to be effective as a motive for reformation of character, and
when there remains only "a certain fearful looking for of judgment"? [12] Perhaps Paul here was speaking as the prophet
which he was; perhaps he here, as God's spokesman, was de-
nouncing the high priest's hypocrisy and giving warning of the
judgment to come. That, too, could well be.

The members of the Sanhedrin were quick to take Paul to
task for having spoken in this manner to the high priest. Paul
was equally quick in replying: "I wist not, brethren, that he
was the high priest: for it is written, Thou shalt not speak
evil of the ruler of thy people." [13]

Here is another saying which we find hard to understand.
Had Paul (due possibly to imperfect eyesight) failed to recognize that it was none other than the high priest who was
sitting in judgment upon him, and who had given the order
that he should be struck on the mouth? And was Paul sincere
in making this apology? Or was all this but so much irony?
Was he refusing to acknowledge that the Sanhedrin, as then
constituted, had any legal or religious status? Was he saying,
in effect: "Who ever would have supposed that a man with so

[11] For Jesus' conduct before the high priest, see John 18:19-23. For
Peter's comment on Jesus' conduct on that and other similar occasions,
see 1 Pet. 2:21-23.

[12] Heb. 10:27.

[13] Ex. 22:28.

little regard for the law would be the high priest?" Paul's words, in themselves, do not hold the answer to our query. What would give us the answer—and it is something which we do not have—is a knowledge of the tone of voice in which Paul spoke.

The hostility of tne Sanhedrin was evident. To escape it, Paul resorted to a dangerous strategem. He called out, in words which were to this effect: "I am a Pharisee, as my father was before me. It is because of my Pharisaic convictions, especially my belief in, and hope of, a resurrection of the dead, that I have been brought to trial." [14] The Sanhedrin, as Paul well knew, was divided very nearly equally between Sadducees and Pharisees. The Sadducees were thoroughgoing materialists. They denied that there was any resurrection of the body; in fact, they denied that there was anything angelic or spiritual. On the other hand, the Pharisees, despite their formalism and aridness of spirit, professed to believe in the resurrection and in other spiritual matters. Paul's words, therefore, injected an issue which often had been heatedly debated by the Sadducees and the Pharisees.[15] The Pharisees had no love for Paul, but they did not propose to let the Sadducees ridicule a man's belief in the resurrection. Accordingly, for their own sake rather more than for his, they declared: "We find nothing wrong in this man. What if a spirit or an angel did speak to him?"

The dissension between the Sadducees and the Pharisees became so violent that it appeared to the tribune, who had been

[14] Paul's statement as to why he was on trial may seem to us to savor of casuistry. We need to remember that he had been trained as a rabbi, and that casuistry played a large part in all rabbinical debates. Skill in its use, far from being condemned, was roundly applauded as evidence of superior cleverness. But it should be noted also that the hostility of the Sanhedrin was not based on a single incident, the taking of Gentiles (as they had supposed) into a forbidden part of the Temple, but was directed against Paul's entire ministry. Paul had declared repeatedly that all he had done, he had done in obedience to Jesus Christ, risen from the dead. He implied that the Pharisees, who claimed to believe in a resurrection, should help him, rather than hinder him, in his efforts to convince the Sadducees.

[15] Paul possibly had seen the Sanhedrin get into just such a snarl on other occasions. For his knowledge of the Sanhedrin, see page 67, note 3.

watching the proceedings closely, that the hapless Paul might be torn to pieces by these contending factions. So far as he could judge, Paul's offense, if any, had been of a religious nature. As such, the issue fell within the jurisdiction of the Sanhedrin. But on the other hand, Paul was a Roman citizen, and it seemed likely that without any proper Roman trial he would be beaten to death then and there by the enraged members of the Sanhedrin. Prompt action was called for. Accordingly the tribune commanded his soldiers to enter the courtroom, rescue Paul from those who were fighting for possession of him, and carry him back to the military barracks, in order that at some later date he might receive a fairer hearing.

### The Lord Encourages His Servant  (Acts 23:11)

Paul's trials were proving heavy, as the Holy Spirit had warned him that they would be; but the Lord had not forgotten his faithful servant. That very night the Lord appeared once again to Paul. The Lord's words must have brought great encouragement to the apostle, for the Lord not only bade him be of good cheer, but also assured him that in return for his faithful witnessing in Jerusalem he was to have the privilege of bearing witness in the city of Rome also. That, above everything else, was what Paul had set his heart upon!

### Another Conspiracy to Slay Paul  (Acts 23:12-22)

The measure of the hostility felt toward Paul may be judged from the fact that on the very next day a company of Jews, more than forty in number, laid plans to slay Paul, regardless of what the consequences to themselves might be.[16] These men bound themselves by a most solemn oath that they would neither eat nor drink till they had accomplished his death. They made known their plot to the chief priests and elders and readily enlisted their co-operation. These chief priests and elders were to request the tribune to bring Paul before the Sanhedrin once more. The Sanhedrin, so they were to say, was desirous of examining into his case more fully. Then,

---

[16] Possibly these men belonged to the political party known as the Zealots. Josephus relates numerous instances of their fanaticism.

when he had been brought out of the barracks and was being taken to the council chamber, at some suitable place along the route, the conspirators would spring upon the unsuspecting guards, overpower them, and quickly put him to death.

The Lord is never without means by which to deliver His servants, when such is His will. In this instance, the plot became known to a young man. This young man, in the providence of God, was none other than Paul's nephew! [17] Perhaps he had overheard the conspirators boasting of what they would do; perhaps, by accident, he had come upon the conspirators as they lay in wait for Paul. However he came by the knowledge, we know that he hastened at once to the barracks where Paul was imprisoned. Inasmuch as Paul was merely being held in what we today would call protective custody, he experienced no difficulty in gaining permission to see his uncle. Paul, on learning of the plot, called one of his guards and requested that his nephew be allowed to tell his story to the tribune. The guard, perceiving that it was a matter of much importance, took the young man to the tribune, and the tribune, wisely, took careful account of all that the young man could tell him. Then, having warned the youth that if he valued his life he should let no one know that he had reported these things to the Romans, he permitted him to depart.

### Paul Is Transferred to the Prison in Caesarea  (Acts 23:23-35)

The tribune, fearful that there might be some disturbance in Jerusalem, took steps immediately to get Paul out of the city. That very night he sent Paul off to Caesarea, the Roman capital; sent him off under heavy military guard—nearly five hundred fully armed soldiers, including both horsemen and footmen. This heavy guard was not to keep Paul from escaping, but to protect him against any enemies that might be lying in wait along the route. By morning these guards, with their prisoner, had reached Antipatris. Then, the greater

[17] We could wish that we had more information concerning the members of Paul's family. This young man, who either lived in Jerusalem or had come to Jerusalem with Paul, is described as "the son of Paul's sister."

danger being past, the footsoldiers turned back to Jerusalem, leaving the horsemen to guard Paul on the rest of the journey to Caesarea.

The substance of the letter which Claudius Lysias, the tribune, sent to Felix, the governor, is given in vss. 26-30. When reading the letter, one can hardly fail to observe that the tribune, in his desire to put everything that he had done in the best possible light, departs considerably from the truth. He makes it appear that he had rescued Paul from the mob because he knew him to be a Roman citizen, whereas he did not learn this until later. He does not mention the embarrassing fact that he had ordered Paul, though a Roman citizen, to be scourged. He states that he had taken Paul before the Sanhedrin merely to ascertain what the charge against him might be; and that, when he learned of the plot against Paul's life (though he had done nothing worthy of death or imprisonment) , it had seemed wise to bring the whole matter to the attention of Felix, the Roman governor. Accordingly, he had sent Paul to Caesarea, where Felix could examine him without the inconvenience of coming to Jerusalem, and he had notified Paul's accusers that they should lay before Felix whatever charges they might have against Paul. (Actually, the tribune had not so notified them, but doubtless he intended to do so. At the time he wrote, his chief concern was to get Paul safely out of Jerusalem without the knowledge of the Jews.)

On reading this letter, Felix inquired of Paul from what province he had come. On learning that Paul was from Cilicia, Felix announced that he would hear the case when Paul's accusers had arrived.[18] In the meantime—so Felix gave commandment—Paul was to be held under guard in Herod's Praetorium.[19]

Only a little more than a week before, Paul had passed through Caesarea on his way up to Jerusalem; now he was back in that Roman city, but it was as a prisoner. So far as the

[18] Inasmuch as Cilicia was an imperial province, the case properly belonged, as Felix recognized, in an imperial court, such as his own.

[19] The praetorium (palace) , where Felix dwelt, had been built by Herod the Great, and took its name from that fact.

book of Acts relates Paul's story, Paul never looked upon the Holy City and its Temple again. He had borne his witness there, and the citizens of Jerusalem, by and large, had rejected it. The prophecy of Agabus had received fulfillment. It had befallen Paul as it had befallen his Lord: he had been rejected, bound, and delivered into the hands of the Gentiles.

## CHAPTER 17

# The Apostle Makes Appeal to Caesar

ACTS 24:1–26:32

$F$OR more than two years, Paul was held a prisoner in Caesarea. That his imprisonment in that city was of such long duration was due chiefly to the unscrupulous character of Antonius Felix, the Roman procurator of Judea. This governor, who despite the corruption and disorders which marked his rule, maintained himself in office from A.D. 52 to 58, is described by the historian Tacitus as cruel, lustful, and unprincipled, as one who "exercised the powers of a king in the spirit of a slave." He is said to have thought that his influential friends in Rome would afford him such protection that he could commit any crime with impunity.

### Paul's First Hearing before Felix (Acts 24:1-23)

After five days, the priests and elders from Jerusalem arrived in Caesarea to press their case against Paul. Leading the delegation was the high priest Ananias.[1] He was determined that this time Paul should be made to pay for his impudence. To that end, he had brought with him an orator (i.e., a professional lawyer) named Tertullus. This lawyer, being a Roman and familiar with the practices of the Roman courts, would know how to present the case against Paul most effectively.

When Paul had been brought into the courtroom, Tertullus, on behalf of the priests and elders, stated the matters whereof they accused Paul. He began his speech by addressing Felix, the procurator, in a most flattering fashion. The people, he

[1] On Ananias, see page 184, note 9.

said, were grateful to him for the peace which he had established. (It is true that Felix had suppressed some robber bands, but his rule had been more marked by turbulence than by quiet. Felix, furthermore, had not been above inciting disorder in order that he might put to death those who engaged in it and confiscate their property to his own personal profit.) Tertullus' words, however insincere, no doubt were pleasing to Felix' ears. Tertullus then assured the procurator that he would present his case quite briefly, so as not to weary him. Paul—so Tertullus said—had proved himself to be a common nuisance. He had stirred up the Jews to resistance against Rome. (Not true, but Felix would have to give consideration to a charge of so serious a political nature.) Paul had been the ringleader of the sect of the Nazarenes. (Up to this time the Romans had considered the Christians to be merely a sect within the Jewish religion, which had a recognized status within the empire. If now the Jews could dissociate the Christians from all connection with the Jewish religion, they would thereby deprive them of whatever protection they enjoyed as a "permitted religion.") Finally, Paul had undertaken to profane the Temple, and would have done so had not faithful Jews prevented him. (Tertullus made no mention of the earlier charge that Paul had taken Gentiles into a part of the Temple which they were forbidden to enter; he had not been able to gather any proof of that!) In conclusion, he asserted that Felix, by questioning the prisoner, could quickly satisfy himself as to the truthfulness of these charges.[2] The Jews thereupon gave their endorsement to all that Tertullus had said.

On being granted permission to speak in his own defense, Paul addressed Felix in terms which were not calculated to give offense, yet avoided such flattery as Tertullus had employed. Paul stated that Felix, having been a judge over the nation for many years, would be able to recognize the truth of what he would say. He had been in Jerusalem too short a

[2] It will be noted that vs. 7 and parts of vss. 6 and 8 do not appear in the best manuscripts, and for that reason they have been omitted from the RSV. The omitted words merely give Tertullus' prejudiced reiteration of facts already stated.

time to have raised any such disturbance as that with which he had been charged. Far from wishing to profane the Temple, he had gone there to worship. The Jews from Asia had been the real instigators of the commotion. If they had any case against him, why had they not come into court to testify? He did acknowledge, and with pride rather than shame, that he was a follower of the Way. Could that be called heresy, he asked, when he served the same God that the fathers of Israel had worshiped, when he believed all that was written in the law and the prophets, and when he held the same hope of a resurrection of both the just and the unjust that his accusers did? At all times, he continued, he had been at pains to have a clear conscience both toward God and toward men. If he had been at fault in any matter at all, it was that when standing before the Sanhedrin he had thrown that court into confusion by loudly declaring that it was on account of his belief in the resurrection that he had been brought to trial. (Ananias and such other Sadducees as were present, remembering what had happened in the Sanhedrin, would not wish to make an issue of that!)

At this point Felix adjourned the hearing. He had some knowledge of the Christians and of their peaceful manner of life, and he had not been misled by the charges which the Jews had made against Paul. It is noteworthy, however, that he does not pronounce any judgment either for Paul or against him. He merely announced that when Lysias the tribune had come and given his testimony, he would give the case further consideration. The absence of Lysias was as good an excuse for delay as any other. As Luke presently makes known, Felix had knowledge of the fact that Paul had brought a considerable sum of money to Jerusalem, and he supposed that Paul had wealthy friends who would pay him well to order Paul's release. Accordingly, he directed that Paul should be held a prisoner, but that he should not be treated with severity. Paul's friends were to be permitted to see him.

## Paul Preaches to Felix and Drusilla (Acts 24:24-25)

Some days later, Felix accorded Paul a second hearing. On this occasion, Felix was accompanied by his wife Drusilla. An

idle curiosity, if nothing more, prompted the pair to listen
while Paul talked of faith in Christ Jesus. Faith in Christ, as
Paul quickly made clear, went beyond verbal assent to theological propositions; faith in Christ was valid only when it
committed the believer to a righteous, Christ-honoring manner of life. When Paul preached of justice and self-control
(qualities of character in which Felix had shown himself
sadly lacking) , and also of the judgment of God which is to
fall upon all unrighteousness, Felix began to feel most un-
comfortable. Paul's sincere and unanswerable words probed
his conscience and greatly upset him. Equally, Paul's preaching reached the conscience of Drusilla. She too had much to
learn about self-control in the Christian sense.

This Drusilla was the youngest daughter of Herod Agrippa I,
hence a Jewess. At this time she was not more than twenty
years of age, and she is said to have been very beautiful. In
order to become the third wife of Felix, the Roman, she had
at his urging deserted her husband, King Azizus of Emesa.

It is difficult to determine what Drusilla's attitude toward
Paul was. One ancient, but not too reliable, manuscript has
an interesting addition to vs. 24. The words, probably only a
gloss, read as follows: "She asked to see Paul and to hear his
word. Therefore, wishing to content her, he [Felix] sent for
Paul." It is possible that the horrible death of her father, in-
terpreted to her as a judgment of God upon him for his treatment of the Christians, may have given her pause and have
awakened within her some interest in the faith of these followers of the Way. Most scholars, however, believe that because she was a Jew her sympathies were wholly with Paul's
accusers; and that it was largely due to her insistence that
Felix did not release Paul, but held him in prison. Paul, in
addressing her, had reasoned of judgment to come. We do not
have to go outside of the recorded history of the period to
learn of one judgment which came upon her. She perished in
the eruption of Vesuvius in A.D. 79.

Felix, undoubtedly, was shaken by Paul's directness. He
"trembled." But instead of following on to a sincere repentance, he abruptly pronounced the hearing at an end. "Go thy
way for this time," he said; "when I have a convenient season,

I will call for thee." Preachers, in criticizing Felix for his pro-
crastination, have sometimes said that no "convenient season"
ever presented itself. The fact is that Felix talked with Paul a
number of times thereafter. God can be surprisingly patient
and longsuffering toward those who resist Him. But Felix was
never again so close to a sincere repentance; he was never
again so near to the kingdom of God. As time went on, he
became more and more interested in securing a bribe, less and
less interested in entering upon a life of righteousness.

*Paul, Brought before Festus, Appeals to Caesar (Acts 24:27
—25:12)*

For two years Paul was held a prisoner in Caesarea. Not the
last part of one year and the beginning of another year (as
the Jews sometimes reckoned), but two full years; Luke's carefully chosen words make this clear. Two years! How easy to
write the words, to read them, to let them slip from the
tongue, but how difficult to endure! And especially for Paul—
for Paul, whose sense of mission prompted him to be always
on the go, who fretted at every brief delay along the road, who
saw his life wearing away with his ministry still incomplete,
for he had not yet preached Christ in Rome!

Had Felix remained in office, there is no knowing how much
longer Paul's imprisonment might have continued. When Paul
had been a prisoner two years, the Emperor Nero removed
Felix and appointed in his stead Porcius Festus. Felix, on
being thus brought to task for his unwise and dishonest administration of the province, made no effort to right the wrong
he had done to Paul. Instead, he added to the injustices of
which he already was guilty. In a desperate effort to placate
somewhat the hostility of the Jews (he could only hope that
they would not be too bitter in their charges when he had to
stand trial before the Emperor), and as his last official act as
procurator, he ordered that Paul should remain a prisoner.
He could not quite bring himself to the point of delivering
Paul into the hands of the Jews, for Paul was a Roman citizen, and that fact might become known to Nero. What his
successor in office might do with Paul was no concern of his.

Of the new procurator, Porcius Festus, history tells us comparatively little. Josephus represents him as a man of nobler
character than his predecessors, and this accords well with
what Luke has written. He seems to have come to his post with
a sincere desire to give the province a just administration. He
found the province to be a hotbed of intrigue. He lived but
two years after assuming office, and is said to have died in
despair over his inability to put an end to the turbulence.
The disorders which he could not put down were due, in
large measure, to the maladministration of his predecessors.

When Festus reached Palestine, he spent but three days in
Caesarea, then hastened to Jerusalem. So prompt a visit to
Jerusalem, he believed, would please his subjects; it would
show his sincere desire to co-operate with their own leaders
and to serve their best interests in all possible ways. But no
sooner had he reached the city than he became caught in one
of their Jewish plots. The chief priests [3] and the principal
leaders of the Jews (i.e., the members of the Sanhedrin) had
lost none of their hostility toward Paul, and they immediately
presented to the new procurator their complaint. The same
complaint which Felix had held under advisement for two
full years! Would Festus, they asked, be so good as to have
Paul brought to Jerusalem for trial? The matter already had
been long delayed, and a trial in Jerusalem, rather than in
Caesarea, would be a great convenience to all concerned.
Doubtless these hostile Jews hoped to take advantage of the
inexperience of Festus, to rid themselves of Paul before Festus had time to inform himself of all the angles of the case.
They had no real desire to bring Paul to trial again, for they
already had determined upon his death. Their real purpose
(as it had been before) was to have a band of cutthroats in
readiness to waylay the military guards who would be assigned
to bring Paul to Jerusalem. These thugs would take the guards
by surprise, murder Paul, and flee away into the hills, before

3 In the best manuscripts the word is plural, not singular as in the
KJV. It is of interest that Ananias, the high priest who previously had
pressed the charge against Paul, had recently been removed from office
by King Agrippa II. The king had appointed Ishmael to take Ananias'
place.

the astonished soldiers fully realized what the commotion was all about. It is possible that for this ambush some of the same assassins were available as had made up that earlier band which had bound themselves by an oath neither to eat nor to drink until they had accomplished Paul's death.[4]

Although Festus was new in office, he was not so unsophisticated as to be taken in by this scheme. These Jewish leaders betrayed the fact that they were up to some trick by their excessive haste and importunity. Festus replied courteously that the many duties of his new office would not permit him to remain in Jerusalem long enough to conduct a proper trial there. He promised, however, that immediately upon his return to Caesarea he would call up Paul's case. Let them send to Caesarea, therefore, responsible men of their own choosing to present their charges against Paul. He would give them a careful hearing at that time.

True to his word, Festus remained in Jerusalem but little more than a week, and on the very next day after his return to Caesarea he summoned Paul to stand trial. The representatives of the Jerusalem priests and rulers were on hand to press their charges against Paul. Luke does not detail these charges, for no doubt they were the same as those which had been advanced at the hearing before Felix. Luke says simply, but impressively, that they "laid many and grievous complaints against Paul, which they could not prove." We catch in these words a suggestion that they had tried to conceal the weakness of their case beneath a multitude of false accusations and exaggerated statements. All their words boiled down, however, to the fast becoming threadbare charges of heresy, sacrilege, and treason. To all three, Paul gave a flat denial. He had not offended "against the law of the Jews" (no heresy), "neither against the temple" (no sacrilege), "nor yet against Caesar" (no treason).

Paul's defense, we may be sure, was made in more detail than Luke's brief summary of it would indicate; and Festus,

---

[4] These would-be murderers, of course, had in the meantime been released from their vow. Such absolution was not difficult for them to secure, for the high priest would recognize the impossibility of their doing anything so long as Paul was held in the prison in Caesarea.

we have good reason to believe, listened to it attentively. He could see that Paul was innocent of any crime against Rome. As for the other charges, those having to do with infractions of Jewish laws and customs—were they not matters which came properly within the jurisdiction of the Jerusalem Sanhedrin? So thinking, he undertook to dispose of the case in a manner which he doubtless thought was fair to all. He proposed, if Paul were agreeable, to declare him innocent of the charge of treason. He would then send him up to Jerusalem to stand trial in the Sanhedrin on those remaining charges which had to do with the Jewish religion. Anticipating that Paul might fear that he would not receive fair treatment at the hands of his Jewish accusers, Festus promised that he personally would go up to Jerusalem and preside at the trial, thereby insuring that the trial would be conducted in a fair and orderly fashion. This plan, he hoped, would please the Jews, dispose of the bothersome case he had inherited from his predecessor, and do no injustice to Paul.

But Paul had no way of knowing how much confidence might be placed in the promises of the new governor. Of one fact, however, he was certain: he would never receive a fair trial at the hands of the hypocritical and already murder-minded members of the Sanhedrin. Paul's response to Festus' proposal was, to Festus at least, wholly unexpected. Though made with dramatic suddenness, it was a move which Paul doubtless had long pondered as a possible last resort. His words were to this effect: "I am being tried in a Roman court, where it is right that I should be tried. If I have committed any crime for which I deserve to die, I shall not seek to escape the death penalty; but if this court judges me to be innocent of the charges which the Jews have brought against me, then it cannot lawfully deliver me into the hands of the Jews to be put to death by them. Therefore, Festus, I must in self defense appeal my case from your court to Caesar's."

We may be certain that Festus was disturbed by this turn of events. To be sure, he was rid of Paul; the responsibility of passing judgment on the prisoner now rested with the emperor. But it did not look well for him, as the new procurator, to have an appeal taken in connection with his very first case.

Festus went into conference with his legal advisers. It was clear to them that Paul was within his rights as a Roman citizen in thus appealing his case to Caesar—the Caesar, at that time, being the young emperor Nero. It was clear to them, also, that it was then too late for anything to be done to change the situation. In the tense stillness of the courtroom, Festus announced his decision. Addressing Paul, he said: "You have appealed to Caesar; to Caesar you shall go."[5]

## Festus Seeks Counsel of King Agrippa (Acts 25:13-22)

Festus realized that when he sent Paul to Rome, he would need to send with him a statement setting forth the charges which had been made against the prisoner.[6] The preparation of a summary of the case, one which would reflect credit upon his conduct of it, would not prove easy. So far as treason against Rome was concerned, Festus was convinced that Paul was innocent; as for the alleged violation of Jewish laws, he was not clear. When, a few days later, King Agrippa and Queen Bernice came to Caesarea to pay him a state visit, he saw in their coming a fortunate opportunity to gain that expert advice on Jewish matters which he felt he needed.

Because this royal pair played an important part in the events which followed, we shall do well to take note of who they were. This was King Agrippa II, the son of Herod Agrippa I, who had executed the apostle James and imprisoned the apostle Peter,[7] and who, in his terrible death, had experienced the judgment of God.[8] At the time of his father's death, he was judged to be too young to receive the kingdom. However, when he had completed his education in Rome, the Emperor Claudius made him ruler over the kingdom of Chalcis, and, later, over the tetrarchies formerly ruled by Philip and Lysanias. At a still later date, the Emperor Nero added to these dominions portions of Galilee and Samaria. As might be expected in the case of one who had enjoyed so much Roman

5 Acts 25:12. (RSV).
6 See Acts 25:27.
7 Acts 12:1-3.
8 Acts 12:20-23.

patronage, his political sympathies were wholly with Rome. Some years later, when his subjects rose in rebellion against Rome, he did not join with them. Upon the fall of Jerusalem in A.D. 70, he retired to Rome, where he died in the year 100.

Despite these strong ties with Rome, Agrippa II, so long as he remained in Palestine, manifested at least a nominal interest in the Jewish religion. This was but natural, for he was for the most part of Jewish blood, being descended, indeed, from the Maccabean priest-kings. On his frequent sojourns in Jerusalem (he had a palace there) he made many lavish gifts to the Temple, and in numerous other ways he sought to show his interest in the religion of his ancestors. But these formal religious exercises must have been performed chiefly as an expedient method of gaining the good will and support of his Jewish subjects. Certainly, in his manner of life he gave no heed to the moral teachings of the law and the prophets. The commandment against adultery had no meaning to him whatsoever. This puppet of Rome was described by his contemporaries as weak, sensual, and pleasure loving.

That this evil characterization was not without warrant appears from his relations with Bernice. One of Agrippa's sisters was Drusilla, the disreputable wife of Felix; this Bernice was another of Agrippa's sisters. She had first married her uncle—a Herod, ruler of Chalcis. Upon his death, she went to Rome to live with her brother Agrippa. And she lived with him in such intimate fashion that there was much talk of scandal. To stop that talk, Bernice married a second time. But when Agrippa came into power as king, she left her second husband to rejoin her brother, at Caesarea, as his queen. Both Roman and Jewish historians charge that her relations with Agrippa were incestuous. This is not difficult to believe when we learn that afterward she became the mistress of both Vespasian and Titus.

On Agrippa's part, a visit of state paid to Festus, the new procurator, was both polite and prudent. Agrippa had been granted considerable authority in purely Jewish affairs, but since he held the throne only through the grace of Rome it behooved him to show himself friendly in every way toward Rome's representative. On Festus' part, Agrippa's visit seemed most opportune. Agrippa, being well versed in all Jewish matters, could give him counsel respecting the charges that had been made against Paul. Festus, accordingly, lost no time in speaking to him concerning Paul. Festus' statement of the situation (vss. 14-21) was made, on the whole, with much fairness. When he concluded, Agrippa expressed a wish to see and hear Paul. Festus quickly declared that Agrippa should have that opportunity. It could easily be arranged. He would have Paul brought up for a hearing in the morning.

*Paul Speaks in His Own Behalf Before King Agrippa (Acts 25:23—26:32)*

The next day King Agrippa, Bernice, and many other prominent persons assembled in Festus' public audience chamber. The chance to hear Paul plead for his life (his case, undoubtedly, had been widely discussed) promised to afford rare entertainment, if nothing more. Festus invited Agrippa to take the central place—the chair of judgment; as for himself, he was content with stating, for the benefit of any who might not know, the purpose of the hearing. When Festus had completed this preliminary, Agrippa, with a lordly air, informed Paul that he was at liberty to speak in his own behalf.

Paul's defense before King Agrippa[9] since it consisted largely of a rehearsal of events which we have considered already in other connections need not be related here in detail. But it would be doing an injustice to one of the most frank, eloquent, and moving addresses ever delivered, not to direct attention to some of its salient points.

The apostle began by expressing the satisfaction which he felt in being able to plead his case before one as well versed in Jewish matters as Agrippa was, and he besought Agrippa to hear him patiently. He declared that the manner of his life, from his youth up, was known to all. His accusers, if they could be induced to testify truthfully, would have to acknowledge that he not only had lived as a Jew, but also had conducted himself in accordance with the regulations of the strictest sect among the Jews, i.e., the Pharisees. Indeed, it was

[9] Acts 26:2-29.

because of his wholehearted belief in the promise which God had made to the fathers of the Jewish nation that the unbelieving Jews had brought their charges against him. In his zeal for Judaism, he had sorely persecuted the followers of Jesus of Nazareth. Indeed, it was while he was bent on such a mission that Jesus had appeared to him, had halted him in his mad enterprise, and had redirected the course of his life. It was because of that vision (how could one do other than be obedient to so heavenly a vision!) and because of the commission divinely given to him at that time, that he had, without neglecting his responsibility to those of his own race, gone as a missionary to the Gentiles. Though he had preached, to Jews and Gentiles alike, nothing but what had been foretold in the law and the prophets, the Jewish leaders had caused his arrest and had sought to have him put to death.

And what had he preached among the Gentiles? What but this, that they "should repent and turn to God, and do works meet for repentance." Paul's *Apologia pro Vita Sua* was finished; but he had something more to do, something that was more important even than his defense of himself. He needed to make clear to his distinguished hearers the nature of the gospel, in order that they might be won, if possible, to belief on Christ. He declared, therefore, that the sufferings of the Christ had been foretold both by the prophets and by Moses; and so also had been the Christ's rising from the dead—that death and resurrection by which light and life were made available to all who walked in the ways of darkness and death, whether Jews or Gentiles.

Paul had no opportunity to continue his summary of the gospel, for Festus, obviously impressed by Paul's learning, yet much confused by reason of his unfamiliarity with the truths he was setting forth, interrupted him. With a loud voice, he rebuked Paul, saying: "Paul, you are mad; your great learning is turning you mad." [10] With commendable patience and restraint, Paul answered that he was not mad, but had been speaking advisedly and truthfully. In support of this fact, he appealed hopefully to King Agrippa. Everything that had

[10] Acts 26:24 (RSV).

been done, had been done openly, as the king well knew. Then, with a holy boldness which could only have been inspired by the God who even then was helping him (vs. 22), Paul addressed a question personally and pointedly to the king: "King Agrippa, believest thou the prophets?" In the presence and hearing of so many Jews, Agrippa could hardly do otherwise than answer affirmatively. But if he did so (Agrippa thought within himself), would not Paul straightway demand to know why he had not acted in accordance with the conclusions which he had so logically deduced from the prophetic Scriptures? While Agrippa was considering how he might handle this embarrassing question, Paul continued his appeal. As though he wished to make it as easy as possible for Agrippa to acknowledge the truth, Paul quickly answered for him: "I know that thou believest."

Agrippa doubtless felt that it was one thing to listen while Paul defended himself, but quite another to be made the subject of Paul's direct preaching. With visible irritation, he spoke up, and, with what he meant to be devastating scorn, said: "Do you, by these few words, think to make a Christian of me?" [11] Paul replied with great earnestness: "Whether I persuade you with few words or many words, my prayer to God is that you (and not you only, but all who hear me this day) may become a Christian, even as I am; except, of course, I would not wish you to wear such bonds as mine" (free paraphrase).

Agrippa would hear no more. He rose to his feet as an indication that the hearing was ended. At this signal the other dignitaries also rose. The rulers then went into conference. There was general agreement that whatever one might think of Paul's teachings, he had done nothing worthy of death or imprisonment. Indeed, Agrippa acknowledged to Festus that Paul might very properly have been set free, if he had not

[11] The Greek text here—we may not have it correctly—is difficult of translation. Agrippa does not say (as a familiar gospel hymn represents him) that he is almost persuaded to become a Christian. He says (if we may freely translate): "Do you, with these few words, think to make me a Christian?" or "Do you, in this short space of time, think to make me a Christian?" On the decision as to the proper translation of this verse depends the translation of Paul's reply, as given in the next verse.

appealed his case to Caesar. Once again a Roman court had heard the charges made against Paul and had refused to sustain any of them.

If Festus had entertained the hope that by means of this hearing before King Agrippa, he could build up a valid case against Paul, a case which would show that he had been justified in holding Paul as a prisoner, he had met with disappointment. Now, he must send Paul on to Caesar; but inasmuch as there was no clear case against Paul, Caesar might resent being bothered with the prisoner. And what would Caesar's opinion be of Porcius Festus, the procurator whom he had but recently appointed?

# The Great Storm and Shipwreck

ACTS 27:1—28:10

*A*ND now Luke's chronicle of the labors, sufferings, and triumphs of those men "on whom the Spirit came" takes us out of the prison in Caesarea, where for more than two years Paul had been confined, and onto the wide and sometimes storm-frequented waters of the Mediterranean.

Along the shores of that Great Sea the early Phoenicians had made their first adventurous and commercially profitable voyages; on that Great Sea the early Greek mariners, sailing cautiously from cove to cove, from island to island, had made their first voyages of exploration and conquest. The Mediterranean's freedom from high tides and from hidden reefs, and its many islands, encouraged navigation. But the boats of those days were small, and when winter descended upon the sea—winter with its fierce gales and dark nights—wise mariners remained in port.

By the time of the Roman Empire, when Rome held sway from Mesopotamia on the east to the islands of Britain, beyond the Pillars of Hercules, on the west, larger and faster sailing ships had come into use. *Mare Nostrum* ("Our Sea," as the Romans proudly called it) competed with their 47,000 miles of solidly built roads for the distinction of being Rome's principal means of transportation.

But even so, travel by sea, save in the fairest weather, was always somewhat hazardous. The ships, being equipped with but one large square sail (or at most, with this one mainsail supplemented by a small foresail or topsail), could not steer very close into the wind; they were in constant danger, therefore, of being blown against any rocky headland that might be near their course. What was even more serious, the Greek and Roman mariners lacked the three inventions which have contributed most to the safety of modern travel by sea. They knew nothing of the compass, by means of which the true north can be determined when neither sun nor stars are visible. Though they possessed a somewhat surprising knowledge of latitude, they lacked the sextant, by which the sun's altitude above the horizon at noonday can be measured, thereby making it possible to compute the ship's position. And they had not yet devised the ship's log, the ingenious mechanism which shows the rate of speed at which the ship is traveling.

*The Journey to Rome Begun—from Caesarea to Myra (Acts 27:1-5)*

The ancients considered it hazardous to sail the Mediterranean after the middle of September. By that time the equinoctial storms were imminent and ship captains exercised caution. Before the middle of November all navigation was suspended, not to be resumed until the following March. It appears to have been early September when Festus finally started Paul on his journey to Rome; that is to say, the season of safe navigation was almost over before the journey was begun! Certain other prisoners were being sent to Rome at this same time—convicted prisoners, most likely, who were to provide entertainment for Rome's multitudes by battling to the death with wild beasts in the arena. Perhaps Festus delayed dispatching Paul to Rome until he had all of these other prisoners rounded up. Perhaps the delay was occasioned by the difficulty of finding a suitable westbound ship at that late season. But whatever the reason for the delay, it had most serious consequences, as we shall presently see.

The ship which Festus chose was engaged in the coastal trade and claimed Adramyttium as its home port. Adramyttium was a Mysian town a short distance to the south and east of Troas. Festus anticipated that at some port in Asia Minor (certainly at Ephesus, if not earlier) it would encounter a ship bound for Italy. To this ship the prisoners could then be transferred.

Thus Paul began his trip to Rome, the trip which he had so long anticipated. His heart thrilled when he thought of what a privilege would be his when he had opportunity to preach the gospel in Rome, the capital of the world. But certainly he was not making the trip in the manner which he had contemplated when, in Corinth, he had first conceived the idea of such a missionary journey. He was indeed going to Rome, but as a prisoner! He was soon to be brought before the emperor to be put on trial for his life. But he felt confident that, whether in bonds or free, he would find some persons in Rome to whom he could bear testimony to Jesus Christ!

Paul and the other prisoners were guarded night and day by a detachment from the Imperial Regiment (the Augustan Cohort). These Roman soldiers were commanded by a centurion named Julius. He seems to have been a man of humane character. He recognized at once that Paul was not of the same sort as his other prisoners. Paul had not been convicted; he was merely being detained for a special hearing before the emperor. For these reasons, the centurion showed Paul special consideration. Indeed, when the ship the next day put in at Sidon, he permitted Paul to visit briefly his Christian friends in that city. They ministered in a practical way to Paul's needs. Paul was further cheered by the fact that he had with him as companions and helpers two of his very best friends, Aristarchus and Luke. Aristarchus was from Macedonia. He had represented some of the churches in that region when Paul had brought their offerings to the church in Jerusalem. It may be that Aristarchus was now returning to his home. We know that Luke was with Paul, for this is another of the "we-sections." Indeed, we have now come to the longest, and one of the most important, of them. It is reasonable to believe that Luke, who also had been a representative of the Gentile churches at the time of the bringing of their gifts to Jerusalem, had remained in Palestine throughout those discouraging years during which Paul was held a prisoner in Caesarea.

How did it come about that Aristarchus and Luke were permitted to accompany Paul on this voyage to Rome? Probably because, as has been explained, Paul had not been convicted of

any crime; and because Paul, being a person of some importance, was privileged to have with him one or more personal
servants. He, of course, would have to pay their travel fare
out of his own funds. The presence of these faithful com-
rades brought comfort and encouragement to Paul. The sun
and fresh salt air would soon remove the prison pallor from
Paul's cheeks.

Upon their first day at sea, the wind being favorable, the
ship made excellent progress. At nightfall, having come seventy or more miles, it put in at the harbor of Sidon. The next
day the ship proceeded on its way, but it experienced more
difficulty. The prevailing winds at that season were from the
west, and the ship could make no headway against them. Consequently the captain, instead of attempting the direct course,
which would have taken his ship to the island of Rhodes at
the southwestern extremity of Asia Minor, continued his
course northward along the coast of Syria until his ship had
come into the sheltered waters behind the island of Cyprus.
Only then, and then only by taking careful advantage of every
land breeze, did the captain succeed in sailing his ship westward. Progress, naturally, was slow.

We can imagine the thoughts which ran through Paul's
mind as the ship skirted the coast of Cilicia. In that direction
lay Tarsus, his birthplace. And then the coast of Pamphylia.
In the distance was Perga. In that low and malarial region,
he once had become ill. Beyond those distant hills were the
Galatian towns which he had visited on his first missionary
journey. How glad he would have been for some late word
from the Christians of Antioch, Iconium, Lystra, and Derbe!
On past Attalia the ship went, until, after more days of difficult sailing, it finally made the port of Myra.

*From Myra to Fair Havens in Crete  (Acts 27:6-12)*

On coming into the harbor at Myra, the centurion was glad-
dened by the sight of a large Alexandrian grain ship. These
ships, in season, plied regularly between Alexandria in Egypt
and the foot of the Italian peninsula. They brought from the
Land of the Nile those huge cargoes of grain without which

the vast population of Rome would soon have gone hungry. Finding that this ship was indeed bound for Italy, the centurion made haste to transfer his prisoners to it. As it was a much larger craft, the centurion anticipated that it would make better time than the boat on which they had come to Myra.

This ship's westward progress, however, proved disappointingly slow. At last, it stood off the island of Cnidus, two hundred miles west of Myra. Then, because the wind was still from the west, the ship sailed southward until it reached the more sheltered waters along the southern shore of the island of Crete. Passing Salmone at the eastern end of that large island, the ship won its way to a little harbor called Fair Havens, not far from the town of Lasea.

The ship had been so much delayed that by this time the "fast" (i.e., the Jewish Day of Atonement) had passed. Winter was at hand. Paul, who knew well the moods of the Mediterranean, sought out the centurion and warned him that the season was so late that the journey, if continued, would certainly result in disaster to the ship and possible loss of life to the passengers and the crew. The centurion discussed the situation with the captain of the ship. The harbor of Fair Havens seemed to belie its name. Being much exposed to the storms, it appeared no safe place for a ship to winter. The owner of the ship, as we can readily understand, was desirous of getting on to Italy, if it could be managed, in order that he might unload his cargo of grain and sell it to the best advantage. The ship's captain, naturally, had to give some heed to the wishes of the ship's owner. He thought it would be the part of wisdom at least to seek a safer harbor. The centurion Julius, who as the representative of the emperor presumably might have taken over the command of the ship, deferred to the judgment of the captain. Paul's warning against putting out to sea, therefore, went unheeded. Not the first time that financial gain has been put ahead of human safety! Not the first time that human prudence has been given priority over a divinely inspired utterance—and with disastrous results! It was decided that when a favorable opportunity offered, they would put out from Fair Havens and sail along the coast of

Crete to the harbor of Phoenix (spelled *Phenice* in the KJV),
some sixty miles farther west. If it then seemed unwise to proceed on to Italy (as likely would prove to be the case), at least
Phoenix would offer a more sheltered harbor in which to
winter than did Fair Havens.[1]

*The Great Storm* (*Acts 27:13-26*)

By and by a day came when the wind blew softly from the
south. Seemingly this was the opportunity they had been
awaiting. They put out to sea. The first problem was to round
Cape Matala, a rugged promontory a few miles to westward.
This called for such close sailing into the wind that it was not
at all certain that they could avoid being blown ashore. They
towed the ship's boat astern, thinking to have it in readiness
in the event that they ran aground. However, they safely
weathered the Cape, and thereafter they had a favorable wind,
one which enabled them to sail westward close along the shore.
All was going well when suddenly a terrific northeaster [2] swept
down upon them. So great was the violence of this storm that
further progress along the shore became impossible. They
found themselves being blown far out to sea.

With the ship carrying only the smallest possible amount of
sail, they ran under the lee of a small island named Clauda
(better, Cauda). They took advantage of that momentary

[1] Vs. 12 in the KJV describes the harbor of Phoenix as lying "toward
the south west and north west." The literal translation is as given in the
margin of the ARV: "down the south-west wind and down the northwest wind." To "look down" a wind is to face in the direction which the
wind is blowing; in this instance, to face northeast and southeast. The
land, then, protected this harbor against the prevailing westerly winds.
An island lying across the mouth of the harbor furnished protection
against a wind from due east. The only exits from the harbor were at
the northeast and the southeast.

[2] The KJV has "a tempestuous wind, called Euroclydon." The ASV,
more correctly, has "a tempestuous wind, which is called Euraquilo."
*Euroclydon* appears to be one of several corrupt forms in which this
word appears. *Euraquilo* is compounded of the Greek word *euros*, meaning east wind, and the Latin word *aquilo*, meaning north wind; hence
the translation of the RSV: "a tempestuous wind, called the northeaster."

respite to hoist aboard the small boat they had been towing. Other preparations for withstanding the storm were hurriedly made. Because already the clumsy ship was straining and groaning and giving evidence that its timbers might soon become sprung, the sailors undergirded it. This heroic feat ("frapping the ship," to use the nautical term) consisted of passing cables under the ship's keel and drawing them taut, so as to hold the hull together.

The storm increased in fury; the sea became wilder; the sky grew darker. With the heavens obscured, the captain lost all knowledge of his ship's position. It appeared to him that his ship might be blown completely across the Mediterranean and driven upon the dreaded Syrtis, sandy shoals lying off the coast of Africa to the west of Cyrene. To stay his ship's progress as much as possible, he gave orders that such sail as the ship had been carrying should be dropped entirely. When this had been done, he no longer had any control over his ship's course. The ship rolled more fearfully than ever in the huge swells.

The next day, since the storm had not abated and the ship was leaking so badly that it appeared it might founder at any moment, the crew undertook to lighten their craft by throwing overboard its cargo. This grain already had been ruined by the salt water which had entered the ship. On the third day, when the plight of the ship had become still more desperate (if that were possible!), the crew threw overboard much of the ship's gear, including, no doubt, the long and heavy yard of the mainsail. Their main concern now was to keep their vessel afloat as long as possible. These extreme measures, however, afforded only slight relief; and when the tempest continued, not for a few days more, but for "many" additional days,[3] the captain and his crew gave up all hope of being saved.

That these veteran seamen despaired is not surprising. They had toiled night and day; the furling of the sails, the securing of the ship's two rudders, the manning of the pumps, and the

[3] A storm of two weeks' duration, such as this was, though not common in those waters, is not unparalleled. Reference books cite numerous Mediterranean storms of equal duration.

throwing overboard of the cargo had been gruelling work. They were wet and cold and exhausted. Furthermore, they had been without food. Much of their food supplies, no doubt, had been ruined by the sea water; and the rolling of the ship had made all cooking impossible. The ship's passengers, both the soldiers and their prisoners, had shared in the labors and privations of the crew; now they shared also in their despair.

There is a hope, however, which does not depend upon human resources, but which is grounded in a knowledge of God's holy will and loving care. Paul more than once, when in some dire strait, had been divinely delivered. He remembered God's power to save, and throughout the storm had been praying for the safety of those upon the ship. His prayers were heard. During the hours of the night an angel of the Lord appeared unto him and made known to him the fact that, though the ship would be lost, all aboard her would escape with their lives. Paul was not to be denied the opportunity of pleading his case before Caesar; he was yet to enjoy the privilege of preaching Christ in the imperial city of Rome. In the morning he communicated this good news to the captain and his crew. "Ye should have hearkened unto me," he said, "and not have loosed from Crete." These words were not spoken as a rebuke, but in the hope that a consideration of the "harm and loss" which they had suffered through disregarding his warning might dispose them to receive the message of encouragement which he now had for them. They were not to lose their lives at sea; they were to be cast upon an island.

### Shipwrecked upon the Island of Malta  (Acts 27:27-44)

The fourteenth night found the ship still laboring heavily across the southernmost portion of the Adriatic Sea, the place where the Mediterranean is its widest. (The captain, of course, had no way of knowing to what place his ship had been driven.) That midnight, however, the practiced ear of a lookout detected, above the roar of the wind and the groaning of the ship, the rhythmic booming of breakers upon rocks.

Soundings were quickly taken. Twenty fathoms! A moment later, only fifteen fathoms! They were being blown upon some shore, and they would have to act quickly if they were to keep the ship from being dashed upon the rocks. At the captain's shouted orders, the sailors dropped four anchors from the ship's stern. Four anchors, for one anchor would never have held so large a ship in such a gale; and from the stern, so as to keep the ship's prow headed toward the land. If the anchors held until daybreak, they would then attempt to beach the ship on whatever shore seemed least dangerous.

Some of the sailors, putting their own deliverance ahead of the safety of everyone else, decided that they would not wait for the dawn to show them where they were. They conspired together to steal the ship's small boat and to escape in it to the land. Under pretext that they would put out anchors from the prow also, they started to lower the boat. Paul perceived their intention, however, and gave warning to the centurion. "Except these abide in the ship," he said, "ye cannot be saved." Julius acted quickly. At his command, some of the soldiers who stood by cut the ropes holding the boat, thereby letting her fall away.

Paul then went among the crew and also among the prisoners, giving them encouragement and counsel. If they were to make their way to the land, they would need all the strength which they could muster; therefore, he urged upon them the wisdom of preparing food and of strengthening themselves by partaking of it. Note the common sense which Paul displayed along with his faith. Once again he sought to cheer these discouraged men. Not one of them, he said, would lose his life. In the presence of all, Paul took up some bread, but before he ate of it he thanked God for such food as they had and for the further fact that the lives of all of them were in God's hand. Some who were present may not have known the God to whom Paul prayed, but they could not mistake his reverent attitude and his confidence of deliverance. When Paul began to eat, the rest of the company, encouraged by his faith, followed his example. At this point in his narrative, Luke introduces an interesting note. Aboard the ship, he says, there were in all two hundred and seventy-six persons.[4]

When they had strengthened themselves with food, all hands set to work to lighten the ship still more. They cast overboard the little that remained of the cargo of wheat. They did this because the less water the ship drew, the farther they would be able to drive the ship on the beach; and the higher it came to rest on the beach, the easier it would be for the passengers and the crew to make their way through the surf to the land.

When at last the morning came, with what eagerness they scanned the shoreline in an effort to determine the character of the place upon which they had been cast! It was the island anciently called Melita or Melitene and now known as Malta, but they did not find this out until some time later. Then, they saw nothing that looked familiar, nothing that they could identify. On looking closely, however, they discerned a small bay, now appropriately named St. Paul's Bay. Since there was a bit of beach there, this inlet seemed to offer them their best chance of driving the ship in really close to the land.

But before they could succeed in running the ship aground at that point, they had a difficult nautical maneuver to execute. First, they made ready to raise a small foresail; then, they unlashed the two wide-sweeping rudders. They would need these means of directing the ship's course. At the last moment, after making sure that every member of the crew was at his post, the captain gave the order to cut the ship free from its anchors.[5] By skillful manipulation of the sail and by hard

4 As stated in a footnote in the RSV, at vs. 37 where most manuscripts have "two hundred and seventy-six," a few have "seventy-six" or "about seventy-six." This variation in the manuscripts may be attributed to an attempt by some copyists to correct what they judged to be an impossibly large number. But such a change is both gratuitous and unwarranted. We have numerous ancient accounts showing the large size of some of these Alexandrian grain ships. One of them, *The Isis*, excited wonder by being 180 ft. in length and 45 ft. in breadth. Its hold had a depth of 43½ ft. The handling of so large a ship would require a considerable crew. Less than a decade after Paul's shipwreck on the island of Malta, the historian Josephus suffered shipwreck in those same waters. The passengers and crew on that occasion numbered six hundred!

5 In vs. 40, where the KJV has "And when they had taken up the

toil at the rudders, the sailors kept the ship from being blown upon the cliffs to leeward.

However, they did not succeed in beaching their ship as intended, for before they came to the chosen place, the ship ran aground upon a shoal. With the ship's bow firmly stuck in the mud and sand, the stern very soon began to break up under the relentless pounding of the pursuing seas. Although the ship now was closer to land than before, and although the waves between it and the land were less high than they were outside this region of shoals, the sea was still too deep to permit of wading ashore. They would have to gain the land by whatever means they could devise.

A new and most serious danger now threatened Paul. As preparations were being hastily made to abandon the ship (it was breaking up rapidly), it occurred to the Roman soldiers that they would be held accountable for the security of the prisoners who had been put in their keeping. If the prisoners were allowed to leave the ship, who could tell how many of them might succeed in swimming to the shore and effecting their escape in the midst of the confusion! The simplest course, so the soldiers thought, and the only course which would relieve them of the possibility of having to forfeit their own lives because their prisoners had escaped, would be to put all their prisoners to death then and there. But Julius, the centurion, had been too much impressed by the bearing of Paul to permit the carrying out of any such plan of wholesale executions. He gave orders that they all, prisoners included, should get to shore as best they could. And this they did, some by swimming, some by means of improvised rafts, and some by clinging to bits of wreckage. Paul's confidence in the promise of God had been justified by the outcome. The ship had been wrecked, but of all those aboard it, not one had lost his life!

## Paul's Sojourn on the Island of Malta (Acts 28:1-10)

The island of Malta is seventeen miles long and about nine miles wide at its point of greatest breadth. Its population

anchors, they committed themselves unto the sea," the RSV has "So they cast off the anchors and left them in the sea."

today is larger than it was in the first century. Luke calls the inhabitants of Malta "barbarians," but he does not mean that they were savages; he means merely that they were not Greeks. They were descended from early Phoenician and Carthaginian settlers. These Maltese spoke a dialect of their own, but the use of Greek was so widespread that Paul and his companions undoubtedly were able to talk with many of them without difficulty in that language. Indeed, human distress speaks in a language which is understood universally. If these ship-wrecked men were troubled by tales they had heard—tales of men being washed ashore, only to be captured and sold into slavery—their fears were soon dispelled. The natives took pity upon them and received them kindly. Because of the cold and continued rain they speedily had a large fire kindled, to which, by friendly gestures, they invited the shipwrecked men to come and warm themselves.

Paul, who was never one to shirk his share of any task which needed to be done, busied himself at gathering wood. But when he was throwing an armful of wood upon the fire, a viper which had been lying dormant among the sticks came to life. Leaping up, it attached itself to Paul's hand. Paul did not lose his presence of mind, but very quickly shook off the viper into the flames. The natives, knowing that the bite of those serpents was poisonous, confidently expected to see Paul's hand begin to swell. His death, they believed, would soon follow.[6]

6 The text does not actually state that this was a poisonous serpent. Note that in vs. 4 of the KJV the word "venomous" is printed in italics, indicating that it does not appear in the manuscripts but has been sup-plied by the translators. It is the same in the ASV. In the RSV, the word "venomous" has been dropped as uncalled for. But that the ser-pent was of some poisonous species may be inferred from the reactions of the natives. Under the circumstances, it is somewhat difficult to de-cide whether or not Luke intends the reader to see something miracu-lous in this incident. We may hold either that Paul shook off the viper before it had injected any poison into the wound, or that God, on this occasion, miraculously delivered Paul from all harm. The latter would be in keeping with the promise given in Luke 10:19. Whichever way it may have been, we have in the incident one more instance of God's providential care. Paul was not to be denied the privilege of preaching Christ in Rome.

A likely explanation of what they had witnessed occurred to them. Paul, they knew, was a prisoner, a murderer perhaps; he had escaped the wrath of the sea, but now, in this unexpected way, justice[7] had overtaken him. But when some little time had passed and Paul still had shown no ill effects from the serpent's bite, they completely changed their minds regarding him. They concluded that Paul, far from being a murderer, was some god who had come down to walk amongst them. Thereafter, these simple, superstitious folk showed Paul a special deference. The apostle, we may be sure, emphatically disclaimed the possession of any divine character, even as he had done at Lystra some years before; but here, as there, while he still had their close attention, he would make the most of his opportunity to tell them of the true God.

The kindly and hospitable natives provided such living quarters as they could for all the members of the shipwrecked company. For three days, Paul and his companions, Aristarchus and Luke, were given shelter by Publius, the "chief man of the island." [8] Publius' estate is said to have been nearby. Perhaps it was through the good offices of Julius the centurion, perhaps it was because Paul already had given evidence that he was the possessor of the miracle-working Spirit of God, that he was thus entertained for a time in the home of the Roman governor of the island.

Publius' hospitality was richly rewarded. It so happened that his father was critically ill of fever and dysentery. A disease known as Malta fever is still common upon the island. Paul entered into the room where the sick man lay. He prayed for him and laid his hands upon him, and the power of God

7 Possibly the word "justice" should be spelled with a capital letter, for the reference may be to the Greek goddess Justice, daughter of Zeus and Themis. This goddess was looked upon as the avenger of crimes.

8 We have no knowledge of this Publius beyond what is given in this passage. The tradition that he later became bishop of the island of Malta is without foundation. The title which Luke applies to him, "first man of the island," is an unusual one; but its correctness has been substantiated by two inscriptions which have been found on Malta. As Roman governor of Malta, he would be subordinate in rank to the praetor who ruled Sicily, for Malta was considered to be a part of the province of Sicily.

came into the sick man's body and made him well. This was but the first of many healing miracles which Paul wrought while dwelling among the friendly people of Malta, for word of what Paul had done for Publius' father spread rapidly, and many persons who had sick relatives or friends brought them to Paul for healing.

Paul, busy with this ministry of healing, and, we may well believe, with a ministry also of preaching and teaching, found the cold winter months quickly slipping by. When the time for his departure drew near, the grateful people of the island supplied Paul and his companions with the clothing and other supplies which they would need while continuing their journey to Rome.

## CHAPTER 19

# The Gospel Is Preached in Rome

## ACTS 28:11-31

*W*ITH the coming of March there was a welcome warmth in the air; blue skies gave promise of fair weather. In the Great Harbor of Malta, eight miles to the southeast of the bay where Paul had been shipwrecked, the many ships which had been tied up there for the winter seemed to come to life. Sailors swarmed over them, repairing whatever damage they had suffered from the storms, replacing worn tackle with new, patching the large sails, and repainting the figures of the gods which adorned the high prows and sterns. Slaves carried aboard fresh stores, or stowed new cargoes within the capacious holds. On the wharfs, merchants and sea captains bargained. The time for the resumption of sailing was at hand.

Julius, the centurion, already had visited the Great Harbor. Among the many ships there, one in particular had met with his approval. It was an Alexandrian grain ship, and, like the one which had been wrecked, it was bound for Italy. He experienced no difficulty in booking passage for himself, the soldiers in his command, and his prisoners. Within a few days —a few weeks, at most—he would set foot on Italian soil. Then a few long marches past familiar scenes and once again he would be in Rome. Old haunts, old companions, days and nights of revelry! His heart quickened at the prospect. Yet he could not put wholly out of mind the things that Paul had said to him—Paul, who not once had been frightened by the storm, and who by prayer and the laying on of his hands had been able to make the sick well; and at times he found himself wondering if Paul, strange Jew that he was, might not

219

have got hold of something more satisfying, more inspiring, more enduring than anything which a career in Rome's legions could offer. And Paul himself, despite the fact that he was still a prisoner and was soon to be put on trial for his life, became more elated in spirit as the passing of each day brought so much nearer the resumption of his journey to Rome.

### From Malta to Syracuse, Rhegium, and Puteoli
### (Acts 28:11-13)

The ship which Paul and the other prisoners were put aboard was named *Dioscuri*, a word for which the most suitable English equivalent is *The Twin Brothers*. The reference in this name was to Castor and Pollux, who, according to the Greek and Roman mythology, were the twin sons of Zeus (Jupiter) and Leda. They were translated to the sky and became the constellation Gemini (The Twins). The poet Horace, in one of his Odes, describes these clear and bright-shining stars (*"lucida sidera"*) as having a calming influence upon the sea. Sailors had come to regard these twin gods as their protecting deities. It is easy to understand, therefore, why this ship had been named in their honor. Not only was the ship so named, but also it carried these gods as its "sign"; that is to say, it bore a representation of them, either carved or painted, as a figurehead on the prow and probably also on the stern.

There were the usual good-bys, a few last commissions called out to the passengers—"Greet my friends in Puteoli"; "Do not fail in the errand I have given you"—a last waving of hands, and the *Dioscuri* slipped its moorings and stood out to sea. The promontory on which the city of Valetta has since been built dropped astern. Ahead of them, some sixty miles northward, they could soon discern (if the weather were clear) the coast of Sicily, dominated by the imposing mass of Mt. Etna, which now and again gave evidence of volcanic activity.[1]

The ship now was following a sea lane so much traveled and so fully described in early writings that it would be pos-

[1] Ancient records tell of eleven eruptions prior to the Christian era. Since then, there have been many more.

sible to tell in detail, if space permitted, of every scene that met the apostle's eyes. It must suffice to say that the ship, having successfully completed a run of approximately one hundred miles, put into the harbor of Syracuse, its first port of call. Here the ship remained for three days; whether because of unfavorable winds or because of cargo to be unloaded, we are not told. Knowing the consideration with which Julius regularly treated Paul, we may believe that he permitted Paul to go ashore. If so, Paul would experience no difficulty in finding a congregation of Jews to whom he could preach. There is a tradition which makes Paul the founder of the first Christian church on the island of Sicily.

Leaving the city of Syracuse—it then was still a great city, though it had lost under the Roman domination much of its former glory—the ship (borrowing the quaint language of the King James Version) "fetched a compass, and came to Rhegium." That is to say, the ship, by dint of much tacking upon a circuitous course, managed to reach Rhegium. Rhegium, the modern Reggio, is on the very toe of the Italian boot. With the wind so unfavorable, the captain did not undertake to sail his ship through the narrow Strait of Messina which separates Sicily from Italy. Instead, he put into port. The next day, however, he was glad to see that the wind was from the south. Therefore he was able, by sailing straight before the breeze, to pass through the Strait. With the most favorable wind possible, he took his ship northward along the coast and late on the following day brought it into the harbor of Puteoli, the most important harbor in southern Italy. Pliny states that none but Alexandrian ships were permitted to enter that harbor with all their sails spread. This distinction was accorded the ships from Alexandria in recognition of their special service in supplying Rome with grain from Egypt. The ship which bore Paul, since it had wintered in Malta, may have been the first Alexandrian ship to enter the harbor that season.

*From Puteoli, along the Appian Way, to Rome*
*(Acts 28:14-16)*

Puteoli (today called Pozzuoli) is located at the northern end of the wide-sweeping Bay of Naples. Eastward across those

blue, sun-kissed waters may be seen the symmetrical cone of
Mt. Vesuvius. When Paul came to Puteoli the volcanic nature
of that mountain was unsuspected. Its western slope was vine
clad. Twenty years later, it was to rain death and desolation
upon the cities of Pompeii and Herculaneum built at its
base.[2]

The town of Puteoli owed its commercial importance in
part to its spacious harbor and in part to its nearness to the
Appian Way. This "Queen of Roads" had been built by Appius Claudius (hence its name: the *Appian* Way) , and it ran
northward from Brundisium (now Brindisi) to Rome. It constituted the busiest and most impressive approach to that city.
Along it, in unending procession, moved Roman officials and
their retinues, soldiers bound for Rome's eastern provinces,
merchants and travelers from every part of the world, and
porters—slaves, for the most part—transporting to Rome the
cargoes that had been unloaded at Puteoli and other southern
Italian ports. Puteoli was not actually on the Appian Way,
but was connected with it by a well-built, much traveled road
(the Campanian Way) which joined it at Capua.

In Puteoli Paul found a considerable number of Christians.
This is not surprising in view of the large population of that
port and its nearness to the metropolis, Rome. What faithful,
witness-bearing Christian—merchant, soldier, or missionary—
had established the church in Puteoli, we cannot say; but Paul
discovered these Christian brethren. He had fellowship with
them, and was much cheered by them. It may be that he,
brave man that he was, needed cheering; for what these Italian Christians told him of the Emperor Nero—his escapades
and crimes—did not indicate that he would hear Paul with
much patience. These Christians besought Paul to remain with
them; to remain for seven days, at least. For "seven days," presumably in order that he might preach to them on the following sabbath. We judge that Julius, because of his high regard
for Paul, permitted this delay upon their journey, and in
explanation of it advanced some pretext or other. Or it may

2 Paul, we believe, arrived at Puteoli in March of A.D. 59. The eruption of Vesuvius which destroyed Pompeii and Herculaneum began on
August 24 of A.D. 79.

be that Julius was under necessity of waiting in Puteoli until the courier he had dispatched to Rome brought back word as to what disposition he should make of his prisoners. We have reason to believe that Paul did remain in Puteoli that length of time, for otherwise there would not have been opportunity for news of Paul's arrival in Italy to have reached Rome or for the Christians of Rome to have come out so far upon the Appian Way to welcome him, as we shall presently learn that they did.

The day was soon at hand, however, when Julius saw that the journey to Rome could not properly be any longer delayed. He gave the order which set the soldiers in his command, and the prisoners in their keeping, to marching on their way. The distance from Puteoli, via Capua, to Rome was at least one hundred and thirty miles. Even assuming that the Pontine marshes were crossed by boat, as was customary, the journey would require nearly a week. But though the way was long, the soldiers set out with light hearts and quick steps. They were on their way to Rome! Even the prisoners—most of them from Rome's eastern provinces—must have experienced a lively sense of anticipation. They were bound for the Eternal City! As for Paul, though he was in chains, he went forward, not so much as a prisoner as in the manner and spirit of a soldier of Christ. He knew in his heart that with Christ was the victory.

When once the Appian Way had come as far as Terracina, it ceased its turnings, and ran on ahead, straight as any surveyor's line, to Rome, the city to which all roads led. This directness of route had been achieved by the builders despite the steep grades in the Alban Mountains and the numerous difficulties encountered in crossing the Pontine marshes. The nearer the road came to Rome, the more impressively was it lined with the tombs of Rome's illustrious dead.

Luke, it may be, was too deeply stirred to enter in his journal anything more than the simple but emotion-filled words: "And so we came to Rome." [3] In this statement we

---

[3] This translation, which appears in the ASV and in the RSV, replaces the weaker translation, "And so we went toward Rome," which appears in the KJV.

have the climax of The Acts, the culmination of Luke's account not only of the life of Paul, but also of the spreading of Christianity in obedience to the divinely given Commission. Yet Luke's eagerness and excitement had, in a measure, betrayed him. The statement, after all, was still somewhat anticipatory; for there were yet many more miles to be trudged, and two interesting happenings along the Appian Way were yet to be related.

When Paul had been brought as far as the Forum of Appius (the place had been named for the builder of the Appian Way and was forty or more miles from Rome), Paul was surprised and much pleased to come upon a band of Christians. These Christians from Rome had learned of his approach, and had come out of the city to welcome him. This town where they met—the Forum of Appius—has been described as a "haunt of thieves, thugs and swindlers," but that day it was the meeting-place of saints! Ten miles farther along the road (i.e., thirty miles from Rome), at a place called The Three Taverns, Paul encountered a second band of Christians. Like the first company, they had come out from Rome to greet him. If Paul had entertained any doubts as to how he would be received by the Christians of Rome, their cordiality completely reassured him. When he had met them and talked with them, "he thanked God, and took courage."

We wonder if there were in these two companies any Christians whom Paul had met previously. Were any of them his converts, men or women whom he had won to Christ during his years of ministry in the eastern provinces, but who now were dwellers in Rome? That would not be surprising in view of the fact that the edict of the Emperor Claudius expelling all Jews from Rome had by this time been repealed. But whether or not he had ever met any of them before, or had even heard mention of their names, they were believers on Christ. They and he served the same Lord; they and he were brothers in the faith.

A few early manuscripts (none of them of much authority) state that the centurion, on reaching Rome, delivered Paul and his other prisoners "to the captain of the guard."[4] Al-

4 This statement, which is included in the text of the KJV, appears in

though there is no good textual authority for this statement, it is probable that the centurion did so. If by "captain of the guard" we are to understand the commander of the Praetorian Guard, we know from Roman records who this was. He was Burrus Afranius, a distinguished Roman general who held that post from A.D. 51 to 62. Other scholars consider it more likely that Paul was delivered to the captain of the Peregrini, the legion which was responsible for maintaining the lines of communication between military headquarters in Rome and Rome's soldiers in the provinces.

Whoever this captain may have been, we know from what Luke tells us that he treated Paul with that consideration which was due to a man who had not been convicted of any crime. Julius, no doubt, had reported to him how Paul, by his encouragement, calmness, and good counsel, had saved the lives of all who had been aboard the ship when it was wrecked on Malta. Because of these facts, Paul was not put in the same place of confinement as the other prisoners. He was permitted to dwell in a house of his own choosing. This was a rented place for which Paul paid either out of his own resources or out of the financial assistance which the Christians of Rome gave him. Yet Paul, though spared such indignities as he had suffered in the prison at Caesarea, was not to be free. Night and day, his wrist would be chained to that of a soldier. He could not work at his trade, but there would be many things that he could do. He could write letters of counsel to his friends in other cities; he could talk with any who might come to see him. Paul would rejoice in these opportunities to bear witness to Christ in Rome, and would make the most of them.

## Paul, Though a Prisoner, Preaches in Rome (Acts 28:17-29)

Paul lost no time in getting started upon the Christian ministry which he had planned to undertake in the city of Rome. Only two days were spent in finding a suitable place in which to live and in getting settled in it. On the third day he called to his house the leaders of the Jews in Rome. These Jews undoubtedly had heard of Paul, and they were strongly op-

the ASV only as a marginal note. It is dropped entirely from the RSV.

posed to all of the things for which Paul contended. But curiosity, if nothing more, prompted them to visit this man who had been so much discussed in Jewish circles everywhere. Here was an opportunity to hear from his own lips whatever startling innovations he might be minded to advocate; here was an opportunity, it might be, to gloat over the predicament in which he now found himself.

On receiving these Jewish elders, Paul related to them the series of events which had brought about his presence in Rome. He stated that although he was a Jew and had done nothing contrary to his nation or its customs, his fellow countrymen had delivered him into the hands of the Roman authorities. He had been closely examined by the Roman governors of Judea and had been found innocent of any offense. But when the Jews had violently opposed his release and when it had become apparent that they might accomplish his death, if they succeeded in their purpose of having him turned over to the Sanhedrin for trial, he had, in a desperate attempt to save his life, appealed his case to the Emperor. It was his hope that the Emperor or his representative would examine all the evidence in the case and reach a decision which would be impartial and without prejudice to anyone. They were the recognized leaders of the Jews in Rome, and it was with respect to a matter of the Jewish religion—Israel's hope of a resurrection from the dead—that he had been made a prisoner. He had summoned them in order that they might have knowledge of these things.

The elders stated that they had heard nothing of these latest developments. They had not received any letters from Jerusalem containing specific charges against Paul; neither had any of their Judean brethren come to Rome to press charges against Paul. Of course, they had heard much, in a general way, about the Christians, and they knew that the sect everywhere was spoken against; but as for themselves, they were quite willing and ready—at least, so they said—to hear Paul in an open-minded fashion.

Accordingly, a day was agreed upon when they would come together again in order that they might hear Paul at greater length. On the day appointed a large number assembled at

Paul's house to hear him preach. Thus it came about that Paul in Rome, as everywhere else that the opportunity afforded, began his work by preaching the gospel to the Jews. From morning till night, Paul addressed them. Not only did he relate his experience, but he showed them, by citing passages in the law of Moses and in the prophets, what the true character of the kingdom of God was, and also what the true nature of Jesus was—He had been proved to be the Christ by many mighty works, and especially by His resurrection from the dead.

To this earnest preaching there was the usual reaction: some who listened, believed; others who heard, would not open their hearts to the truth. Before the meeting broke up, Paul gave to those who were intent upon continuing on their self-willed course a solemn word of warning. It was nothing less than the warning which the prophet Isaiah had given to the wicked and impenitent of his day. The passage which Paul quoted, Isaiah 6:9-10,[5] was one which the Lord Himself had cited when discussing the failure of Israel to hear and heed His teachings.[6]

Once again Paul had offered the gospel to the Jews, and once again, speaking generally, they had rejected it. Once again they had given evidence of the truthfulness of the prophetic description of the hardness of their hearts, and had shown how fully justified God was in throwing open to all the Gentiles the precious privileges which might have been theirs as the Chosen People.

The Jews, unable to agree among themselves, departed from Paul's house.[7] With the exception of the few who had believed, they would give ear to Paul no more. But Paul, as an ambassador of Christ, had now fully discharged his responsibility to them; he thereafter was at liberty to devote his full energy to the preaching of the gospel to the Gentiles of Rome. Judging

[5] As customarily, Paul quoted the passage as it is found in the Septuagint, the Greek translation of the Old Testament.

[6] For Jesus' use of this passage, see Mark 4:12 and John 12:40.

[7] Vs. 29, not found in the most important manuscripts, is rightfully omitted from the ASV and the RSV. The statement it makes, however, is not inappropriate in this context.

from his experience on other fields, they would receive the gospel more cordially than had the Jews. There were many of them who would believe on Jesus Christ, and in believing on Him find their salvation.

### Paul's Two Years in His Own Hired House  (Acts 28:30-31)

The Acts contains but two verses more. These closing verses indicate that at least two years passed before Paul's case was called up for trial. During all of that time, Paul was permitted to dwell in his own rented quarters. He was not allowed to leave them, but he enjoyed as much freedom as is possible to one whose wrist is chained to that of a guard. He could write letters, and he could receive and talk with all who might come to see him. Luke sums it up by saying that Paul spent those two years (as we who have learned his character would expect of him) in "preaching the kingdom of God and teaching those things which concern the Lord Jesus Christ."

Paul carried on this Christian work courageously, confidently, and happily. No one forbade him to do so; no one seriously hindered him. It appears from what Paul wrote at this time in a letter to the church at Philippi that his ministry during these two years was extremely fruitful. Converts were won from among the soldiers sent to guard Paul; converts were won also from among the men and women who were connected with the imperial palace. "I would ye should understand," Paul wrote the Philippians, "that the things which happened unto me have fallen out rather unto the furtherance of the gospel; so that my bonds in Christ are manifest in all the palace, and in all other places; and many of the brethren in the Lord, waxing confident by my bonds, are much more bold to speak the word without fear." [8]

### And What Thereafter?

Luke here brings his second volume, The Acts, to its conclusion. Although its closing verses tell us much, they leave much untold. They do not answer some of the questions which come insistently to mind. What happened, we ask, when those

[8] Phil. 1:14.

two years were ended? Was Paul then put on trial? And what was the outcome of his trial? Although Luke's final words, "no man forbidding him," have been likened to "a trumpet blast of triumph," there is in this conclusion, admittedly, a certain abruptness.

Although any further discussion carries us beyond the termination of Luke-Acts, and is involved, unfortunately, in some obscurity, it may be well for us here to take account of the various possibilities.

First, there is the view set forth by Harnack (and since ably defended by the late A. T. Robertson and many other competent scholars) that The Acts stops at this point because that was as far as the course of events had progressed at the time Luke wrote. In other words, Luke had brought his chronicle down to date. In support of this view, it is argued that Luke nowhere reveals any knowledge of the destruction of Jerusalem (which took place in A.D. 70) or of the events leading up to it. He makes no reference to Paul's letters, which late in the first century came to be highly regarded and widely circulated. The book describes the Roman authorities as indifferent toward Christianity, not hostile, as they became in the later decades of the first century. Finally, it is argued that if Luke had known of the martyrdom of Paul, he would most certainly have told of it. It has been said that "the blood of the martyrs is the seed of the church," and certainly no martyrdom was more memorable than Paul's.

Those scholars who hold that Luke-Acts was written quite late in the first century account for the abrupt ending in one or the other of two ways. Some suggest the possibility that Luke, in his writing, had come to the end of his second scroll or codex (book) and, because of limited space, was under necessity of bringing the work quickly to a conclusion. It was his intention, however, to write a third volume. This third volume, which would have contained an account of Paul's martyrdom, for some reason, was never written, or, if written, became lost before it had received any wide circulation. Ancient tradition knows nothing of it. Others suggest the possibility that Luke had set definite limits for The Acts, and that he, in telling how the early disciples, in obedience to the

Great Commission, had carried the gospel from Jerusalem to Judea and Samaria and on to Rome, had fully accomplished his purpose. A few have thought that Luke knew of Paul's martyrdom at the hands of the Romans, but because he was writing to commend Christianity to Roman readers, he, for political reasons, avoided charging the Romans with having put to death Christianity's foremost exponent, and sought rather to show that the Romans at first had at all times been favorably disposed toward Christianity. This proposed explanation does not do much credit to Luke as a straightforward historian.

Although we have every reason to believe that Paul eventually did become a martyr, it is incredible that at the end of these two years he should have been found guilty and put to death. The charges which had been preferred against him were too indefinite and too poorly substantiated to admit of such an outcome. Luke implies in his closing verses, if he does not explicitly state it, that two years went by without any responsible person or persons having come from Jerusalem to Rome to support the charges which had been brought against Paul. Professor Cadbury, who carefully investigated the Roman practice in trials such as this, found that if no accusing witnesses presented themselves within a year or two, the case was thrown out of court and the prisoner released.[9] Perhaps Luke, by the words with which he concluded The Acts (i.e., "no man forbidding him"), meant us to understand that all the charges against Paul were dropped, and that Paul accordingly was set free to continue his ministry. In other words, The Acts concludes with Paul's complete vindication.

In harmony with the view that Paul was released from prison is a remarkably uniform, widespread, and persistent tradition. According to early church writers, Paul had opportunity, following his release, to preach Christ again in the East and also in the West.[10] Indeed, apart from such a period of renewed

[9] H. J. Cadbury, writing in *The Beginnings of Christianity*, edited by Foakes-Jackson and Lake, vol. V, pp. 319-338. (Macmillan, 1920-33.)

[10] Clement, who wrote in the last decade of the first century, states that Paul, before his martyrdom, journeyed to "the farthest bounds of the West" (i.e., Spain), thus achieving the purpose he had expressed in Rom. 15:24.

missionary activity, no place is left in the record for the writing by Paul of 1 and 2 Timothy and Titus, and many of the references in these epistles are inexplicable. To be sure, numerous modern scholars deny the Pauline authorship of the Pastoral Epistles (as 1 and 2 Timothy and Titus are called)'. These epistles, so these scholars maintain, reveal a much advanced stage of church organization, and also a conflict with late heresies (Gnosticism in particular) of which Paul could have had no knowledge. Although the problems raised by these scholars are difficult, two facts seem clear. First, there is no place within the historical framework provided by The Acts for the events mentioned in the Pastoral Epistles. Either these events came *after* the activities related in The Acts or they are completely unhistorical. Second, if Paul had suffered martyrdom at the end of the two years of imprisonment described in The Acts, it is difficult to imagine why any writer, however much he may have admired Paul, should have invented circumstances and happenings contradicted by the known facts in the case.

Paul's period of freedom, however, could not have lasted more than a few years. Hostility toward the Christians developed to such an extent that when in A.D. 64 a large part of the city of Rome was destroyed by fire, the Christians were charged with having set the conflagration. The unpopular and unarmed Christians made an excellent scapegoat! Furthermore, during those years, the character of the Emperor Nero steadily degenerated; he became more and more sensual, more and more bestial. It is not surprising, therefore, that immediately following the burning of Rome a severe persecution should have broken out. Hundreds of the Christians, having been subjected to indescribable tortures, suffered martyrdom. During this Neronian persecution, so it is believed, Paul was again arrested. Perhaps, contrary to an imperial edict, he had returned to Rome to give comfort and encouragement to the persecuted Christians of that city. This time Paul's incarceration, if the tradition is correct, was in the Mamertine Prison. During this second imprisonment in Rome he wrote his second epistle to Timothy. Those acquaintances who had not suffered martyrdom feared to come to his assistance. Only Luke was with him.[11]

Clement, Caius of Rome, Dionysius, Tertullian, Origen, and Eusebius all state that Paul suffered martyrdom in Rome. The tradition is that when he had been convicted, he was led out of the city and along the Ostian Way to a point about three miles distant. There (the place subsequently became known as *Aquae Salviae,* i.e., "The Healing Waters") he was put to death. Because he was a Roman citizen, he was not crucified, as the apostle Peter is said to have been, but was beheaded. The church of *San Paolo alle Tre Fontane* is said to mark the spot; the church of *San Paolo* (St. Paul's without the Walls) is said to have been built over the catacomb where the mutilated body of Paul was laid to rest.

Paul had indeed fought a good fight; he had finished his course; he had kept the faith. A crown of righteousness awaited him.

*In Conclusion*

Now that the entire book of Acts has been surveyed, a few concluding observations may be in order. The first has to do with what may be termed the supernaturalism discovered in The Acts.

One cannot honestly say that he has read The Acts if all the while he has kept his eyes shut to the many indications of a divine power operating in the lives of the apostles and in the activities of the early churches. Luke took full account of these spiritual phenomena. To have omitted mention of them, or to have minimized their importance, would have completely discredited him as a historian. They were an essential part of the historical development which he was describing. The apostles were courageous, determined, and resourceful men, but they could not have accomplished all that they did if they had not received that significant empowering by the Holy Spirit. Luke was but showing himself a competent historian when in his account of early Christianity he recognized the spiritual, as well as the sociological, factors.

11 2 Tim. 4:11.

This recognition of the supernatural is not limited to The Acts. It is to be found everywhere in the Scriptures. The Gospels report the mighty works of Jesus. They present Jesus Christ Himself as the greatest miracle of all. The Gospel by Luke relates more miracles than does any other Gospel, but only six of the miracles are peculiar to Luke. That is to say, the miracles do not stand solely on Luke's word. The Acts likewise tells of many miracles, and this despite the fact that in certain passages Luke seems to be endeavoring to avoid implying a miracle where it is not certain that a miracle actually took place. We may use of the miracles in The Acts the expression which Luke employed when telling of Jesus' miracles.[12] They were "glorious things" (Greek, *eudoxa*) ; i.e., manifestations of the glory of God—Father, Son, and Holy Spirit.

Some years ago William Sanday wrote: "If ever there was a manifestation of the supernatural, it was in the condition of things out of which arose the New Testament. We have only to take up the epistles of St. Paul and we find him surrounded, penetrated, permeated with the supernatural. It is, as it were, the very atmosphere which he breathes. He does not assert it. He does not need to assert it. . . . St. Paul assumes it as a fact everywhere present to the consciousness of his readers as much as to his own." To the same import are the more recent words of the Reverend Arthur John Gossip, who writes: "For the New Testament is the happiest book in the world, written by men who had heard news too good to be true, yet it was true; who had had spiritual experiences so extraordinary that plainly they were just impossible, and yet they had happened to them. . . ."[13]

Perhaps it is because we today have lost so much of this awareness of the supernatural, perhaps it is because of some deep-seated and wholly perverse antipathy to everything savoring of the supernatural, that we sometimes are puzzled by what we read in The Acts.

The second observation has to do with Luke's comments

12 Luke 13:17.
13 Arthur John Gossip, in *In the Secret Place of the Most High*, Copyright, Charles Scribner's Sons, 1947.

concerning the Holy Spirit. He points out that the rapid increase in the number of Christian believers was due, in large measure, to the presence and power of the Holy Spirit in the hearts of the members of that first Christian company.

Luke does not write as a systematic theologian, but as a historian. He proposes no definition of the Holy Spirit, but he reports in welcome detail what the Holy Spirit did. Although this is not enough to satisfy curiosity, it is sufficient to direct attention to the practical aspects of the matter. He shows that the Holy Spirit produced in the lives of the apostles a confident and overcoming spirit unprecedented in history. If Christians are to conduct themselves becomingly amid the perplexities and perils of this present age, they must seek the help of the Holy Spirit. Nothing short of this will avail.

What does it mean to be filled with the Holy Spirit? What but this: to be filled with that spirit (mind, disposition, will) which we behold in Jesus Christ our Lord. His holy spirit is the Holy Spirit. What again but this: to manifest that spirit (patient, loving, just, courageous, peace-seeking, and forgiving) which we behold in these men "on whom the Spirit came." Their spirit, when they were living at their best, was the Holy Spirit. Truly, "the fruit of the Spirit is love, joy, peace, longsuffering, gentleness, goodness, faith, meekness, temperance." [14] When a life manifests these Christian graces, we have indubitable evidence of the presence in it of the Holy Spirit. The absence of these graces can only mean that the individual is not obedient to the Spirit's promptings. We must not, dare not, "grieve . . . the holy Spirit of God." [15]

If, then, anyone desires to be filled with the Spirit, we have this promise from the lips of Christ Himself: "If ye then, being evil, know how to give good gifts unto your children: how much more shall your heavenly Father give the Holy Spirit to them that ask him?" [16] But let him who asks bear in mind that in so doing he is requesting much more than an ecstatic experience; he is requesting that his will shall be brought into conformity with the holy will of God. He is asking for a readi-

14 Gal. 5:22-23.
15 Eph. 4:30.
16 Luke 11:13.

ness to endure persecution, to serve unceasingly, and to make great personal sacrifices for the sake of the kingdom of God. To receive the Spirit, one must be willing to "endure hardness, as a good soldier of Jesus Christ." [17]

The third observation which may be made has to do with the universal outlook which is characteristic of The Acts. Indeed, this breadth of sympathy and this wideness of horizon are discernible throughout the entire New Testament. Edward Shillito has written: "The New Testament deals not with any section of humanity, but with mankind. It claims the world for its scale. It is in its design neither Jew nor Gentile, but human. And since it is human it is also missionary, for the missionary is simply the servant of a kingdom which includes in its range all the peoples of the world. He believes that a word which is meant for all men should be offered to all men."[18] This point of view is nowhere more obvious than in The Acts. In it we see Spirit-directed men carrying the gospel to Gentiles and establishing Christian churches in Gentile cities. Whereas The Acts begins in Jerusalem, it comes to its close in Rome. Whereas Paul, when he began his missionary work, had Christian Jews for his fellow-workers, when he ended his career he was accompanied by Christian Gentiles— Luke, Aristarchus, and Trophimus, to name only three.

Although conditions upon the world's mission fields are constantly undergoing change, human needs the world around are much the same as in the first century. The missionary's task, in its essential character, is the same today as then. There is still need to bear witness to the risen and ever-living Lord, for only in Him does the world—its individuals and its nations —have hope of deliverance. It is not surprising, therefore, that The Acts should be counted a major missionary document for study today.

Now, in a very significant sense The Acts is but a sequel to the Gospels. In the Gospels we learn of the activity of our Lord prior to His resurrection; in The Acts we learn of His activity after His resurrection—His activity in the lives of those

17 2 Tim. 2:3.
18 Edward Shillito, in *The Way of the Witness: A New Testament Study in Missionary Motive.* Copyright, Friendship Press, 1936.

who believed on Him. We see countless Spirit-directed and Spirit-empowered men going out into the world with a joyous, glorious, and life-transforming message. They announced everywhere: "Jesus is risen; Jesus, therefore, is Lord!" These men were the missionary pioneers, the vanguard of the thousands of witnesses who have followed them. If men continue to heed the voice of the Spirit, countless thousands more will yet show themselves obedient to the Great Commission which Christ has given.

In this sense, the Acts of the Apostles (the book telling of the deeds of the sent-ones) is still unfinished. It recounts but the first thrilling chapter. It tells of the faithfulness of only the first company of apostles. The last chapter will not be written until account can be taken of the labors and sacrifices of all the vast throng "who follow in their train." The story will not be ended until all the kingdoms of this world have become the kingdom of our Lord and of His Christ.

# A Chronology for The Acts

*L* UKE, like the eminent Greek historians who had preceded him, regarded history as an art rather than as a science. He was more interested in the meaning of events than in their precise dates. Although he was not so date-conscious as a modern historian, he nevertheless recorded his events in an orderly sequence, and in many instances he gave precise time measurements. For example, Acts 18:11 states the length of one of Paul's ministries. Acts 20:3 states the length of another of his ministries. Acts 20:15 shows the time spent in making each of certain stages of a sea voyage.

Furthermore, close examination of The Acts reveals that Luke arranged his literary material in accordance with an outline which is chronological as well as geographical. The missionary commission given by Christ to His disciples demanded that the gospel should be preached first in Jerusalem, and then—in ever-widening concentric circles—throughout Judea and Samaria, and on to the ends of the earth. In the apostolic spreading of the gospel, Luke perceived six distinct steps. These steps (stages or periods) may be discerned without difficulty by the reader, due to the fact that at the conclusion of each period Luke has given a summary of its character. Each summary sounds a note of triumph. These summaries, which the reader will do well to examine, are as follows: Acts 6:7; 9:31; 12:24; 16:5; 19:20; 28:31. By taking account of them, we arrive at the following outline:

Period 1. The Witnessing in Jerusalem (Acts 1:1—6:7).
Period 2. The Witnessing throughout Palestine (Acts 6:8 —9:31).

Period 3.    The Witnessing in Antioch  (Acts 9:32—12:24).
Period 4.    The Witnessing in Galatia  (Acts 12:25—16:5).
Period 5.    The Witnessing in Greece  (Acts 16:6—19:20).
Period 6.    The Witnessing in Rome  (Acts 19:21—28:31).

It will be recognized that these brief designations are un-
equal to the task of indicating all that occurred within each
period. To illustrate, Paul's important ministry in Ephesus—
a ministry lasting three years—falls within Period 5 which
takes its name from the farthest point westward which Paul
had reached up to that time. Included in Period 6 is Paul's
imprisonment in Caesarea and his voyage to Rome, with its
shipwreck, as well as his witnessing in the city itself. The period designations are but names for the important milestones
passed by the Spirit-filled witnesses as they carried the gospel
farther and farther from Jerusalem.

When calendar dates are assigned to these six periods, as is
done below, an interesting fact emerges. Each of the six periods is found to be approximately five years in length. This
uniformity is too great to be wholly accidental. Here then is
justification for the statement previously made that Luke's
outline is chronological as well as geographical. It is now in
order to consider briefly the process by which the year-dates
are determined.

We have observed in our study of The Acts that certain of
the events mentioned occurred in connection with, or at the
same time as, other events of which we have some knowledge
through the annals of secular historians. Chief among these
synchronisms are the following:

1. Aretas ruling over Damascus (Acts 9:25 read in connection with 2 Cor. 11:32-33).
2. The famine in the reign of Claudius (Acts 11:28).
3. The death of Herod Agrippa I (Acts 12:20-23).
4. Sergius Paulus proconsul in Cyprus (Acts 13:7).
5. Jews expelled from Rome by Claudius (Acts 18:2).
6. Gallio proconsul in Achaia (Acts 18:12).
7. The procuratorship of Felix (Acts 23:24).
8. Festus succeeds Felix (Acts 24:27).
9. The reign of Herod Agrippa II (Acts 25:13).

For such dates as are available for this period, we are in-

debted principally to the Roman historians, Tacitus and Suetonius, and to the Jewish historian, Josephus. But inasmuch as
these historians are not always clear and sometimes are in contradiction, an unfortunate element of uncertainty is introduced into the reckoning. The most important date, so far as
a knowledge of the life of Paul is concerned, is that on which
Felix was recalled, to be succeeded in the procuratorship by
Festus. This is the most important date, because it is the date
from which events in the life of Paul can be most satisfactorily reckoned. But whereas our ancient sources are in almost
complete agreement on such a date as that of the death of
Herod Agrippa I (A.D. 44), they are in considerable confusion concerning the date on which the procuratorship of Felix
terminated and that of Festus began. Scholars studying the evidence have reached conclusions ranging from A.D. 55 to
A.D. 61. The weight of probability favors A.D. 58.

Working back from A.D. 58, and making use of such incidental statements as are to be found in The Acts and in the
Pauline epistles, we arrive at A.D. 35 as the year of Paul's conversion. Figuring ahead from A.D. 58, it appears that Paul
reached Rome early in A.D. 59 and that his first Roman imprisonment ended in A.D. 61. This date fits in with the widely
accepted tradition that Paul suffered martyrdom during the
Neronian persecution, which began in A.D. 64. The other
events in Paul's life may now be fitted into this framework.
When this has been done, it is found that all of Luke's statements fall well within the tenable limits fixed by the secular
historians.

The dates given below, accordingly, are not to be thought
of as fixed with finality; but they are approximately correct,
and the table will serve as a convenient chronological outline.
For a fuller discussion of these matters, the student is referred
to the carefully written article, "Chronology of the New Testament; Part 2, The Apostolic Age," by C. H. Turner, in *A
Dictionary of the Bible*, edited by James Hastings (Charles
Scribner's Sons, 1911). See v. 1, pp. 415-425.

*Preceding The Acts*

A.D.

29 (30?)  The Crucifixion  (Luke 23:33-56)
29 (30?)  The Resurrection, Post-resurrection Appearances, and Ascension  (Luke 24:1-53)

## THE ACTS

| | | |
|---|---|---|
| I | 29 (30?) -35 | **THE WITNESSING IN JERUSALEM** (Acts 1:1—6:7) |
| | 29 (30?) | The Post-resurrection Appearances and the Ascension |
| | 29 (30?) | The Bestowal of the Holy Spirit |
| | 29 (30?) | Peter and John Bear Witness |
| II | 35-39 (40?) | **THE WITNESSING THROUGHOUT PALESTINE** (Acts 6:8—9:31) |
| | 35 | The Martyrdom of Stephen |
| | 35 | The Conversion of Paul |
| | 38 | Paul's First Visit to Jerusalem |
| | 38 | Paul in Tarsus |
| III | 39 (40?) -45 (46?) | **THE WITNESSING IN ANTIOCH** (Acts 9:32-12:24) |
| | 41 | Peter's Vision |
| | 41 | Claudius Becomes Emperor |
| | 42 | Barnabas Sent to Antioch |
| | 44 | Barnabas Brings Paul to Antioch |
| | 44 | Death of Herod Agrippa I |
| IV | 45 (46?) -50 | **THE WITNESSING IN GALATIA** (Acts 12:25—16:5) |
| | 46 | Paul's Relief Visit to Jerusalem |
| | 47-48 | Paul's First Missionary Journey |
| | 48 (49?) | The Council in Jerusalem |
| | 49 | The Second Missionary Journey Begun |
| | 49 | The Jews Expelled from Rome |
| V | 50-55 | **THE WITNESSING IN GREECE** (Acts 16:6—19:20) |
| | 50 | Paul in Philippi, Thessalonica, and Athens |
| | 50 | Paul Reaches Corinth |
| | 51 | Gallio Becomes Proconsul |
| | 52 | Second Missionary Journey Completed |
| | 52 | Third Missionary Journey Begun |
| | 52-55 | Paul's Three Years in Ephesus |
| | 54 | Nero Becomes Emperor |
| VI | 55-61 | **THE WITNESSNG IN ROME** (Acts 19:21—28:31) |
| | 56 | Paul's Arrival in Jerusalem |
| | 56-58 | Paul's Imprisonment at Caesarea |
| | 58 | Felix Replaced by Festus |
| | 59 | Paul Reaches Rome |
| | 59-61 | Paul's First Roman Imprisonment |

*Beyond The Acts*

61-64  Paul's Later Missionary Labors
64  The Christians Persecuted by Nero
64  The Martyrdoms of Peter and Paul
66  The Jews Declare War on Rome
70  The Destruction of Jerusalem

## APPENDIX B

# *A Bibliography for The Acts*

*T*HE literature dealing with The Acts is voluminous; furthermore, it is supplemented by the even more voluminous literature dealing with the life of the apostle Paul. The multitude of books makes for bewilderment. Of these books, the critical works (i.e., those dealing largely with such speculative issues as those of text, date, and sources) frequently are found to be in disagreement. They differ not only in their interpretation of details, but also in their basic presuppositions and in their manner of approach to the problems under consideration. It is not surprising, therefore, that sometimes they arrive at widely different conclusions. Some of the books which are mines of information can be read profitably only by those who have some acquaintance with the critical processes employed by the scholars. In addition, certain of these books are based upon the Greek text, and a knowledge of that language is a prerequisite to the reading of them.

All that is attempted here is to list some of the major scholarly works (these for the advanced student) and some of the less pretentious, but nevertheless very helpful, works which the layman or young person may read with interest. Books which are out of print, as a few of these are, frequently may be borrowed from a public library or picked up at nominal cost in shops dealing in second-hand books. It will be understood, of course, that the listing of a book does not imply an endorsement of all its contents. Every book—this book no less than others—needs to be read with discrimination.

*The Acts in English Translation*
The New Testament, Revised Standard Version. Copyright,

International Council of Religious Education, 1946; Thomas Nelson & Sons, publishers. This authorized revision of the American Standard Version of 1901 is the work of a large committee made up of America's foremost biblical scholars. It incorporates the changes demanded by advances in scholarship and seeks to combine the simplicity and beauty of the King James Version of 1611 with the greater accuracy of the American Standard Version.

## The Major Scholarly Works

Harnack, Adolf von. *The Mission and Expansion of Christianity in the First Three Centuries;* tr. by James Moffatt; 2 ed. Putnam, 1904.

Knowling, R. J. *The Acts of the Apostles;* in *Expositor's Greek Testament;* v. 2. First published, 1917; reprinted by Wm. B. Eerdmans Pub. Co. Has critical notes on the Greek text and much helpful comment.

Cadbury, H. J. *The Making of Luke-Acts.* Macmillan, 1927. An important study of Luke's sources and methods.

Lake, Kirsopp and Foakes-Jackson, F. J., eds. *The Beginnings of Christianity*. Part I, 5v., by Kirsopp Lake and H. J. Cadbury. Macmillan, 1920-33. Volumes 4 and 5, containing the English translation and commentary, are especially helpful.

Weiss, Johannes. *The History of Primitive Christianity;* completed after the author's death by Rudolf Knopf; tr. by four friends; ed. by Frederick C. Grant. Wilson-Erickson, 1937. 2 v.

Lietzmann, Hans. *The Beginnings of the Christian Church;* tr. by B. L. Woolf. Scribner, 1937.


## Commentaries on The Acts

Lumby, J. Rawson. *The Acts of the Apostles,* in the *Cambridge Bible for Schools and Colleges* series. G. P. Putnam's Sons. First published, 1882; many editions. An older work which frequently is still helpful.

Rackham, R. B. *The Acts of the Apostles,* in the *Westminster* series. Methuen, 1901.

Carver, William Owen. *The Acts of the Apostles,* in the *Con-*

*vention* series; I. J. Van Ness, ed. Sunday School Board, Southern Baptist Convention, 1916. A convenient handbook combining good scholarship, devotional spirit, and clarity of statement.

Blunt, A. W. F. *The Acts;* in the *Clarendon Bible* series. Oxford University Press, 1922.

Foakes-Jackson, F. J. *The Acts of the Apostles,* in *Moffatt New Testament Commentary* series. Harper, 1931.

*On the Life of Paul*

Coneybeare, W. J. and Howson, J. S. *The Life and Epistles of St. Paul.* First published in two volumes in 1854. Doran. Many editions. Though written long ago, it is still useful.

Ramsay, W. M. *St. Paul the Traveller and the Roman Citizen.* Doran, 1896. Sir William Ramsay's patient investigations need always to be taken into account. Much helpful material concerning Paul will be found in Ramsay's other writings.

Smith, David. *The Life and Letters of St. Paul.* Doran, 1920. This work takes account of Sir William Ramsay's epochal discoveries and incorporates many of his interpretations.

Foakes-Jackson, F. J. *The Life of St. Paul, the Man and the Apostle.* Boni and Liveright, 1926.

Robinson, B. W. *The Life of Paul.* University of Chicago Press, 1928. Brief, dependable, very useful.

Patterson, Harriet-Louise H. *Around the Mediterranean with My Bible.* W. A. Wilde Co., 1941; reprinted by The Judson Press, 1947. A fascinating travel book telling of a trip to the scenes of Paul's labors.

Klausner, Joseph. *From Jesus to Paul.* Tr. from the Hebrew by William F. Stinespring. Macmillan, 1943. An informing study by an eminent Jewish scholar who states that he has sought to write, "not as a Jewish or Christian theologian, but, above all, as a historian, to whom theology is only an auxiliary subject."

Goodspeed, Edgar J. *Paul.* John C. Winston Co., 1947. A scholarly, yet popularly written, account of Paul's life and work. As primary sources, Dr. Goodspeed rates the Pauline epistles above The Acts.

## On the Holy Spirit

Brightman, E. S. *The Spiritual Life.* Abingdon-Cokesbury, 1942. The nature and work of the Holy Spirit stated in the terms of religious philosophy.

Dana, H. E. *The Holy Spirit in Acts.* 2 ed., revised; Central Seminary Press (Kansas City, Kans.), 1943. A helpful gathering up of the teaching of The Acts with respect to the Holy Spirit, considered in the light of present-day Christian experience.

Dillistone, F. W. *The Holy Spirit in the Life of Today.* Westminster Press, 1947. Sane, understandable, and helpful.

## On the Christian Mission

Shillito, Edward. *The Way of the Witnesses.* Friendship Press, 1936. A New Testament study in missionary motive. Readable and inspiring.

Kraemer, Hendrik. *The Christian Message in a Non-Christian World.* Harper, 1938. A thought-provoking study of the theological foundation of the Christian mission.

Latourette, K. S. *A History of the Expansion of Christianity.* 7 v. Harper, 1937-45. A monumental work on the history of Christian missions. See especially v. 1, *The First Five Centuries.*

## On the Literary and Archeological Background

Deissmann, Adolf. *Light from the Ancient East;* tr. by Lionel R. M. Strachan. 4 ed., revised. Harper, 1927. The New Testament illustrated by recently discovered texts of the Graeco-Roman world. Gives much help on the language and on the social and religious background.

Finegan, Jack. *Light from the Ancient Past.* Princeton University, 1946. The archeological background is helpfully shown. Recent, authoritative, and well illustrated.

## Maps

Wright, Filson, and Albright. *The Westminster Historical Atlas of the Bible.* Westminster Press, 1945. New and authentic. See especially the maps and text on "The Journeys of Paul," pp. 87-92; and on "The Expansion of Christianity," pp. 93-96.

APPENDIX C

# Questions and Projects

*T*HE following questions, based on the chapters of this
book, should not prove difficult. Answers, as a rule, can
be found either in the chapter indicated or in the Scripture
material there considered. Included with these questions are
a number of study or service projects. They call for some independent research, some formulating of judgments, and some
planning and action. Such projects are profitable from the
point of view of learning and also from the point of view of
practical service to others.

## Chapter 1

1. What are the reasons for believing that The Acts was
written by Luke?
2. What is known certainly about Luke and his life?
3. What was Luke's purpose in writing The Acts?
4. What reasons are there for believing that The Acts was
written during or immediately following Paul's first imprisonment in Rome?
5. How reliable a historian has Luke been proved to be?
6. Read Luke 1:1-4 and Acts 1:1-5 in one of the modern
speech translations, then write out in your own words all that
Luke states in these two passages. What indications do they
contain that Luke and Acts are two parts of a single literary work?

## Chapter 2

1. With what events does the Gospel by Luke conclude?
With what events does The Acts begin? What events are re-

lated in both Luke and Acts? Why this repetition?

2. Which apostle figures most prominently in the early chapters of The Acts? In the later chapters? But is the account limited to the activities of these two apostles?

3. What did the apostles do following Jesus' ascension?

4. Who was chosen to take the place made vacant by the defection and suicide of Judas?

5. In how many Gospel passages do we find statements (variously worded, of course) of the Great Commission? In how many Gospel passages do we find promises of the giving of the Holy Spirit?

6. At the present time, is it more important that the churches should greatly increase their missionary giving, or that they should seek more of the power of the Holy Spirit? What is the relationship between these two aspects of the missionary task? Does increased spirituality prompt greater giving? Does increased giving develop greater spirituality?

## Chapter 3

1. Why was the day of Pentecost a fitting time for the bestowal of the Holy Spirit?

2. What outward signs made the bestowal of the Holy Spirit evident to all? What effect did the bestowal of the Holy Spirit have upon the apostles?

3. What were the apostles, when filled with the Spirit, straightway impelled to do? What divine help did they have in their witnessing?

4. What were the principal points which Peter made in his sermon on the day of Pentecost? What did he call upon his hearers to do? How effective did his witnessing prove?

5. After studying 1 Corinthians, chapters 12-14, write a paper in which you give Paul's judgment respecting such speaking with tongues as was going on in the church at Corinth. Did he regard it as a true gift of the Holy Spirit? How did he rate it in comparison with other spiritual gifts? Have there been any genuine and really edifying instances of speaking with tongues in recent centuries?

## Chapter 4

1. Describe the early Christian fellowship.

2. What was the purpose of the eating together? Of the praying together? Of the sharing of possessions? What impression did this manner of living make upon all who beheld it?

3. What responsibility does each Christian bear respecting the poor and physically handicapped persons in the community?

4. Wherein did Peter's sermon following the healing of the lame man resemble his sermon on the day of Pentecost? What same facts did he emphasize? What did he call upon his hearers to do? What was the result of his faithful preaching of Jesus Christ?

5. After studying Acts 2:41-47, list the principal characteristics of a true church. Can you frame a definition of a church? Compare your definition with those prepared by other members of the class.

## Chapter 5

1. Discuss the spirit and content of the prayer of thanksgiving offered by the church on learning of the safety of Peter and John. In what respects did this prayer resemble the apostolic preaching? What was the only thing asked? What answer did God give?

2. Why were there so many poor persons in the Jerusalem church? What plan of caring for them had the church adopted? Would such a plan work successfully today?

3. Of what sin were Ananias and Sapphira guilty? In the light of all the circumstances, how great was their sin?

4. Acts 5:12-16 tells of the ministry of healing carried on by the apostles. To what extent did it contribute to the growth of the church?

5. Are churches today manifesting more interest in the healing of sick bodies and minds than they did a generation ago? If so, in what ways is the new interest being manifested? Does moral and religious health contribute to mental and physical health? Is your church discharging its full Christian responsibility in the area of health?

## Chapter 6

1. Tell of the arrest and divine deliverance of the apostles. Why did they resume their preaching? When they were arrested again, what charges did the Sanhedrin bring against them? What answer did Peter give to these charges?

2. How wise was the advice Gamaliel gave the Sanhedrin?

3. What commendable things had Stephen done? Why did he, when brought before the Sanhedrin, say so little about himself and so much about the history of Israel?

4. What were the duties of the deacons in the early days of the church? What are the proper duties of deacons in the church today?

## Chapter 7

1. What part did persecution play in the spreading of the gospel?

2. Tell of the activities of Philip. What significance is there in the fact that he witnessed for Christ in Samaria?

3. What part did Peter and John have in the evangelization of Samaria? What significance is there in the fact that the Holy Spirit came upon the Samaritan believers?

4. What is the sin of simony? How did it get that name?

5. What part did Philip have in the conversion of the Ethiopian? What part did the Scriptures have in it? What part did the Holy Spirit have in it?

6. In this chapter three types of bestowals of the Holy Spirit are described. How helpful are these distinctions? Can you find additional Scripture verses in support of each type?

## Chapter 8

1. What is known of Paul's early life?

2. How many accounts of his conversion do we have? Where are they found?

3. What commission did Paul receive from Christ?

4. Who was Ananias? What did the Lord call upon him to do?

5. Where did Paul begin his Christian preaching?

6. Under what circumstances did Paul leave Damascus?

7. How was Paul received on his return to Jerusalem?

8. How successful was Paul's preaching in Jerusalem?

9. Write a paper telling of the manner and significance of Paul's conversion. Be sure to include in it your answers to these questions: In what respects was Paul's conversion wholly unprecedented and exceptional in nature? In what respects was it typical of every conversion today as well as then?

## Chapter 9

1. In what respects did Peter's raising of Dorcas give indication that Jesus Christ, risen from the dead, was still active for good in the world?

2. Had Peter already largely overcome his Jewish prejudice against Gentiles, or did he greatly need such a vision as came to him when on the housetop? What bearing did that vision have upon the missionary task?

3. Is baptism essential to receiving the Holy Spirit?

4. Tell of Peter's deliverance from prison. Did prayer play any part in it?

5. What strong racial prejudices exist today? How do you account for them? Why is racial prejudice always unchristian? If Christians want to break down an existing racial prejudice, how may they set about it most tactfully?

6. What strong religious prejudices exist today? Why do different Christian groups find it so difficult to have fellowship and to co-operate? To what extent are today's denominations due to actual differences of belief? To what extent are they due to misunderstandings and prejudices? When is tolerance a vice, and when is it a virtue?

## Chapter 10

1. How had it come about that there was a Gentile church in Antioch? How did Barnabas come to be connected with it?

2. What responsibility does a church have for sending relief to those in distress outside its own community? Can a church by its charitable giving show its sincere friendliness and Christian purpose? Does a church impoverish itself by giving to those in need? How would the generosity and helpfulness of

the Antioch church make for better feelings between the Jewish Christians and the Gentile Christians?

3. What constitutes a call to missionary service?

4. How are missionaries commissioned and sent forth today?

5. How seriously does your church take its missionary responsibility? How seriously have you considered your personal responsibility in connection with the missionary enterprise?

## Chapter 11

1. When there were so many unconverted people in Antioch, how could a mission to Cyprus be justified?

2. In what ways was the conversion of Sergius Paulus important?

3. Why is it that teachers of pseudo-religions and false cults, such as Elymas the sorcerer, can win such large followings?

4. Does every missionary encounter opposition similar to that which Paul encountered from Elymas? What does Paul's experience show concerning the power of the gospel to overcome ignorance, superstition, and evil?

5. Discuss Paul's sermon in Antioch in Pisidia from the point of view of a message based upon the Scriptures. Was this a tactful approach to his hearers? Why was his preaching at first well received, later rejected?

6. Trace on a map the course of Paul's first missionary journey. Be prepared to tell briefly what happened at each place Paul visited.

## Chapter 12

1. Why was Paul so insistent that the Gentile converts not be required to observe the Mosaic law?

2. What agreement was reached at the Jerusalem conference? Was it a compromise, or a full vindication of Paul's position?

3. Who was Paul's companion on his second missionary journey? Why did not Barnabas accompany him?

4. Can you think of any reason why the Holy Spirit should have been unwilling for Paul to preach at that time in the provinces of Asia and Bithynia?

5. Trace Paul's second missionary journey from Antioch in

Syria as far as Troas. What indication is there that Luke joined Paul at Troas?

## Chapter 13

1. Is the evangelization of the great cities as important in kingdom strategy today as it was in Paul's time?

2. Paul's work in Europe began with the conversion of Lydia. How large a part have women played in the spreading of the Gospel?

3. Why was Paul thrown in prison when in Philippi?

4. What charges were brought against Paul when he came to Thessalonica?

5. Paul seems to have felt that his preaching in Athens was largely a failure. Was the difficulty in himself, in his sermon, or in his hearers? But was his sermon all in vain? Is any gospel sermon ever a failure?

6. Trace Paul's journey from Philippi to Corinth. What conditions made Christian work in Corinth difficult? What challenge did that great city offer?

## Chapter 14

1. What events put a stop to Paul's ministry in Corinth?

2. Trace the return portion of Paul's second missionary journey, i.e., from Corinth back to Antioch in Syria.

3. Trace the first portion of Paul's third missionary journey, i.e., from Antioch in Syria to Ephesus.

4. What were some of the severe trials which Paul endured during his years in Ephesus?

5. Are there still those who would make profit out of man's belief in magic? What is the difference between belief in magic and belief in the power of God? If there should be a genuine and widespread revival of true religion in your town, what businesses would it interfere with?

## Chapter 15

1. What cities did Paul visit on his return to Europe? What was the purpose of these visits? What plot was made against his life? How did he escape it?

2. What happened when Paul preached at Troas? Tell of Paul's conference at Miletus with the elders from Ephesus. Why was Paul so determined to go up to Jerusalem?

3. Who at Caesarea warned Paul against going up to Jerusalem? Did Paul do wrong in not heeding this warning?

4. Trace the remainder of Paul's third missionary journey, i.e., from Ephesus into Europe and then back to Jerusalem.

## Chapter 16

1. How was Paul received by the leaders of the Jerusalem church? What did they propose that he do?

2. Why was Paul mobbed and arrested when worshiping in the Temple? Had he violated any law? What fact saved him from being scourged?

3. Can Paul's conduct when brought before the Sanhedrin be justified? With what statement did he throw that body into an uproar?

4. What new plot was made against Paul's life? How was it discovered? To what place was Paul transferred for greater security?

## Chapter 17

1. Who made the charges against Paul at his first hearing before Felix? What were those charges?

2. Why did not Felix, after hearing Paul's story, order his release?

3. Who, after two years, replaced Felix as governor? What was the character of the new governor? Why did Paul appeal his case to Caesar?

4. Of whom did the new governor seek counsel respecting Paul? What effect did Paul's preaching have upon them?

5. Acts 26:2-29 is a stirring oration. Practice reading it aloud.

## Chapter 18

1. Trace Paul's course from the time he was removed from the prison in Caesarea until he was shipwrecked upon the island of Malta.

2. How did it come about that Paul, who was taken aboard

the ship as a prisoner, came to have so much influence with his guards, the crew, and the ship's captain?

3. How was Paul treated by the natives of Malta? What services did he render them? When was the journey to Rome resumed?

## Chapter 19

1. Trace Paul's journey from Malta to Rome.

2. What happened at Puteoli? At the Forum of Appius? At the Three Taverns?

3. Tell of Paul's conference with the Jewish elders in Rome. How successful was he in preaching to them?

4. What opportunities for Christian witnessing did Paul have while a prisoner in Rome?

5. What reasons are there for believing that after two years Paul was released and permitted to resume his missionary efforts?

6. When and where did Paul suffer martyrdom? What is your estimate of his character?

7. Now that you have studied the entire book of Acts, what do you consider to be its principal teachings?